Charles Taylor

For Sue

Charles Taylor

Meaning, Morals and Modernity

Nicholas H. Smith

Polity

First published in 2002 by Polity Press in association with Blackwell Publishers Ltd

Editorial office:
Polity Press
65 Bridge Street
Cambridge CB2 1UR, UK

Marketing and production:
Blackwell Publishers Ltd
108 Cowley Road
Oxford OX4 1JF, UK

Published in the USA by
Blackwell Publishers Inc.
350 Main Street
Malden MA 02148, USA

ISBN 0-7456-1575-9
ISBN 0-7456-1576-7 (pbk)

A catalogue record for this book is available from the British Library and has been applied for from the Library of Congress.

Typeset in 10.5 on 12 pt Palatino
by Best-set Typesetter Ltd., Hong Kong
Printed in Great Britain by MPG Books Ltd, Bodmin, Cornwall

This book is printed on acid-free paper.

Key Contemporary Thinkers

Published

Jeremy Ahearne, *Michel de Certeau: Interpretation and its Other*
Peter Burke, *The French Historical Revolution: The* Annales *School 1929–1989*
M. J. Cain, *Fodor: Language, Mind and Philosophy*
Michael Caesar, *Umberto Eco: Philosophy, Semiotics and the Work of Fiction*
Colin Davis, *Levinas: An Introduction*
Simon Evnine, *Donald Davidson*
Edward Fullbrook and Kate Fullbrook, *Simone de Beauvoir: A Critical Introduction*
Andrew Gamble, *Hayek: The Iron Cage of Liberty*
Graeme Gilloch, *Walter Benjamin: Critical Constellations*
Karen Green, *Dummett: Philosophy of Language*
Phillip Hansen, *Hannah Arendt: Politics, History and Citizenship*
Sean Homer, *Fredric Jameson: Marxism, Hermeneutics, Postmodernism*
Christopher Hookway, *Quine: Language, Experience and Reality*
Christina Howells, *Derrida: Deconstruction from Phenomenology to Ethics*
Fred Inglis, *Clifford Geertz: Culture, Custom and Ethics*
Simon Jarvis, *Adorno: A Critical Introduction*
Douglas Kellner, *Jean Baudrillard: From Marxism to Post-Modernism and Beyond*
Valerie Kennedy, *Edward Said: A Critical Introduction*
Chandran Kukathas and Philip Pettit, *Rawls: A Theory of Justice and its Critics*
James McGilvray, *Chomsky: Language, Mind, and Politics*
Lois McNay, *Foucault: A Critical Introduction*
Philip Manning, *Erving Goffman and Modern Sociology*
Michael Moriarty, *Roland Barthes*
Harold W. Noonan, *Frege: A Critical Introduction*
William Outhwaite, *Habermas: A Critical Introduction*
John Preston, *Feyerabend: Philosophy, Science and Society*
Susan Sellers, *Hélène Cixous: Authorship, Autobiography and Love*
David Silverman, *Harvey Sacks: Social Science and Conversation Analysis*
Dennis Smith, *Zygmunt Bauman: Prophet of Postmodernity*
Nicholas H. Smith, *Charles Taylor: Meaning, Morals and Modernity*

Geoffrey Stokes, *Popper: Philosophy, Politics and Scientific Method*
Georgia Warnke, *Gadamer: Hermeneutics, Tradition and Reason*
James Williams, *Lyotard: Towards a Postmodern Philosophy*
Jonathan Wolff, *Robert Nozick: Property, Justice and the Minimal State*

Forthcoming

Maria Baghramian, *Hilary Putnam*
Sara Beardsworth, *Kristeva*
James Carey, *Innis and McLuhan*
Rosemary Cowan, *Cornell West: The Politics of Redemption*
George Crowder, *Isaiah Berlin: Liberty, Pluralism and Liberalism*
Thomas D'Andrea, *Alasdair MacIntyre*
Eric Dunning, *Norbert Elias*
Jocelyn Dunphy, *Paul Ricoeur*
Matthew Elton, *Daniel Dennett*
Nigel Gibson, *Frantz Fanon*
Espen Hammer, *Stanley Cavell*
Keith Hart, *C. L. R. James*
Sarah Kay, *Žižek: A Critical Introduction*
Paul Kelly, *Ronald Dworkin*
Carl Levy, *Antonio Gramsci*
Moya Lloyd, *Judith Butler*
Dermot Moran, *Edmund Husserl*
Steve Redhead, *Paul Virilio: Theorist for an Accelerated Culture*
Chris Rojek, *Stuart Hall and Cultural Studies*
Wes Sharrock and Rupert Read, *Kuhn*
Nicholas Walker, *Heidegger*

Contents

Acknowledgements

I am grateful to the Humanities Board of the British Academy and to the Research Office at Macquarie University for help in funding the research for this book. My research took me to many libraries, and it is a pleasure to thank the librarians at Middlesex University, McGill University, London School of Economics, Macquarie University, the British Library and the excellent National Library of Canada for their help. The research leave granted me by the Division of Society, Culture, Media and Philosophy at Macquarie University in the second semester of 2000 was invaluable in allowing me to complete the manuscript. Jay Bernstein offered me useful advice at the beginning of the project; I also thank Michael Kenny, Guy Laforest, Rüdiger Bubner and Matthew Smith for various acts of generosity related to the book. I have learned much from discussions of Taylor's work with Shane O'Neill, Hartmut Rosa, Paulo Costa, Jonathan Rée, Neil Levy, Nigel DeSouza, Irma Levomaki, and others I do not have space to mention. I am particularly grateful to Arto Laitinen, David Macarthur and Shane O'Neill for invaluable comments on draft chapters. Damion Buterin helped me format the bibliography. Thanks are due to Rebecca Harkin and Gill Motley at Polity for their great patience, and to Charles Taylor for his cooperation. Most of all, I would like to thank Susan Best for her love and support, as well as for suggesting all sorts of improvements to the text. The book is dedicated to her.

List of Abbreviations

Citations from the works listed below are referenced in the text. As a rule, when I cite a work included in Taylor's collections of philosophical papers for the first time, I give the original place and date of publication in the notes.

CM   *A Catholic Modernity?* ed. James L. Heft (Oxford: Oxford University Press, 1999).

EB   *The Explanation of Behaviour* (London: Routledge and Kegan Paul, 1964).

H   *Hegel* (Cambridge: Cambridge University Press, 1975).

HAL   *Human Agency and Language. Philosophical Papers, 1* (Cambridge: Cambridge University Press, 1985).

HMS   *Hegel and Modern Society* (Cambridge: Cambridge University Press, 1979).

MM   *The Malaise of Modernity* (Toronto: Anansi Press, 1991). Republished as *The Ethics of Authenticity* (Cambridge, Mass.: Harvard University Press, 1992).

MPR   *Multiculturalism and 'The Politics of Recognition'* (Princeton: Princeton University Press, 1992).

PA   *Philosophical Arguments* (Cambridge, Mass.: Harvard University Press, 1995).

PHS   *Philosophy and the Human Sciences. Philosophical Papers, 2* (Cambridge: Cambridge University Press, 1985).

PP   *The Pattern of Politics* (Toronto: McClelland and Stewart, 1970).

RS   *Reconciling the Solitudes: Essays on Canadian Federalism and Nationalism* (Montreal: McGill-Queens University Press, 1993).

SS   *Sources of the Self: The Making of the Modern Identity* (Cambridge: Cambridge University Press, 1989).

Introduction

Charles Taylor's reputation as a leading philosopher of his generation is based on his contributions to a wide range of fields. He has written influentially on the limits of mechanistic approaches to the study of human behaviour, on the role of interpretation and cross-cultural judgement in social science, on the contemporary relevance of German Romantic philosophy, and on the connection between the self and broadly speaking 'moral' concerns. Taylor is also a chief protagonist in the debate between liberals and communitarians in political theory, he is an influential figure in contemporary discussions of multiculturalism and democracy, and he has developed an original and provocative diagnosis of the maladies of the modern age. In the course of this book I shall consider Taylor's contributions to each of these areas. But I shall also present them as strands of a unified philosophical project. The project turns on an idea formulated by Maurice Merleau-Ponty, one of the philosophers most admired by Taylor, as follows: 'because we are in the world, we are *condemned to meaning*'.[1] We are condemned to meaning in the sense that human life generally, and modern life in particular, is structured by inescapable layers of meaning or significance. While in essence a simple thought, it is of enormous consequence for philosophy and the human sciences. Let me begin by spelling out how Taylor's complex project germinates from this simple core idea.

The Project

To understand Taylor's project we must first distinguish various levels at which the world appears meaningful or significant to human beings. Perhaps the most rudimentary level at which meaning appears is through *perception*. Like other animals, human beings have perceptual fields in which certain items stand out from the background. Generally, this happens when something relates to the desires and purposes of the perceiver. So, for instance, when the prey of an animal enters its sensory field, it stands out, it is significant to the predator as a potential source of satisfaction for its hunger. Human perception seems to have a similar structure. The mere fact that our perceptions are bound up with desires and purposes means that we perceive a world that is 'non-indifferent' for us,[2] and we refer to features of the world to which we are non-indifferent as bearing meaning or significance. Again like other animals, we *act* in ways that are directed by some desire or purpose, and we think we understand the meaning of an action when we grasp the desire or purpose it serves. But rather than 'perceiving' the meaning of an action, we often have to *interpret* it. Typically, we resort to interpretation when the purpose or desire directing an action strikes us as complex, opaque, strange or elusive. If we are to grasp the meaning, we must reflect and interpret creatively, perhaps under the guidance of a theory, or another person's point of view.

When we do submit a course of action to creative interpretation, we may find that it contains more (or perhaps less) significance than we initially supposed. But desires and purposes seem to have more or less significance in another way: some *matter* more, are deemed to be more *worth* having or more worth acting upon (or less worth having and less worth acting upon) than others. A fulfilling desire is more worth having, an enduring purpose more worth living by, than a superficial or whimsical one. Moreover, some desires and purposes also seem to function as *moral* standards. For example, if a close friend tells me something in confidence, I want to be true to my word, though I may well have a burning desire to tell someone else. I do not want to let my friend down, but I also do not want to let myself down by succumbing to the temptation. The thought that I would be letting myself down if I broke the confidence, like the thought that I would be wasting my life if my dominant desires and purposes were unfulfilling, suggests that something about my very identity is at stake here: the desires and purposes I seek to cultivate and act upon, and the standards that I recognize, reflect something about the kind of person I am and the person I aspire to be. In such cases we seem to be dealing with a qualitative difference between desires, purposes and ways of life: one kind of purpose or desire stands 'above' the other, it has its place in a 'higher', or more fully human, or more fully *my* way of life. In comparison to this higher mode, other, incompatible ways of living may seem empty, futile and shallow, or perhaps fraudulent, pious and hypocritical. Otherwise put, there seems to be an important class of desires and purposes that also serve as ideals: we seek them out – we are really motivated by them in our lives – but they are also normative for us, they set standards for us to live by. And in playing this joint role they help define our identity.

If some desires have more significance than others, if a life oriented by some purposes is more worthwhile than a life oriented by others, then it seems to make sense to ask what our highest desires and purposes might be. That is, we can reflect upon the nature of our highest values, of what we most aspire towards and strive for. Such reflection is notoriously difficult. It is not just that the content of these values – the things that most make a life worthwhile – is characteristically vague, elusive and resistant to precise formulation; though this is true and important enough. It is also complicated by the fact that they seem to vary enormously, and on at least three levels. An individual person might strive for different things at different stages in her life, and even at any one stage there may – and probably will – be some conflict between her ideals. At a second level, a particular culture is likely to contain diverse standards that are normative for the individuals within the culture. This, at any rate, seems to be the case in modern cultures, which are characterized by many different conceptions of what is most worthwhile in life. At a third level, different cultures seem to embody distinct, and often incompatible, standards. Within an individual's life, between individuals who share a culture, and between cultures themselves, there is conflict over the desires and purposes that are most worth pursuing.

At the same time, underlying this diversity, for many individuals – and in most, if not all, cultures – the meaning which a meaningful life enjoys seems to involve a sense of belonging to or participating in some life larger than the individual's own. For example, many people find meaning from a sense of being part of God's creation, from living in accordance with God's commands.

Others find it from living in a way which brings them close to nature, with or without God. And perhaps most pervasively, people find meaning from their sense of belonging to a particular group or community – be it a family, tribe, profession, trade, tradition, church, class, nation or whatever – with its own history and way of life. Subtract this sense of participating in or belonging to a reality beyond their own, and you take away what is most precious, or most highly valued, in these people's lives.

So meaning is not just something that objects in the world have when they relate to our desires and purposes: it is something that human beings seek *of* their desires and purposes, and more generally, their lives as a whole. We desire meaning in our lives, we find it natural to distinguish between a desirable, meaningful life and a life empty of meaning. Moreover, if we perceive there to be a radical gap between the meaning that exists in our actual lives – both taken in isolation and as part of the larger life of a society or culture – and the meaning that is *potentially* available to us as human beings, we can turn against this life in the hope of achieving a better future. That is to say, the conception we have of a truly worthwhile goal or purpose can be used to criticize the life that surrounds us, and it can help us imagine alternative forms of life in which these goals are realized. Our conception of what it is to lead a fulfilled life provides a *standard* for the surrounding form of life to meet. At the same time, the desire for meaning seems to take us outside ourselves: to another person, a family, a community, an idea, nature, God. Furthermore, to the extent that the 'higher' life is available to us – if not as actuality, then as a horizon of hope – it seems to require mediation. That is to say, it needs to be kept alive or nourished by some practice. Acts of creative imagination, experiences of wilderness and communion with nature, philosophical contemplation, rituals of remembrance, or, for believers in God, prayer would be examples of such practices. The point about them is that they enable people to live their lives by higher standards, or at least to keep those standards alive as real possibilities for the future.

We have been reflecting on some familiar ways in which the world appears meaningful to us. We began with perception: our perceptual field presents us with things to which we are 'non-indifferent', things that carry meaning for us by relating to our desires and purposes. Then we moved on to the level of action: our actions are directed by desires and purposes and as such appear meaningful or significant. The meaning often requires interpretation, and for this we use languages that can disclose or unravel more or less meaning. Meaning also appears at the ethical level: it is integral to the *good* life for human beings. This in turn took us to the political level, partly because we are dependent on non-familiar others for the good we have, partly because the good life can appear absent, as requiring a transformation of the larger social and cultural life that provides the context for, and in part constitutes, individual lives. And to this we can add one more level, where meaning is found not so much in the good life, or in hope for it, as in suffering and death. We could call the apprehension of meaning in suffering and death – that is, in things that go beyond or transcend the human desire for fulfilment and self-realization – the religious location of meaning.

But if this is how the world *appears* to us, is it how things stand in *reality*? Does the mere fact that we *do* talk of objects, thoughts, actions, language, values, and forms of life, even death, as bearers or potential bearers of meaning *entitle* us to talk that way? If we familiarly deploy the notion of meaning to make sense of human experience, *must* we do so? Is the concept of meaning really indispensable for understanding human existence, or can – indeed ought – we do without it?

Such questions can be raised at each of the levels of meaning we reflected upon. We might ordinarily talk as if perception picks out objects or happenings in the world that mean something to a perceiving subject, but are we really, say from a strict scientific point of view, entitled to use such language? Are we able to give an account of perception that dispenses with concepts of meaning and subjectivity? If mechanistic theories of perception are correct, and perceptions are no more than neural firings or complex computational processes, might not the idea of a perceiving subject open to a field of meanings be an illusion? In the case of actions, do we really need to apprehend them as realizers of desires and purposes in order to understand and explain them correctly? Or are such notions rather hindrances to a proper understanding of behaviour? And in the case of languages, does it really make sense to say that they have variable 'disclosive' powers? How is that possible? As we shall see in chapters 1, 2 and 3, these are the key issues at stake in Taylor's work in philosophical psychology, the philosophy of action and the philosophy of language.

When we move onto the ethical level, the controversy thickens further. Is it really the case that desires and purposes differ qualitatively? Or are all desires and purposes fundamentally homogeneous – say, as quantities of pleasure and pain – and hence, in principle, commensurable? And even if they can be qualitatively distinguished, can they really be ranked? If the goals people admire and strive for, or alternatively condemn as base and worthless, vary as much as we noted – that is, within individuals, between individuals within a culture, and between cultures – how can they be assessed objectively? What entitles any one individual, or any one culture, to criticize the standards of another individual or culture? Do such criticisms ever have rational backing? Even if goals and purposes can be ranked rationally in terms of their worth, does this tell us anything about morality? Or are moral values of a different kind again, with a force wholly independent of whatever it is that contributes to the good life for human beings? Is our self-realization at all relevant for understanding our obligations to others? We shall deal with Taylor's treatment of these questions, which are decisive for his moral philosophy and hermeneutic philosophy of social science, in chapters 4 and 5.

At the political level, is the idea that human community possesses intrinsic significance, independent of its utility for individuals, well-founded? Does it really make sense to say that the worth or meaning of a human life is 'constituted' by the community in which the individual is set? And even if it does, ought it to inform conceptions of how to transform human life for the better? Is it not rather an extremely dangerous idea, even an implicitly totalitarian one? Finally, are we justified in believing that some 'larger reality' is capable of conferring meaning or significance on human life? Or does modernity destroy such beliefs, exposing them as mere projections of our own subjective desires for meaning onto an objectively meaningless world? And what are we to make of the idea of a meaning that transcends life? What kind of justification can be given to the claim that there is such a meaning? Taylor's political philosophy, as well as his theory of modernity, are shaped by his thinking on these matters, as we shall see in chapters 6, 7 and 8.

So these are some of the big issues that will concern us in the forthcoming chapters. But merely having raised them, we are in a position to glean the thrust of Taylor's project. It has what we might call a negative element, and two interrelated positive components. The negative part is critical of a certain philosophical outlook or 'mindset' Taylor believes to be commonplace in the modern world. His name for it is 'naturalism'. For naturalism, the meaning-dimension of human existence is ultimately a realm of subjective illusion. It assumes that the layers of pragmatic, linguistic, moral, social and religious meaning that appear to constitute human agency are really something else, something that is only properly understood when considered from the point of view developed by modern natural science. The naturalist outlook, according to Taylor, motivates all sorts of still-born attempts at reducing meaning to non-meaning in psychology, linguistics, anthropology, sociology and political science, as well as in philosophy. Yet despite its failures, naturalism holds many in its grip. To be released from it, Taylor will argue, is to see that the undeniable advances in the natural sciences since the seventeenth century do nothing of themselves to alter our entitlement to think of human reality as bearing meaning, be it at the level of perception, action, ethics or politics. Taylor will try to convince us that there really is such a naturalist mindset at large in modernity, and that to expose it is to shift the burden of proof in much philosophical debate. This is the 'therapeutic' aim of Taylor's project.

The critique of naturalism feeds into a positive or constructive project, which Taylor calls 'philosophical anthropology'.[3] It involves two tasks which Taylor considers to be complementary: one transcendental (not to be confused with the religious meaning of the 'transcendent' introduced above), the other historical. The first, transcendental task is to investigate whether we are not only entitled but *required* to account for human reality in terms of the meanings made manifest in it. And Taylor will argue that in certain cases we are. He will argue that meanings have an *indispensable* place in human perception, action, ethics and politics. This will become the first principle of Taylor's philosophical anthropology. Then, having shown *that* meaning is a constitutive component of human reality, it remains to show *how* it is. But this question, Taylor maintains, can only be given a historical answer. Transcendental analysis must be refracted through historical understanding. The *historicity* of the meanings that inescapably structure human reality is the second central principle of the constructive project. The manner in which meanings appear is historically conditioned, hence historically variable. These two principles provide the framework for Taylor's investigations of the particular meanings that help shape the modern identity.

However, Taylor does not always distinguish clearly between the transcendental and historical levels of his project. And this lack of clarity, we shall see, is a source of confusion. Indeed, there is something confusing about the very expression 'philosophical anthropology' as a designation of the second of Taylor's constructive tasks. While it makes clear sense to call transcendental analysis of human subjectivity 'philosophical anthropology', perhaps a more apposite name for the investigation of historically specific features of subjectivity would be 'philosophical history'. When doing philosophical history, Taylor, like Foucault before him, is interested not so much in general truths about the human condition as in contingent constellations of human self-understanding, specifically those that prevail in the modern world. Furthermore, one of the reasons for engaging in such historical study is to correct the anthropological or universalist *mis*representation of contingent modes of self-understanding as invariable truths. While there is no reason in principle why transcendental and historical analysis must be at odds with each other, there is clearly a danger of conflict here. In following through his project, Taylor runs the risk of 'anthropologizing' or 'ontologizing' historically contingent features of subjectivity. Taylor is fully aware of this risk; indeed he is an adept at diagnosing the ontologizing fallacies of his naturalist opponents. But it is questionable whether he takes sufficient steps to avoid it himself. It is not always clear where Taylor's philosophical anthropology ends and where his philosophical history begins.

What about the relationship between the therapeutic and constructive components of Taylor's project? They are complementary in two important respects. First, Taylor's historical investigations try to locate the philosophical suspicion that meaning is an illusion within a broader cultural development stretching back to the onset of modernity. Taylor strives to reach an 'effective historical consciousness' of naturalism, to use Gadamer's expression,[4] and so to expose it as one possibility for human self-understanding amongst others. To see it that way is already to be considerably released from its grip. The second way in which Taylor's historical studies feed back into the therapeutic aspect of his project is by attempting to *retrieve* at least some of the aspirations that underlie naturalism. In Taylor's view, the culture of modernity, of which naturalism is a partial and inarticulate expression, is spiritually very demanding. The modern age measures itself against standards of human worth and fulfilment undreamed of in previous epochs; and its religions, its philosophy and especially its art provide a veritable powerhouse of moral energy for meeting those standards. At the same time, these sources of moral energy lie buried, and discontent brews over the shallowness of modern life, its flattened and impoverished modes of experience, its domination by technocratic and bureaucratic forms of rationality, and its amoral individualism. For Taylor, if we are to be cured of these maladies, we have to find ways of retrieving forgotten and neglected sources of meaning, of harnessing a suppressed potential for self-realization at a higher level.

Taylor's organizing idea, then, is that human reality is structured by layers of meaning. These layers inescapably shape how we perceive and act in the world. They also shape how we govern, criticize and transform ourselves. Contrary to naturalism, meaning persists even in the disenchanted world of modernity. But in crucial cases it does so in hidden, misunderstood and suppressed forms. Much modern philosophy contributes to this suppression, but philosophical reflection can also help recover the self-defining meanings of modernity. Taylor's own philosophical reflections – the melange of therapeutic and constructive argumentation, of transcendental and historical analyses that make up his philosophical work – are directed at such recovery. His aim is to understand the present within a horizon of possibilities of how the human spirit might more fully realize itself.

Style

I should now say something briefly about the manner in which Taylor undertakes his project. The first point to make is that Taylor's mode of philosophizing is problem-oriented rather than system-oriented. That is to say, he will write on a particular topic in accordance with what he takes the subject-matter to demand, rather than in accordance with the exigencies of systematization. Systematic philosophers – like Kant, Hegel or Sartre – must invent a special vocabulary, an armoury of technical terms, to differentiate the concepts which form the scaffold of their system. Of course they will also address specific problems. But the problems will be formulated in the vocabulary imposed by the requirements of the system, that is to say, in technical terms constructed by the philosopher for systematic purposes. This can make the writings of systematic philosophers difficult to understand. They call for reconstructive exegesis in a more familiar language. No such exegesis is required of Taylor's writings. Taylor is not a systematic philosopher: for better or worse, he has no interest in system-building, and there is no need for him to deploy a technical philosophical vocabulary. Taylor's writings are thus highly accessible and can be read with profit by anyone interested in the subject-matter. For someone with a project as philosophically ambitious as the one I have just outlined, this is quite unusual.[5]

The problem-centred, relatively jargon-free style of writing we find in Taylor's work is sometimes said to be a characteristic of analytic or Anglo-Saxon philosophy, as opposed to Continental philosophy. Taylor himself received the formal training of an analytic philosopher: after studying history at McGill University in Montreal, from 1952 to 1955 he studied philosophy, politics and economics at Oxford University, where he remained, as Fellow of All Souls College, until completing his doctorate in 1961. Whatever can be said of analytic philosophy in general, it is certainly true that in the Oxford milieu of the fifties philosophy was done in plain, unembellished English, with precisely defined terms and transparently sequenced arguments. The Oxford house-style suited Taylor and he would adopt it for his own purposes. But in other ways the Oxford environment was less commodious. Most notably, its philosophical culture was deeply hostile to the very traditions from which Taylor had to draw: broadly speaking, the phenomenological and dialectical traditions of Continental Europe. Against the Oxford grain, Taylor familiarized himself with the work of Hegel, Husserl, Heidegger and Merleau-Ponty. He was convinced that these Continental thinkers had much to offer his Oxford colleagues. Alas, his attempts at persuading them had little success.[6] Frustrated by their unwillingness to engage in dialogue with other traditions, Taylor rebuked the Oxford philosophers for their long-standing 'cultural solipsism' and for the 'contempt' in which they often held the Continentals.[7] On the other hand, Taylor also believed that the ideas of the Continental philosophers would need clarification and refinement to be of use. He would have to reformulate them in the analytical style of argumentation he felt comfortable with and respected. The upshot was that during the 1960s and 1970s Taylor came to assume the paradoxical role of the leading analytic exponent of Continental philosophy. He held this reputation both in the English-speaking world (particularly Britain) and, through translation of his works, in Continental Europe.

But it was not just the sidelining of Continental philosophy that Taylor had to contend with at Oxford. In the post-war period, philosophy began to establish itself as a specialized academic discipline with its own set of problems and procedures for answering them. As a result, it became cut off from traditionally allied modes of enquiry. The professional philosopher now had his own field and could get by, indeed ought to get by, without meddling amateurishly in the affairs of the social or behavioural scientists. The emergence of philosophy as a specialized discipline separated from the human sciences – by no means unique to Oxford but acutely manifest there – was a hindrance to Taylor's investigations. His interests did not fit the grid of the nascent academic bureaucracy, something that would remain true throughout his career. For instance, the publication that resulted from his doctoral dissertation – his first book, *The Explanation of Behaviour* (1964) – is as much a study in psychology as philosophy. The first part develops a conceptual framework for dealing with the general problem of explaining human behaviour; but the second, larger, part investigates the actual empirical evidence for a particular psychological theory. *Hegel* (1975) combines philosophical exegesis with historical and sociological reflections on the nature of modern society. *Sources of the Self* (1989) begins with an analytic framework for thinking about the self, but the bulk of the text consists of studies in the history of ideas, ideas of selfhood drawn from modern literature, art and theology as well as the conventional history of philosophy. None of these works is easy to classify. They are all 'philosophical', yet none of them is pure 'philosophy', as that term is used by bureaucrats of knowledge at least in the English-speaking world.

But if Taylor was uncomfortable with the Oxonian professionalization of philosophy on account of its isolating philosophy from other disciplines within the academy, he was even more uneasy with the professional philosopher's cultural and political isolation. From the beginning, Taylor has endeavoured to produce a living philosophy, one that has a purchase on the key issues of the times. It matters to Taylor that his ideas are able to connect with the concrete concerns of ordinary thinking people. He has written extensively for a non-specialized, non-academic readership. And he has been involved in several projects aimed at fostering open philosophical debate on issues of public interest. These activities are driven by the conviction – to his critics overly optimistic – that human beings have a capacity to transform themselves, and the societies in which they live, in the light of a deepened self-understanding. But they also serve as a reminder that Taylor's philosophy is fundamentally conceived in light of its *practical* goal: the realization of vital human goods in accordance with the best available interpretation. There are some goods, or desirable human goals, Taylor believes, that can be realized by the very act of authentic philosophical reflection, contemplation or interpretation. But most require a lot more: they are objects of struggle, they have to be fought for in the realm of praxis, not theory. One of these goods is democracy. Taylor has committed a good deal of his time to its realization, particularly in his native Quebec. Indeed, the practical goals of Taylor's philosophical project are bound up with a whole life's engagement in the political realm. I shall now say something about Taylor's life in politics.

Life in Politics

A twelfth-generation Quebecker, Taylor was born in Montreal in 1931. His mother's family was French-speaking, his father's English-speaking, and Taylor was raised bilingually: 'I am half-francophone, half-anglophone', he says.[8] Taylor recalls how, as a child, he found the two languages playing very different roles. The anglophones regarded English-speaking as a useful skill to possess, which enabled them to do lots of other things. But they saw nothing intrinsically important about English-speaking as such. This was not the case for the francophones. For them, speaking French had intrinsic, one might say 'existential', significance: it was indispensable to their sense of 'identity', to their own 'way of being' in the world.[9] It could not be replaced without destroying that identity and way of being. As we shall see, the idea, rooted in this childhood experience, that language 'expresses' and 'constitutes' identity will play a key role in Taylor's philosophy. So will the notion of plural identity, of identity constituted or expressed in multiple ways. Early on, it struck Taylor that even one's identity as a philosopher should be shaped by this idea. As a student of philosophy at Oxford University, Taylor had 'a spontaneous affinity with those people who had multiple ways of belonging (*appartenances*), who straddled two or more worlds'.[10] This was a quality he found in the two teachers who would have the most enduring influence on him, Isaiah Berlin and Iris Murdoch. It was also a characteristic of his own he could draw on for political advantage.

Taylor showed a knack for politics from a young age, as is nicely illustrated by the following episode. In 1954, while still an undergraduate at Balliol College, Taylor launched one of the first campaigns for banning the hydrogen bomb in Britain. As reported in *The Times* of London on 3 May 1954, Taylor framed a petition calling on the British government immediately and unilaterally to ban the bomb because the bomb was 'morally wrong' and banning it 'would reduce tension between east and west and could be a practical first step towards total disarmament'. The petition was distributed around the university. A week later, as also reported in *The*

Times, it was the subject of a 'heated two-hour discussion' amongst representatives of the university's student political, cultural and religious organizations. The terms of the petition were accepted, albeit in the slightly modified form proposed by the delegate of the 'right-wing Blue-Ribbon club', who had objected to Taylor's original formulation on the grounds that it would be treated as a 'near-communist smear'.[11] The Blue-Ribbon club representative, whom Taylor had wisely brought on board to pre-empt University obstruction of his campaign, was Michael Heseltine, future minister of defence and deputy prime minister of the United Kingdom.[12] On 21 June the petition, signed by 1,140 undergraduates of Oxford University, was presented by the Conservative member for Oxford at the House of Commons. It urged the Conservative government to make 'ever more vigorous efforts in securing disarmament, including the abolition of the hydrogen bomb and other such weapons of mass destruction through effective international control and inspection'.[13] This outcome was all the more remarkable considering that the left wing of the Labour opposition was at that time struggling with its own Party leadership for support of a similar petition. Three years later, aged just 26, Taylor became the first president of the Oxford University Campaign for Nuclear Disarmament.[14] In the first and arguably most successful years of CND this was a particularly effective branch of the organization.[15]

Upon the Soviet invasion of Hungary in October 1956, Taylor left Britain to spend six months with Hungarian student refugees in Vienna. On returning to Oxford in April 1957, he helped to establish the independent socialist journal *Universities and Left Review* (ULR).[16] The journal ran for seven issues before amalgamating with the *New Reasoner* to become the *New Left Review* in 1960. These journals and their associated clubs were the pivot of the New Left movement that flourished in Britain in the late 1950s. The ULR helped organize the first Easter march from London to Aldermaston (where research into nuclear weapons took place) in 1958, an event which was later to acquire key symbolic significance for the CND.[17] The ULR clubs gave active support to the establishment of CND and were responsible for what one historian described as London's 'second act of civil disobedience in the cause against the bomb' on the night of CND's launch in February 1958.[18] Taylor was adamant that the British New Left provide international leadership, and on Bastille Day 1958 the ULR organized a meeting which 'united on its platform representatives of the West German anti-nuclear mass campaign and the French neutralist Left, spokesmen

from the crushed Hungarian revolution and the anti-fascist generation of Spain'.[19] The event packed St Pancras Town Hall in London.
Such was the public support and enthusiasm for the New Left clubs,
discussion groups, rallies and other activities that a revolutionary
situation even suggested itself, at least to those involved. However,
by the time the golden age of the New Left came to an end in summer 1961 – a period which coincided exactly with Taylor's involvement – few of the movement's goals had been achieved.

In any case, Taylor's roots lay in 'Canada, Quebec, and Montreal',[20] and in 1961 he returned there. He immediately took up
teaching posts, lecturing in politics and philosophy at McGill University and the Université de Montréal, positions he occupied con-
tinuously over the next ten years. He also resumed his journalism,
working as an editor and correspondent for both francophone and
anglophone independent political journals throughout the 1960s.[21]
In 1961 the New Democratic Party (NDP) was formed in Canada,
and as the main party of the democratic left, Taylor joined with
enthusiasm. The NDP provided the institutional structure within
which Taylor pursued his political ideals throughout the 1960s. By
1963, Taylor had already stood as candidate for the NDP in two
federal elections, the second with the support of the future prime
minister of Canada, the late Pierre Elliott Trudeau.[22] Neither campaign was successful, but the NDP was weak in Quebec – indeed
at this stage it had no official party base in the province at all.
Quebec lacked a tradition of democratic socialist politics and its
emergent nationalist aspirations posed particular problems for a
party committed to preserving the Canadian federation, problems
the founding convention of the federal NDP had failed to resolve.
The NDP in Quebec therefore needed its own policy and ideological framework. In 1963 a provisional committee for the organization of NDP-Quebec was set up with Taylor on board.[23] In 1964,
Taylor composed a document that was to be used as the basis of the
federal party's platform on constitutional questions – in particular
relations between federal and provincial powers – in its campaign
at the forthcoming federal elections. Those elections took place in
November 1965 and Taylor once again stood as NDP candidate
for the Mont Royal riding in Montreal. Taylor was now one of the
NDP's four biggest hopes of making a breakthrough in Quebec. But
his campaign suffered a setback when it was announced that a
prominent left-of-centre Quebecker was to stand against him as
Liberal Party candidate: friend and former ally Trudeau, whom the
Liberal Party had recruited just weeks before the plebiscite with

the promise of a 'safe' seat.[24] Despite gaining more than twice the number of votes he received in 1962, and a percentage of the total vote well above average for the NDP in Quebec, Taylor could only manage second.[25] Hopes were high when Taylor ran for office one more time in the federal elections of 1968. But again Trudeau was to prove his undoing. This time it was Trudeau's appointment as leader of the Liberal Party just prior to the election, and the cult of personality of the 'New Young Leader' that characterized the campaign, that contributed to the most disappointing of Taylor's defeats.

In fact, the 1968 election was disastrous for the NDP as a whole. Its leader resigned and a successor had to be found. Taylor certainly seems to have had the credentials for the post: 'young, bilingual, attractive and articulate in a slightly academic way', as one historian of the NDP put it, Taylor 'was the favourite of the party leaders'.[26] And there was substance behind the image. On account of several documents he had drafted on a number of important issues – such as economic independence, nationalism, constitutional matters and urban revival[27] – by the end of the sixties Taylor was considered 'number one policy consultant within the New Democratic Party'.[28] Taylor's reputation was consolidated and broadened with the publication in 1970 of his book *The Pattern of Politics*, at once a stinging critique of Trudeau's liberalism and a powerful call for a socialist transformation of Canadian politics through the mediation of the NDP. Taylor's contribution to the party was not just intellectual: he had helped set up NDP-Quebec, he had been its vice-president for five years, and he had campaigned on the ground in four federal elections. But if Taylor were to accept the nomination for presidency of the federal party, a safe seat would have to be found for him. And that meant – given the results of the previous election – a seat outside Quebec. Taylor was reluctant to make such a move. Besides, by this time there was other business to sort out. Since his days at Oxford, Taylor had been working on a project he now wanted to bring to fruition: an extensive study of the work of Hegel. In 1971 he resigned as vice-president of NDP-Quebec, declined to stand for leadership of the federal party, and effectively withdrew from party politics. In 1973 he became professor of philosophy and political science at McGill, and in 1975 he published the six-hundred-page volume *Hegel*.

The book was a resounding success. In 1976 Taylor returned to Oxford as Chichele Professor of Social and Political Theory, but after three years political events again brought him back to Quebec. In

1979 the separatist Parti Québecois gained power in Quebec, and
a referendum on sovereignty association between Quebec and the
rest of Canada was summoned for the following year. Taylor returned to campaign against secession, and though the Quebeckers
voted 'non' to independence on that occasion, the question of
Quebec's constitutional status remained unresolved. In the twenty
and more years since, Taylor has contributed tirelessly to the
ongoing debate surrounding Canada's constitutional crisis. He gave
submissions to two Royal Commissions: the MacDonald Commission in 1985 on the Economic Union and Development Prospects
for Canada, and, between 1990 and 1992, the Bélanger-Campeau
Commission on the Political and Constitutional Future of Quebec.
During the two-year consultation period for the latter, Taylor
appeared twice before the National Assembly and prepared two
important documents on the nature and legitimacy of the Quebeckers' demands.[29] Taylor's apparent capacity for grasping and
mediating the conflicting claims and aspirations of Quebec's distinct cultural groups led to his recruitment onto the Conseil de la
Langue Française, the body responsible for advising the Quebec
government on its controversial language laws. Though sympathetic to the francophones' cause, Taylor – who resigned from the
Conseil at the end of 1996 – was by no means uncritical of attempts
to push French language rights too far.[30] But Taylor's opposition to
excessive and irrational Québecois militancy is most evident in the
impassioned polemic he launched against Jacques Parizeau, leader
of the Parti Québecois, in the aftermath of the 1995 referendum on
sovereignty. In Parizeau's mind, blame for his narrow defeat lay
squarely with the 'ethnic vote'.[31] Taylor ruthlessly dissected the prejudices and pathologies lying behind this view, and later, together
with a number of other Quebec intellectuals, publicly called for a
more open and honest post-referendum debate.[32]

I will consider Taylor's political views in chapters 6 and 7. Let me
bring this introduction to a close with a comment about the unity
of Taylor's political theory and political practice. As a number of
commentators have remarked, Taylor brings theory and practice
together in an unusually vivid way. He draws on his considerable
philosophical learning to illuminate key contemporary issues. And
his understanding of theoretical matters is informed by his considerable practical experience in politics. Taylor emphasizes the value
of the latter when he says that 'the unity of theory and practice is
true for me, in the sense that I have learnt enormously from my
involvement in politics. There are things I have learnt that I never

could have learnt in books.'[33] Yet Taylor's life in politics is strewn with defeats and disappointments. The radical hopes of the New Left vanished into air, the New Democratic Party failed to gain power, and Canada looks likely to disintegrate. However admirable, Taylor's political projects have been strikingly unsuccessful. While Taylor has gone as far as any contemporary intellectual in marrying theory and practice, theory has certainly done better out of the relationship.

1

Linguistic Philosophy and Phenomenology

At the core of Taylor's project is the conviction that human reality is structured, and in some sense constituted, by layers of meaning. This is the first principle of his philosophical anthropology. But how is it to be made compelling? What resources are available to Taylor for exploring, refining and vindicating this idea? When Taylor arrived at Oxford in 1953, he found himself in the midst of the 'linguistic revolution' in English philosophy. The revolutionary idea of the Oxford philosophers was the discovery of what they took to be the authentic method of philosophical enquiry. The cornerstone of the method was the mobilization, as P. F. Strawson put it, of 'a refined, thorough, and, above all, realistic awareness of the meaning of words'.[1] Such awareness would be secured by careful analysis of the ways in which words are used in ordinary language. The name given to the method was 'linguistic analysis' and the movement which practised it became known as 'ordinary language philosophy' and 'linguistic philosophy'. We have already seen that Taylor found the analytic style of Oxford philosophy to his liking. But what else did it have to offer him? Besides the manner of its philosophizing, what more was there to learn from the linguistic movement that flourished at Oxford in the fifties?

Linguistic Philosophy

The idea that philosophy was properly a matter of linguistic analysis seemed plausible given a certain conception of the objects of human enquiry. The linguistic philosophers inherited from the British empiricist tradition the view that human enquiry divides into two great branches: the empirical and the conceptual. According to this distinction, empirical enquiry concerns 'matters of fact'. It generates knowledge of facts and in this way it is informative about the world. Conceptual questions, by contrast, concern the meanings that thoughts and sentences must have in order to be able to convey facts at all. The focus of conceptual enquiry is the medium through which things appear in the world rather than the world itself. To be sure, this medium – language and thought – can also be the subject of empirical investigation: philology, for instance, is concerned with certain facts about language; psychology with facts about the mind.[2] But conceptual enquiry is distinct in that it aims to elucidate the ways in which we are able to mean things even in such factual accounts. And it is this clarification of sense-making activity that demarcates philosophy, as well as logic, from the empirical sciences. For Gilbert Ryle, J. L. Austin and the other pioneers of linguistic analysis, philosophy was circumscribed as conceptual enquiry. The specific task of philosophy was to elucidate the 'logic of language', to clarify the ways in which language users are able to make sense.

The linguistic philosophers were not alone in thinking that the aim of philosophy was the clarification of 'meanings': the view was common to all the philosophers of the analytic movement, from Russell and Moore to Wittgenstein and the logical positivists. But the Oxford philosophers of the fifties had a distinctive conception of how that aim was to be achieved and why it mattered.[3] It was to be achieved in the first place by recognizing the diversity of the ordinary sense-making activities of language users. Such acknowledgement, they believed, was fatal to the belief that all meaningful expressions had something in common – an 'essence' of meaning – that analysis could serve to display. In the second place it was to be achieved by taking heed of the particularity of the ways in which meaning is conveyed in ordinary language. Just as previous philosophers tended to view meaning as if it possessed an essence, they were also inclined to believe that a single model of analysis would suffice for conceptual clarification. The models elaborated by Russell and the young Wittgenstein, for instance, had been inspired by the exacting clarity and precision displayed by the discourses of mathematics and formal logic. But as the later Wittgenstein – another key figure in the linguistic movement – had shown, they were inappropriate as tools for elucidating the meaning of many ordinary linguistic expressions. Far from clarifying their meaning, such models ended up either obscuring or distorting them. The problem was even more evident in the approach to meaning taken by logical positivism. The logical positivists put forward a simple test for telling whether a proposition conveyed sense: if the proposition claimed to say anything about the world, it was either empirically verifiable or else literally nonsense. But again, this approach took a feature of one type of discourse – in this case natural science – and generalized it into a theory of meaning that rode roughshod over the particularities of ordinary language use.

By attending to the particular details of the diverse forms of speech, without prejudice about how language *must* be in order to be able to convey sense, the linguistic philosophers would avoid the errors of their predecessors. But Russell, the young Wittgenstein and the logical positivists were not the only ones to be misled by inappropriate models of the logic of language: the whole field of metaphysics had succumbed to them. Metaphysical discourse, as the linguistic philosophers understood it, begins with certain puzzles and paradoxes thrown up by the attempt to think generally and systematically about fundamental concepts such as 'truth', 'knowledge', 'mind' and 'reality'. In order to resolve the paradoxes, the metaphysician constructs a theory; say, a theory of Truth or a theory of Mind. But such theories invariably end up being 'shocking to common sense', and worse, they distort the very concepts that philosophy seeks to understand. There thus arises the need for vigilance: to identify and to correct the conceptual distortions that creep into metaphysical thinking. The linguistic philosophers did not suppose that alertness to the full range of meanings a concept ordinarily conveys would solve the problems that gave rise to metaphysics. The point was rather to 'dissolve' the problems, to remove the source of puzzlement and paradox by bringing the metaphysically troublesome concept back to its 'home' usage in ordinary language. Linguistic philosophy provided a kind of antidote to an intellectual disease – the construction of metaphysical illusions.

The revolutionary thrust of linguistic analysis owed much to this 'therapeutic' conception of the tasks of philosophy. The primary goal of Ryle's *The Concept of Mind* (1949) – one of the classic texts of the linguistic movement – was to dispel a long-standing philosophical myth about the nature of the mind by showing how it arises from confusion over the function of mental concepts. The myth in question was mind–body dualism: the idea that the mind is an entity, distinct from the body, which somehow resides invisibly within the body like a 'ghost in a machine'. According to Ryle, the myth was one of the main legacies of the seventeenth-century philosopher Descartes. In Ryle's view, it had since become so widely accepted that it even deserved to be called the 'official doctrine' of the mind. The dualist theory – or, as it is also called, 'Cartesian dualism' – maintains that every human being possesses both a mind and a body. The body belongs to the physical world, is open to external or public inspection, and is subject to the causal laws that determine the behaviour of physical objects. The body thus has an essentially machine-like existence. The mind, by contrast, has a spirit-like existence. The life of the mind is not accessible from the outside: it consists of a series of mental events or conscious episodes that are privately and incorrigibly witnessed 'from within', as it were, by whoever it is that experiences them. These mental events do not follow each other in the causally determinate way in which physical events unfold. They are not subject to mechanistic laws. The mind and body, according to the dualist doctrine, occupy different worlds and exist in fundamentally different ways. At the same time, they manage to interact and to be united in each individual human being. Each human being is an amalgam of the distinct entities of body and mind.

Ryle sought to show that the dualist theory of the mind was a paradigm case of metaphysical illusion. It is a commonplace of ordinary language, Ryle noted, to do things like communicate thoughts, express feelings, and ascribe intentions and motives to people. We do this without supposing that our interlocutor possesses an inner mental world, with its distinct mode of existence, in addition to a physical visible body. The idea that thoughts, feelings and intentions are properties of some invisible mental entity is a metaphysical construction designed to address questions like 'what kind of stuff is the mind made of?', 'what are its chief attributes?', or 'how does the mind enter into causal relations with other kinds of thing?'. But such questions, Ryle suggests, only make sense if we suppose that what we do when we ordinarily use mental concepts is describe states of affairs, or ascribe properties to things, or denominate particular kinds of object. And this is a mistake; a mistake in the categorization of the concepts we use, or as Ryle put it, a 'category-mistake'. It is a category-mistake because it involves allocating a set of concepts – in this case mental concepts – to the wrong 'logical type'. The mistake can be seen at work, Ryle argued, in a certain way of construing the difference between a statement that describes an action and a statement that ascribes a motive to the action. The mistaken construal is to take the latter as reporting a further fact, or as describing a 'mental' event that takes place in addition to the physical, observed event reported in the former statement. The confusion misleads the philosopher, who unlike the ordinary language user builds theories on the basis of conceptual categorization, into thinking that there is an inner series of mental events accompanying the publicly observable series of physical events. It then seems natural to posit the existence of an invisible entity, the mind, as their locus. According to Ryle, the very idea of the mind as an inner entity could only occur to someone who had failed to get the 'logical geography' of motive-ascription and kindred concepts clearly in view. Once it is in view, the questions that give rise to the Cartesian theory disappear, and with them the temptation to believe in anything like a 'ghost in the machine'.

The justification of the linguistic method did not lie solely in the therapeutic exposition of conceptual confusion. It also pointed the way to a new, constructive philosophy based on an appreciation of the semantic nuances at play in ordinary language. But enough has been said now to consider how Taylor situated himself in relation to his Oxford professors. In 'Phenomenology and Linguistic Analysis' (1959), an article Taylor published while preparing his dissertation at Oxford, he expresses ambivalence towards them.[4] The main lesson to be learned from the linguistic movement, he thinks, is the need for caution in adopting *reductive* modes of analysis. Reductive analysis attempts to translate the items of one language into those of another, in a way that brings out the true meaning of those items more fully, while eliminating the actual terms used in the original language. Clearly, the procedure is more likely to work if the meaning of the original terms is fairly straightforward. But the more complex, subtle and diverse the range of meanings conveyed in the original language, the less plausible the reductionist programme starts to look. By revealing the complexity of ordinary language, the linguistic philosophers helped to uncover deep problems facing reductionist theories of meaning, such as the one advanced by logical positivism. And as we shall see later, Taylor would deploy the same strategy when dealing with reductionist analyses of human action put forward by behaviourism. More generally, Taylor applauds the linguistic philosopher's reluctance to use *a priori* models of analysis. Rather than assuming in a dogmatic manner that language *must* be constituted in a certain way – that is, in accordance with some *a priori* model or requirement, like the capacity to name things or designate objects – we are properly enjoined by linguistic philosophy to look without fixed preconceptions at the language itself, at how it actually works. The linguistic philosophy rightly recommends alertness to the multiplicity of ways in which language is used and guardedness against the tendency to impose a single, homogenizing model. Taylor also has sympathy for the linguistic philosopher's diagnostic thesis that ill-conceived, theoretically motivated constraints about how things *must* be can be a grievous source of error. The identification of such *a priori* constraints, Taylor agrees, gives philosophy an important therapeutic role. It enables us to see how implausible philosophical theories go wrong. Finally, Taylor emphatically concurs with Ryle that the Cartesian theory of the mind is one such theory. That is, he agrees with Ryle that the 'ghost in the machine model' is popular yet wildly implausible, and that the way to tackle it is to expose, through a kind of therapeutic reflection, the source of the error that makes us vulnerable to it.

On the other hand, Taylor had at best a sanguine view of what the linguistic method alone could achieve. In the first place, the grounds of its anti-metaphysical stance seemed shaky. Taylor observed that if linguistic analysis were to deliver a genuine alternative to metaphysics, it would have to proceed in a manner that was free from metaphysical presuppositions itself. It might meet this requirement in one of two ways: either by being neutral with respect to substantive conceptions of the world, or by justifying – and not just leaving to dogma – the view of the world it does favour. It was clear to Taylor that linguistic analysis was not free from metaphysics in the former sense, as Ryle's account of the mind demonstrated. Ryle's method licenses him to discount conceptions of the mind that are inconsistent or absurd by the standards of ordinary linguistic usage. But it only makes sense to do this, Taylor pointed out, if it is already assumed that the use of mental terms in ordinary language provides the framework for a consistent theory. And this itself is a metaphysically loaded, and far from self-evident, conception of language. Moreover, even if a consistent theory could be extracted from ordinary language, there is little reason to think it would be a neutral one in the required sense. The idea that ordinary language clothes a neutral, common-sense view of the world that can serve as an arbiter between theories simply ignores the ways in which common sense is marked by traces of substantive scientific, metaphysical and theological belief. Common sense is not a repository of neutral or 'natural' beliefs and practices. It is a historically contingent way of interpreting and dealing with the world. The fact that it is a contingent product of history does not of course make it false. But it does make it metaphysically partial. Taylor concluded that the linguistic method was not free of presuppositions as the Oxford philosophers claimed. It was not without prejudice on the issue of how the world is constituted.

So if the linguistic method was really free of metaphysics, it had to be because the substantive views it does favour are not posited dogmatically. But this is just what does seem to happen when common sense or ordinary language usage is summoned to arbitrate disputes. The point of linguistic analysis is to uncover conceptual confusions, which it does by identifying discrepancies between ordinary usage and the revisionary one. But why assume, Taylor remarks, that conflict with common sense amounts to confusion? *Prima facie* arguments can be given for siding with common sense: for instance, that ordinary language has to prove itself in countless acts of communication, or that it embodies the practical knowledge of past generations. But such arguments themselves have to be proved against other rival claims and theories. And then, as Taylor points out, we are no longer engaged in linguistic analysis, but in some other form of argumentative discourse. Whether common sense can be vindicated at this level or not, the point is that linguistic analysis alone will not provide the answer. We have to move beyond the standards of argument warranted by the linguistic method itself. Without such argument, common sense is taken on trust, and the method rests on a dogma. With such argument, the method has recourse to other, non-linguistic forms of reasoning. But linguistic analysis tells us little about how such reasoning proceeds.

This is a serious weakness, in Taylor's view, because we ought to be concerned not just with the meaning of fundamental concepts but with their *validity*. It is a major concern of Taylor's that, in limiting itself to the description of the use of concepts in ordinary language, linguistic analysis is insufficiently *critical*. By leaving language 'as it is', it made it impossible to assess the concepts embedded in given linguistic practices or 'language games'. Neither the mere description of the varieties of linguistic usage, nor the 'dissolution of paradox' that the proper classification of concepts is supposed to bring, allows us to focus on the decisive issue of validity. Consequently, as Taylor put it, the linguistic method generated a 'strange permissiveness and tolerance as to the content of belief'.[5] Any violation of ordinary usage – say, of 'the language of religious worship in its appropriate place in the proper "language game"' – is left 'not above, but beyond reproach'.[6] But validity that is earned so easily – by simply having its own place in a linguistic practice – is 'hardly an interesting kind of validity'. For it simply bypasses the fundamental problem that many of the concepts and beliefs that feature in different forms of linguistic usage are incompatible with each other. It is here, with *competing* bodies of doctrine about the constitution of reality, with *rival* models of knowledge, and the inflection of such doctrines and models in common-sense belief, that most philosophical problems arise. They do not typically arise, as the linguistic philosophers maintained, from paradoxes arising from the misunderstanding of the logic of language as such. If philosophy has a therapeutic role – and the widespread grip of Cartesian dualism suggests it does – then it will have to take these features into account and not just confused models of conceptual anatomy.

The linguistic method was thus hardly well suited for Taylor's project. First, it made the question of human subjectivity accessible only indirectly through what we are entitled to say about it in ordinary language. It therefore imposed arbitrary limits on how the constitution of human subjectivity could be explored. Second, it failed to think historically. This flaw was evident in the naturalization of common sense. Third, its model of argumentation was insufficiently precise. It was implicitly committed to a certain ontological or metaphysical view but was unable to justify it. Moreover, the linguistic method left it a mystery how argument over such issues is to proceed at all. It seemed to leave them in an argumentative limbo: they were neither purely conceptual questions (and so philosophical) nor purely factual questions (and so scientific ones). In Taylor's view, these drawbacks were all symptoms of a fundamental 'lack of reflection' about method. To be sure, linguistic philosophy had taken some steps in the right direction. It avoided the hasty reductionism and apriorism of earlier models of analysis. And it had identified deeply mistaken interpretations of philosophical concepts, such as the Cartesian account of the mind. But it was unable to identify the proper source of the mistaken conception – its diagnosis was inaccurate – and it failed to provide a viable, convincing alternative. If Taylor was to make good his own project he would have to draw on richer resources than the linguistic method could provide.

Merleau-Ponty's Phenomenology

He found one such resource in existential phenomenology. Taylor was especially drawn to the work of the French phenomenologist Maurice Merleau-Ponty. Here, the young Taylor found a philosopher addressing the issues that most concerned him with a directness and profundity unlike anything coming from the analytic school. In his first published philosophical article, Taylor attempted to convey to an audience acquainted with linguistic philosophy the neglected insights of Merleau-Ponty's masterpiece, *Phenomenology of Perception*.[7] In doing so, Taylor sketched an approach to the theory of human subjectivity, or philosophical anthropology, that would go on to serve him throughout his writings. While this approach is arrived at largely by way of an exegetical reconstruction of Merleau-Ponty's text, it is also not without criticism of certain general claims made on behalf of the phenomenological method. Taylor is convinced that once it is freed of these questionable methodological assumptions, phenomenology is a vital resource for the theory of subjectivity.

The phenomenological method is the name Merleau-Ponty gives, following Edmund Husserl, to a set of procedures aimed at reaching an undistorted description of experience. The first principle of the method is the 'phenomenological reduction', otherwise known as the 'eidetic reduction' or *epoche*. The phenomenological reduction addresses the following problem: how are we to reflect in a manner that is true to the experience being reflected upon? It is important, if we are aiming at a description of experience as it is prior to reflection, that the model our reflection brings to the experience comes from the original experience itself, and not some extraneous source. But such sources are what we do rely on when we ordinarily engage in reflection: we draw, for example, on common sense, on everyday uses of language, and on what we deem prevailing scientific theories entitle us to believe. If we are to be genuinely open to the content of original experience, if we are to arrive at an undistorted or 'pure' description of it, we have to be prepared to 'bracket' or 'suspend' the natural assumptions of ordinary reflection. And this is what the phenomenological reduction enjoins: we are to put on hold our 'natural attitude' in order 'to make reflection emulate the unreflective life of consciousness'.[8]

According to the phenomenologists, the *epoche* yields a fundamental principle about the nature of conscious life – its intentionality. The intentionality thesis is often formulated as the idea that consciousness is always consciousness 'of' something. Consciousness, according to this formulation, is essentially 'directed towards' something. It is about some object, and this relation of 'aboutness' gives content to specific conscious states. Phenomenologists do indeed propound such a thesis, but as Taylor notes, they give it a distinctive twist by further claiming that 'whatever is an object of consciousness has "significance" '.[9] To say that consciousness is intentional is thus to say more about it than that it is directed towards an object: it implies a relation not just of mere aboutness, but aboutness 'for' something. This interpretation of intentionality – we might call it 'intentionality-as-significance' – is elaborated in detail by Merleau-Ponty. In the unreflective life of the perceiver, Merleau-Ponty observed, objects and events appear in a 'phenomenonal field'. The phenomenal field is not just whatever is present to consciousness, like shapes, sizes, sounds or colours. It also includes things that, in the very act of being perceived, 'refer' beyond themselves. So, for instance, we perceive objects or events as 'hiding' others or 'bringing them into view', as being 'in front of' or 'behind' other things, as 'the beginning of' or 'end of' some object or event. Such percepts refer to or 'announce' other things that are not actual or present. The mere fact that we are able to use such terms as 'announce' and 'refer' to describe percepts suggests that perception has intentionality-as-significance. Taylor is fond of citing Merleau-Ponty's formula that 'each part (of the phenomenonal field) announces more than it contains and . . . thus is already laden with significance'.[10] But a further crucial determinant of the 'logic' or 'syntax' peculiar to the phenomenonal field is the purposes of the perceiver. A phenomenonal object will appear, for example, as 'a means to' or 'in the way of' an end desired by the perceiving subject. In this sense, perception is closely tied to the way in which perceivers are 'at grips' with their environment. Perception is thus intimately connected to behaviour. Indeed, according to Taylor's interpretation of the intentionality thesis, 'perceptual and behavioural space are one . . . our behavioural know-how enters into what we see' and this too 'invests the phenomenonal field with significance'.[11]

Merleau-Ponty's intentionality thesis attempts to capture an essential structure of lived experience. He proposes it as a corrective to the two classical accounts of perception found in empiricism and Kantianism. He first considers the empiricist theory. According to this theory, the basic units of experience are sensations, or, as they are also called, 'impressions' or 'sense-data'. Sense-impressions are allegedly discrete atoms of experience that provide the raw material for our empirical knowledge. When we see something like a red patch, or smell the odour of a petal, we seem to be in touch with a primitive realm of 'mute' experience furnished directly by the senses. Such sense-data seem to present themselves immediately – the perceiving subject seems quite passive in relation to them – and they seem to give to the perceiver self-contained, fully determinate pieces of sensory information. According to the empiricist theory, the perceptions we commonly experience are combinations of sense-impressions processed by complex psychological mechanisms, such as memory, learning and association. So, for instance, I may perceive the red patch as a flag on account of its combination with other sense-data, such as shape and movement, which, through psychological association, memory and the like, I have learned to identify and respond to in certain ways.

But is this what perception is really like? Merleau-Ponty first pointed out – as, incidentally, did J. L. Austin over in Oxford – that it is hard to identify anything in our perceptual experience with the properties allegedly possessed by the sense-data. Sense-data are supposed to be discrete and determinate, but it is extremely difficult to establish the precise boundaries of our perceptions. We perceive particular objects against a background with no definite limits. The perceptual field is not rigidly framed like a tableau. It is bounded more in the manner of a horizon: indeterminate, out of focus, shifting with the eye of the viewer and never quite caught up by it. At the centre of the perceptual field, where we are able to focus, we find objects with hidden aspects, objects that present themselves as open to perceptual exploration, and so as not fully *present* to any one point of view. Taking these points into account, the sense-data theory seems to distort the quality of the phenomenon in two basic ways. On the one hand, it distorts by making the phenomenon an element of consciousness rather than something before consciousness (treating the phenomenon 'as a mute impression when it always has a meaning'); and on the other hand, it misconstrues the object or meaning as 'always fully determinate'.[12]

Merleau-Ponty then considers the classical alternative to empiricism – the so-called 'intellectualist' or 'rationalist' theory of the Kantian school. The Kantian view grants that the objects we perceive possess meaning, in the sense that they stand in logical, and not just contingent psychological, relations to each other. In perception, we apprehend objects, properties and events *as* something. But the ground of the meaning-bearing quality of perception, on the Kantian view, is our faculty of *judgement*. Perceptions possess meaning because they display the logical form of judgements. According to this view, a perception has sense in the same way a proposition does. We grasp objects and events *as* something on account of the fact that whatever is given in perception is submitted *a priori* to the conceptualizing activity of the mind – a view Kant expressed in the famous formula 'intuitions without concepts are blind'.[13]

But while Kantianism marks some advance on empiricism, Merleau-Ponty is far from satisfied with it. One obvious weakness with the theory is that we often perceive, and perceive 'as', without being able to put what we perceive into words. So it would seem that prior to any conceptualization of experience, prior to experience assuming the form of a judgement 'that', perception gives us access to a world, a pre-predicative or pre-objective world. But the problem with the Kantian view is not just that it rules out the possibility of such access to the world. It overlooks the radically perspectival nature of perception, on account of which it differs fundamentally from judgement. Percepts, like propositions, convey information about what we perceive. But unlike judgements, they are also essentially informative about where the subject stands in relation to what is perceived. Furthermore, the propositional model of perception – like the sense-data account – fails to appreciate the richness of the phenomenonal field, a richness and diversity 'that no finite series of statements can do justice to'.[14] There is always an excess, surplus or remainder to the described content of a perception. The perceptual field provides a 'background' against which particular perceptions can be thematized or predicatively described. But that thematization and predicative description cannot be extended to cover the background itself. Descriptions of the predicative world are based on a never fully describable, never fully explicit, perceptual, pre-predicative or pre-objective world. This failure to acknowledge the dependence of the explicit on the implicit, of the predicative on the pre-predicative, is a serious shortcoming of the intellectualist theory.

The phenomena of perception are thus poorly described by both the classical accounts. If we attend to the phenomena, we see that the perceptual field presents meaningful relations, a world, to the perceiving subject prior to any non-perceptual input. Drawing on its *own* resources – and not by relying on some non-perceptual mechanism of psychological association, conceptual schematization or interpretation – the perceiving subject finds itself *in* a world, that is to say, in the midst of phenomena that bear meaningful relations to each other and to the subject of perception. The classical accounts can miss all this, Merleau-Ponty suggested, because they allow considerations that are appropriate for scientific *theorizing* about perception to intrude into and to distort the description of perception itself. They take it for granted that perception will deliver knowledge of itself in the same way it reliably delivers knowledge of physical objects, without noticing that physical objects and percepts have very different appearances. This is particularly evident in the empiricist theory. Our physiological knowledge suggests that visual perception involves a causal process by which light strikes the retina, triggering a neural response transmitted via the optic nerve to the visual cortex, where it is decoded and 'experienced' as, say, a patch of white. Impressed by this, the sense-data theorist is then led into depicting the percept as possessing properties belonging to causal processes generally. But it only takes a moment of 'pure' reflection to see that our experience does not possess these properties. Blinded by the natural attitude, the classical account freezes the perception of a meaning – which in its essence is indeterminate, multiply expressible, and in normal cases practically orienting for a subject – into a discrete, inert, self-contained sensory datum. As Taylor puts it in a formulation I shall return to in the next chapter, the empiricist theory *reifies* the mind. Not only is this false, but to the extent that it helps shape the experience it purports to describe, it is oppressive.

Taylor is wholly sympathetic to Merleau-Ponty's critique of theories of perception that unwittingly objectify, and thereby falsify, lived experience. He also shares Merleau-Ponty's view that a phenomenology of perception is needed as a reminder that lived experience is intelligible as a field of meanings and not, as the standard accounts maintain, as a series of causally related entities or events. Taylor agrees that the pre-objective world of lived human experience has a different kind of intelligibility from the objective world presented by scientific theory, a point that the dominant modern philosophies of perception overlook. But Merleau-Ponty goes further by saying that the objective world, or the world disclosed to common sense and scientific reflection, has its *genesis* in the pre-objective world. He claims that the pre-objective or pre-predicative mode of being in the world is in some sense originary or primordial. The objective apprehension of things, including scientific representations, is in this sense conditioned or derivative. The phenomenological reduction suggests we should see objective representations as one amongst many ways of making human experience explicit, rather than as the primary or essential mode of experience. One of the tasks of Merleau-Ponty's genetic phenomenology, then, is to show how the idea of an objective fact or experience, the kind of fact and experience made explicit in everyday discourse and the theoretical languages of science and philosophy, presupposes the pre-predicative, pre-objective experience of the world. According to Merleau-Ponty, the pre-objective world is the 'condition of possibility' of the known world. It functions, as Taylor puts it, as the 'transcendental implicate' of objective discourse.[15]

Taylor is wholly sympathetic to this idea too. Indeed, much of Taylor's own work on epistemology will simply recapitulate, from various angles, Merleau-Ponty's thesis that objective experience is only intelligible when set against a background, pre-predicative disclosure of the world. But he will also try to overcome a difficulty he sees in Merleau-Ponty's construal of the status of phenomenological descriptions. Ideally, the phenomenological reduction would bracket everything that does not belong to the original experience itself. The phenomenologist aims at a 'pure' description of the original experience, that is, a description of the pre-objective, pre-propositional, presuppositionless world inhabited by the pre-reflective subject. Only such a putatively pure and presuppositionless description would be able to give voice to the world as it is prior to objectification. If we are really to reach back to the origins or genesis of the structures that underwrite ordinary language and scientific discourse, we would seem to require a kind of *self-authenticating* descriptive vocabulary, one that owed nothing whatsoever to the everyday and scientific languages that presuppose it. But as Taylor notes, there is something inherently paradoxical about the very idea of a presuppositionless description. Certainly, Merleau-Ponty's own phenomenological descriptions are by no means presupposition-free: 'they are inescapably on the predicative side of the "predicative"–"pre-predicative" boundary line'.[16] They therefore take for granted the applicability to experience of at least some categories. The fact that they do take certain categories for granted should not be interpreted as a fault in Merleau-Ponty's *application* of the phenomenological method. For the suspension of one set of categories for the sake of describing an original experience will always put into play other modes of expression, which in turn can be submitted to a phenomenological reduction. It follows that no description is ever immune from revision, a point affirmed by Merleau-Ponty himself when he writes that 'no phenomenological reduction is ever complete'. But if descriptions of original experience are never complete, if they are always revisable in the light of a further phenomenological reduction, then no description of original experience is ever really 'pure'. 'Applied to itself', Taylor remarks, 'the theory of phenomenological reduction underlying the claim that description can be "pure" leads to a vicious regress.'[17]

Taylor is thus sceptical of the very enterprise of pure pre-suppositionless description. It seems to presume that some self-authenticating descriptive vocabulary is there to be found if only the phenomenologist looks hard enough. It is as if there were some foundational, self-evidently true way of talking about experience that can be settled, with certainty, once and for all. Admittedly, Merleau-Ponty himself typically turns away from such a foundationalist understanding of the phenomenological enterprise. He speaks, for instance, of the phenomenologist's predicament as that of a perpetual beginner. And this would suggest there is no way of reaching some final purity. But the concession has implications which Taylor – at least in his early writings – claims Merleau-Ponty does not adequately address. For if the originary content given to the pre-objective experience is intrinsically open to revision, what entitles us to reach any philosophical conclusions about the nature of the subject who experiences? It is one thing to say that the pre-objective world is a necessary presupposition of objective descriptions. But it is quite another to say that the concrete description of the pre-objective world offered by the phenomenologist itself enjoys philosophical necessity. For it to have such necessity, it would have to possess a finality and purity it can never obtain. We should therefore not look to phenomenology for the 'authentically true categories' in which human reality is described once and for all. Simply in virtue of being possible objects of a further phenomenological reduction, the descriptive categories are revisable and corrigible. And if they are always open to revision they have no strictly necessary status.

Furthermore, the phenomenological method does not provide us with a guide for dealing with *conflicts* of description. If several different and conflicting descriptions can plausibly be given of some phenomenon, how are we to choose between them? The phenomenological method as such does not seem to offer much help here. It does not clarify how the validity of competing basic descriptions is to be determined. The argument will be 'genetic', it will involve tracing categories back to phenomenologically more primitive ones. But again, it is not clear what *ontological* conclusions can be established by such argument. Phenomenology may be well-suited to clarifying the structure of lived experience. But it does not make it clear why the structures of experience it discloses should be the ultimate consideration for determining what the experiencing subject really *is*.

We might recall that Taylor expressed a similar reservation about linguistic analysis. By attending to the details of actual language use, the linguistic philosophers had demonstrated the irreducible diversity of meaning-making activity. This was an important correction to the homogenizing tendency of previous theories of meaning, especially logical positivism. But the downside of this approach was that having shown the plurality of language games it was unable to say how we can arbitrate between them. This is no small drawback from Taylor's point of view, for if philosophical anthropology is to have any credibility it must have something to say about what makes one theory of subjectivity better than another. We must have some standards for accepting or discounting rival accounts. Likewise, the phenomenological method rightly enjoins us to attend to the rich and inexhaustible details of lived experience. In doing so it corrects the implausibly static constructions of experience found in the classical empiricist and Kantian accounts. But it fails to make clear how the purity or primordiality of phenomenological categories is to be decided. It too fails to reflect adequately on how validity is possible in the theory of subjectivity.

This problem would not be so pressing if it were not for the fact that a powerful rival to *all* accounts of subjectivity that deploy categories of meaning has emerged in modern times. The rival theory insists on the one hand that our ontological commitments should be decided by what is ultimate at the level of *explanation*. On the other hand, it claims that what is ultimate at the level of explanation is not at all like the way things appear either in ordinary language or in primordial lived experience. Rather, it is the way things look to the modern natural scientist. Modern science explains nature without taking into account the 'meaning' nature appears to have from the standpoint of common sense or phenomenology. And why, proponents of the rival account argue, should human nature be different? Are not the meanings objects have for us redundant from a scientific point of view? If they are, they have no place in the ultimate order of explanation and so no role to play in an ontology of the human or philosophical anthropology. This is the central thesis of mechanism. Taylor's chief philosophical preoccupation in the sixties was to be a kind of settling of accounts with mechanism.

2

Science, Action and the Mind

In the first part of *The Explanation of Behaviour*, Taylor argues that the scientific revolution changed the way we think about the sciences of nature in two fundamental respects. Both concern the procedures by which we judge the legitimacy and appropriateness of scientific explanations. If we are to appreciate the challenge modern science poses for the thesis that human reality is structured and constituted by dimensions of meaning, Taylor thinks, we must first get these procedures into focus.

For Taylor, the first relevant feature of modern natural science concerns *the form of the laws* invoked in its explanations. According to pre-eighteenth-century, 'Aristotelian' science, there are two kinds of answer to the question 'why did something happen?'. They correspond to two fundamentally different kinds of change. First, there are changes that take place 'naturally'. Naturally occurring change takes place in accordance with a 'normal' pattern of development. Events of this kind are explained in terms of an intrinsic tendency to result in a given end-state. This end-state, the *telos*, is the reason why the event happened, its 'final' cause. Explanations that invoked such end-states, so-called teleological explanations, were integral to Aristotelian astronomy, physics, chemistry and biology. The second kind of change is explained 'mechanistically', that is, in terms of the causal 'push' of the antecedent state of affairs, or the 'efficient' cause. A change explained in this manner was 'accidental' in the sense that it departed from the normal, intrinsic – and in that sense necessary – unfolding of the phenomenon. The mechanistic explanation works by invoking 'interfering factors' that disrupt the inherent tendencies of the system under investigation.

The applicability of a metaphysical – not just metaphorical – distinction between normal and abnormal, natural and unnatural, proper and improper states of a physical system, states in which the telos of the system is either realized or not, is a defining characteristic of Aristotelian science. There is thus a basic asymmetry of explanation built into that science. Aristotelian science thereby bestows a kind of ontological privilege on certain end-states of natural systems: it distinguishes between end-states occurring 'by design' and those occurring 'by chance'. It supposes there to be a natural order – a press of events, so to speak – in the mould of which phenomena unfold. Since particular phenomena cannot be explained without invoking the larger order in which they are naturally set, the science brings with it a holist ontology. That is to say, since the *explanans* (the thing doing the explaining) of teleological explanations makes reference to the whole of which the *explanandum* (the thing to be explained) is a part, the whole in a sense possesses a greater, or more fundamental, degree of reality than the part.

It therefore makes no sense, on the Aristotelian view, to think of reality as an aggregate of atoms interacting according to mechanistic laws. But this changes with the scientific revolution of the seventeenth century. For Galileo, all physical changes are intelligible according to the same mechanical principles. Galilean science allows us to talk of a difference between natural and unnatural states of physical systems only metaphorically. It warns us against supposing there is any *real* distinction between them. The Galilean scientist assumes that once all the mechanical laws at work in the universe have been discovered, no more explaining needs to be done. Taylor illustrates this key difference between Galilean and Aristotelian science by contrasting the former's principle of inertia with the latter's doctrine of natural and violent motion. Unlike the principle of natural and violent motion, the principle of inertia performs its explanatory task without the assumption of a privileged end-state. It does not, as Taylor states, 'single out any particular direction in which bodies naturally tend to move', and in this sense it is neutral between the different states of the system (*EB* 23). Explanations by the principle of inertia do not posit any particular end-state as privileged, one bound to arise 'by design' unless blocked by contingent countervailing factors. An ontologically differentiated teleological science is replaced 'by a homogeneous science of nature' in which all differences are explained 'in terms of the same set of antecedent variables' (*EB* 25).

In Taylor's view, the eradication of explanatory asymmetry had two effects that proved decisive for the long-term success of Galilean science. First, it rendered superfluous attempts to preserve established teleological laws by *ad hoc* modifications in the light of new observations. The new science requires no *further* explanations in terms of necessary 'intrinsic tendencies' and contingent 'external factors'. Why complicate explanations by adding final causes when efficient causes suffice? Why add 'intrinsic tendencies' to the furniture of the universe if its behaviour can be explained without recourse to them? Second, debunking the assumption of asymmetry opened up established baselines of teleological explanation to renewed mechanistic scrutiny. The asymmetry between the normal and the abnormal, between the proper and the improper, served to protect the putative 'normal' or 'proper' states of physical systems from rigorous scientific investigation. The normal state was after all the baseline in terms of which observed phenomena were explained. But as soon as its 'natural' status is lost, a presumed baseline state becomes as amenable to explanation in terms of universal mechanistic laws as any other state of affairs. An unprecedented expansion of systematic empirical enquiry thereby became possible.

So the first aspect of the scientific revolution highlighted by Taylor is the subsumption of teleological explanations under mechanistic ones. But this change in the form of the laws invoked by the new science also came packaged with new conceptions of scientific *evidence* and *objectivity*. According to Taylor's account, only 'discrete units of information, each of which could be as it is even if all the others were different', are allowed to count as evidence for the new science; each piece of scientific information 'must be identifiable independently of its connections with any others' (*EB* 11). This stringently atomistic standard of evidence was tied to an exacting new ideal of objectivity, which found expression in the distinction between 'primary' and 'secondary' qualities. Roughly speaking, primary qualities – like mass, velocity and number – inhere in physical objects themselves. They are the way they are independently of any subjective point of view on them. Accordingly, a correct description of the primary qualities of an object is bound to draw the agreement of all competent – that is to say, fully objective – enquirers. Following Thomas Nagel, Taylor refers to this understanding of the objective point of view as the 'view from nowhere'.[1]

And following Bernard Williams, he calls the account of reality articulated purely in primary quality terms the 'absolute conception'.[2] The view from nowhere is a totally subject-independent, absolutely neutral perspective on the world. The 'requirement of absoluteness', in Taylor's words, is that 'the task of science is to give an account of the world as it is independently of the meanings it might have for human subjects, or how it figures in their experience'.[3] In striving for an absolute conception of reality, science eschews subject-related properties and so divests the laws of nature of all traces of human partiality and subjective significance.

The standard of absolute objectivity is all the more difficult to meet because human enquirers – so advocates of the new science believed – are disposed to construe elements of their own subjectivity as if they were intrinsic features of the objective world. This is true of the so-called secondary qualities. By contrast to primary qualities, secondary qualities – like colour, sound and warmth – are not independently subsisting qualities of objects at all. Rather, they exist only as objects of experience for conscious subjects. There would be no such thing as colour, for instance, if it were not for the existence of beings (like humans) with certain kinds of functioning sensory apparatus. A rose petal reflects light of a certain wave length and looks red to the human eye. If there were roses but no humans (or animals equipped with similar sensory apparatus) to see them, the petals would still reflect light, they would still possess primary qualities, but they would have no redness. Secondary qualities are therefore 'subject-dependent' and as such are not a legitimate feature of objective accounts of reality. They seem objective only because human enquirers are prone to project their own subjective states onto the world itself. And this is how the champions of the new science diagnosed the mistakes of their Aristotelian predecessors. The putative 'intrinsic purposes' of Aristotelian science were retheorized as projections of human designs onto nature. The 'enchanted' character of the Aristotelian depiction of nature arose from this projection of human meanings onto the world. In order to foreclose the 'spiritualization' of nature perpetrated by pre-modern science, genuine scientists must adopt a resolutely disengaged perspective on the world.

The shift to an absolute conception of objectivity is of course closely linked to the priority ceded to mechanistic explanation. On the old, 'enchanted' conception of nature, the universe embodies purposes which recur throughout nature as 'Ideas' or 'archetypes'. The universe, or more accurately the cosmos, has a 'meaning' constituted by these purposes. But as Taylor puts it, 'the idea of a meaningful order is inseparably bound up with that of final causes since it posits that the furniture of the universe is as it is and develops as it does in order to embody these ideas; the order is the ultimate explanation' (H 5). The idea of nature displaying a meaningful order is bound up with the 'semiological ontologies' that formed the basis of the European world view dominant right up to the scientific revolution. The new science, with its eschewal of teleological explanations, its method of disengagement, and its aspiration to an absolutely subject-independent language, eventually submitted this outlook to overwhelming cognitive pressure. While this pressure may not have been the decisive factor in the success of the new scientific world view – indeed Taylor was later to argue emphatically that it was not – Taylor seems to have few doubts that mechanistic explanations from an absolute point of view have proved their cognitive worth. He finds it impossible to deny that the procedure adopted by post-Galilean science is the appropriate one at least for understanding the laws of nature.

Having outlined the basic shape of modern scientific explanations, Taylor's next step is to examine their appropriateness for determining how things stand with human beings. But before we turn to that, it is worth pausing for a moment to consider what exactly Taylor is claiming about the modern natural sciences. If we take Taylor to be offering a sketch of how, in general terms, modern science actually proceeds, he seems to be guilty of a considerable oversimplification. Clifford Geertz has made this kind of complaint.[4] He is astonished that Taylor – who in other ways is alert to the historical contingency of human practices – can propose a conception of the natural sciences that is so insensitive to the details of historical change. Taylor's conception is at best, as Geertz puts it, a 'temporally frozen' sketch of the natural sciences as they appeared at the opening stages of the scientific revolution, one which Taylor assumes without argument is applicable to all subsequent scientific developments. Geertz has little trouble showing that the guiding image of Taylor's reconstruction – a 'once-and-for-all foundational act' separating Galilean science from its pre-revolutionary precursors – does not stand up to the historical evidence. But in addition to being historically inaccurate, Taylor's depiction also ignores the present state of the natural sciences. If he were to attend to this, Geertz submits, he would see that recent developments in the sciences, especially in biology and physics, do not fit the stereotype of the post-Galilean paradigm. It is hard to argue with Geertz on either of these points. In Taylor's defence, it could be said that his account is narrower in ambition than the one Geertz attributes to him, as it is concerned only with a transition in the general form of acceptable scientific theories rather than wholesale changes in scientific practice. After Galileo, Taylor is saying, theories proposing mechanistic explanations of nature, couched in absolute terms, tended to be more successful than teleological explanations, until they eventually became the norm in science. But this does not mean there is no room for variation around the mechanistic norm. This interpretation makes Taylor's view more plausible, but it does not make it less vulnerable to the objection that it is put forward with scant support from the history of science. Even here, there is something peculiarly formal and ahistorical about Taylor's approach to science.

A different kind of objection could be made to Taylor's account: that science not only does not fit Taylor's description but could not do so. For there is something incoherent, it could be said, in the idea that science adopts a 'view from nowhere'. Richard Rorty has made an objection of this sort.[5] For Rorty, scientific enquiry, like any other kind, is radically perspectival. Scientific theories are tools for meeting human purposes and these purposes vary with the perspective of the enquirer. The validity of theories is to be measured in terms of their success in getting things done rather than their approximation to some chimerical absolute conception of the world. For Rorty, Taylor's model is not so much empirically inaccurate as conceptually or philosophically confused. But up to a point, Taylor is prepared to embrace Rorty's idea. Taylor can draw on Merleau-Ponty's genetic phenomenology to argue that the language of scientific theories (as well as observations) arises out of a background of practical concerns from which it is impossible to disengage fully. The terms of the absolute account should be considered as a 'refinement, development, and correction of our ordinary understanding', an understanding which emerges through a practical engagement with things, rather than as designative of pure, absolutely disengaged observations.[6] But this does not entail that validity is just pragmatic, or that modern science differs from its predecessor merely in the different purposes it serves. In Taylor's so-called 'realist' view of science, scientific theories emerge from a sphere of practical concerns. But they succeed as theories by identifying the real causal powers inherent in different kinds of substance. Incidentally, this realist view leaves it an open question whether causal powers are teleological or mechanistic. It is not up to the philosophy of science to decide what causal powers there are in the world. However, Taylor is convinced that a certain *kind* of teleology, one that ascribes subject-related properties to physical substance, is no longer credible. Taylor's philosophical realism leaves open the possibility of a teleological science of nature that neither regresses to the old Aristotelian 'enchanted' view nor intrudes into the human sciences in a destructive way. Having said that, it is not a possibility Taylor himself explores.

There is another way of reading Taylor's depiction of the scientific revolution worth mentioning. It could be that Taylor's primary concern is not so much with reconstructing actual developments in scientific practice as with articulating an 'imaginary' of what the scientific revolution achieved. Its purpose, perhaps, is to capture something about how science has been imagined in modern culture – by philosophers and perhaps scientists themselves – rather than to represent how things actually stand with science. More specifically, Taylor's account could be read as a presentation of the image of science possessed by those who take up a mechanistic approach to the study of human reality. So, for instance, the atomistic conception of evidence is not to be read as Taylor's own view of how modern science works. It is rather a feature of a dominant image of scientific enquiry. But on the one hand, if this were the case, we would expect Taylor to be more critical of mechanism even in the sciences of nature. And on the other, there are features of the image Taylor presents that certainly do correspond to his own views. Most notably, he accepts that science did advance on the basis of its adoption of the absolute standpoint. This is actually what happened in science and it helps explain its success. If Taylor is just sketching an image of science, then, he does not do enough to distinguish those features of it to which he subscribes from those he rejects. Taylor does not clearly differentiate his reconstruction of the image from his reconstruction of the reality, and this generates confusion.

Explaining Behaviour

Whatever the limits of Taylor's model of the natural sciences, it is widely agreed that the substitution of teleological explanations for mechanistic ones was a decisive step in the evolution of modern physics. And it can hardly be doubted that the success of modern physics has encouraged the belief that all the sciences, in their mature form, ought to be able to account for their object-domain exclusively in mechanistic terms. The behaviourist movement in psychology, pioneered early in the twentieth century by J. B. Watson and later developed by psychologists such as C. L. Hull and B. F. Skinner, set out to apply this principle to the study of human behaviour. A mature science of human behaviour, in their view, would be mechanistic at its most basic level of explanation. It would account for behaviour in terms of laws that share the same form as those invoked so successfully in mechanistic explanations of nature. If behaviourism were to prove itself as a science, it would destroy the idea that purposiveness, intentionality and meaning had any real explanatory value, and so any role in determining the ultimate nature of human beings. Taylor thus felt compelled to tackle the claims of behaviourism head on. Was behaviourism borne out by the evidence? How successful was it as a scientific research programme?[7]

Behaviourism attempts to give a mechanistic account of behaviour at the 'molar' level, that is, at the level of the gross movements of an organism and the organism's environment. As such, it is not a science of the physiological mechanisms that determine behaviour. It just assumes that correlations holding at the molar level have a material basis in the operations of the brain and the nervous system. The most distinctive characteristic of mechanistic correlations at the molar level is that they make no reference to any 'inner' process that appears to take place 'behind' the behaviour. Behaviourists include phenomena like purpose and intention in this class. Purposes and intentions, according to behaviourism, are part of a hypothetical 'inner world' of organisms. This inner world may have a role to play in everyday, so-called 'folk-psychological' explanations of behaviour, but a mechanistic science can have no recourse to it. Instead of explaining the behaviour of organisms in terms of redundant purposes or intentions, behaviourism attempts, as Taylor put it, 'to link the environment, characterized non-intentionally as the "stimulus", and behaviour, characterized non-intentionally in terms of movement as the "response", in a series of law-like correlations'.[8] According to so-called 'S–R' theory, animal behaviour is best explained in terms of non-intentionally or 'intrinsically' describable responses to stimuli. Animals learn to behave in one way rather than another, according to this theory, because one kind of movement or response rather than another to an environmental stimulus is favoured by 'positive reinforcements' or rewards. The aim of psychological science, on the behaviourist view, is to identify the S–R connections on the basis of which animals learn to behave. In principle, all behaviour could be explained in terms of this basic model, that is, as functions of laws holding between kinds of stimulus and kinds of effect. For behaviourism, the determinants of behaviour reside not in the goals of a purposive subject but in contingently operating S–R mechanisms.

Taylor's case against behaviourism rests on three principal contentions. The first is that behaviourism does not establish on *a priori* grounds that the form of the laws governing human behaviour – indeed the behaviour of any animate being – is mechanistic. The second is that while it *is* true *a priori* that explanations of behaviour in terms of purpose – that is, the particular class of teleological explanation behaviourism wants to supersede – are *incompatible* with mechanistic explanations, this consideration alone does not rule out the *possibility* of a mechanistic science of behaviour. These two contentions converge on the thesis that we must look to the experimental sciences themselves to see whether behaviour is better explained in mechanistic or teleological terms. Taylor's third contention is that if we do this, we see that the scientific evidence provided by behaviourist research fails to support the hypothesis that the laws governing animal behaviour are, as a matter of fact, mechanistic. As almost no one now subscribes to behaviourism, much of Taylor's critique is of antiquated interest.[9] However, the structure of Taylor's argument is worth rehearsing for a couple of reasons. First, while behaviourism is long dead, the belief that the laws governing human behaviour *must* be mechanistic in form is still very much alive. The very idea that teleological explanations might have a place in the science of behaviour is no less an anathema to many philosophers and psychologists now than it was in the heyday of behaviourism. Taylor's defence of teleology from *a priori* attack therefore retains contemporary relevance. Second, Taylor's argument is as much about the relationship between scientific explanation and conceptual analysis as it is about behaviourism narrowly defined. And this issue remains of central interest to philosophy. Without going into too much detail then, let us consider Taylor's three main claims in turn.

Taylor attributes the behaviourist conviction that behaviour *must* be explicable in mechanistic terms to its underpinning empiricist epistemology. According to this epistemology, a statement or doctrine must be empirically verifiable if it is to count as genuine knowledge. Scientific concepts should avoid reference to anything non-observable: if, as in the case of theoretical concepts, they do not designate observables directly, they should be translatable via 'correspondence rules' to an 'operational definition' which would give them a definite and unambiguous empirical content. We are entitled to talk of cause and effect in cases where we observe constant conjunctions of unambiguous empirical data. On this view, no observed empirical event, no 'matter of fact', entails another. We can always imagine the facts to be otherwise; thinking the facts to be otherwise does not embroil us in logical contradiction. But in the world as we observe it, events of one type are regularly, in some cases invariably, succeeded by events of another type. In such cases, we legitimately speak of the antecedent event as the cause of the consequent.

The empiricist theory of knowledge rules out purposive explanations of behaviour at a general and particular level. First, it puts in jeopardy the whole class of teleological explanations. This is because teleological explanations do not seem to be verifiable in the required sense. On the one hand, goals – or that for the sake of which something happens – are not observable as antecedent entities. And if they are not observable as antecedent entities, it is impossible, on the empiricist view, to verify explanations purporting to identify them. However, Taylor points out that this particular objection to teleological explanations rests on a misunderstanding. For the 'purpose' invoked in a teleological explanation, the inherent tendency of a system towards some end which does the explanatory work, is not a distinct entity functioning as a causal antecedent. Only on the assumption that ends feature as efficient causes of mechanistic explanations do they take on occult, non-observable characteristics. But this is to miss the point about the distinctive *form* of teleological laws. As Taylor puts it: 'a teleological explanation is marked out as such by the form of its laws and not by reliance on some special type of antecedent variable' (*EB* 98). A teleological law is in play whenever the occurrence of an event is 'dependent on that event's being required for some end' (*EB* 9). The cause of an event which conforms to a teleological law is the state of a system relative to a certain goal. And whether the state of a system does require a given event if a certain goal is to be obtained is quite observable. Taylor also examines some attempts at reformulating teleological correlations in non-teleological terms, but finds them all wanting. He concludes that the idea that the telos or purpose of a system, which refers simply to a property of an integrated whole or irreducible totality, must be translatable out of explanatory laws remains unproven.

It follows that we need more than the empiricist theory of knowledge to justify the abandonment of teleological explanation. But the behaviourist's *a priori* rejection of the explanatory function of consciousness or intentionality – that is, the particular sub-class of teleological explanation it aims to supersede – rests on similar epistemological considerations. A science of behaviour, on the empiricist theory, will have a maximally clear and unambiguous observation language. There can be no room for disagreement on the meaning of the terms that make up such a language. The data must be describable in a manner that is neutral with regard to the theories under observational test. Indeed, only if there is such a language are differing 'theory-languages' testable. For the behaviourists, intentional psychological concepts like 'expecting' or 'desiring' are like the concepts of a theoretical language: lacking a clear, unambiguous empirical content, they are not directly and incontestably verifiable. There is no neutral, non-question-begging or interpretation-free way of testing propositions containing them. Whether a given state of affairs is a case of expecting or wanting is never self-evident. It always requires a degree of interpretative input from the observer. But genuine evidence ought not to leave room for such input. Indeed the whole point of scientific evidence is that it decides between the different interpretations scientists or observers give to phenomena. Hence a major task of behaviourism is to show how psychological concepts ordinarily used to identify behaviour can be translated into a language with a clear and unambiguous empirical content. But in this, Taylor argues, they are no more successful than in the general task of reducing teleological to non-teleological relations. The translation of psychological terms into standardized or operationalized 'physical thing' definitions always involves a revision of the meaning of the psychological concept. It transforms the empirical content of the psychological concept because it has to 'cut off the empirical implications of the concept at a certain point, and thus to alter its meaning' (*EB* 82). The meaning of psychological concepts is thus never equivalent to their operationalized or translated revisions.

The empiricist epistemology behind psychological behaviourism, Taylor maintains, leads it to *assume* that a successful reduction can be carried through of teleological to mechanistic forms of law, and of psychological or intentional terms to a 'physical thing', non-psychological language. However, the further Taylor examines the details of the reductionist proposals the more implausible they begin to look. Behaviourism can overlook or side-step the difficulties facing the various reductions because of an overriding confidence in empiricist epistemology: if empiricism is valid, we *must* be able to prosecute the reductions no matter what the difficulty. Hence it is not the outcomes of the reductionist project that engender conviction. Rather, it is the steadfastness of the empiricist model of knowledge – and its associated concept of experience – that stands behind the project. But behaviourism does not argue for its empiricist premises, and it certainly has not established their truth. Taylor's point is that to the extent that the empiricist theory of knowledge and experience goes unargued for, behaviourism rests on a dogma.

So much for Taylor's first contention, that behaviourism does not succeed in ruling out *a priori* teleological and intentional modes of explanation. What about the second? We noted that behaviourism is hostile not just to teleological explanations in general, but specifically to that type of teleological explanation in which the 'telos' or goal is defined in terms of purpose or intentionality. Now according to Taylor, it is a defining characteristic of the concept of *action* that it is applied to cases of behaviour explicable in terms of intentionality. By analysing the concept of action as it features in ordinary language, Taylor shows that behaviour counts as action whenever the presence of an intention or purpose plays a role in bringing about the behaviour. Action, as opposed to non-action or mere movement, is behaviour directed towards a goal that is intended or desired by an agent. The occurrence of movements that bring about an end does not normally suffice for us to speak of an action taking place. Action involves an intention to realize that end-state as a goal. Of course, actions need not succeed in bringing about the end for the sake of which they occur. The goal towards which the behaviour is directed is not always achieved, and may not even be conscious. But at least in ordinary language, the concepts of 'achieve', 'attempt' and 'goal' are closely connected and always have application in the sphere of action rather than 'non-action' or mere movement.

In so far as we speak of a piece of behaviour as action, then, we are committed to explaining the behaviour in terms of an intention for the sake of which it occurs. But, according to Taylor, that means ruling out another kind of explanation – namely, an explanation that accounts for the behaviour in terms of laws governing movement. A piece of behaviour cannot at the same time be subject to laws governing action and laws governing movement, for if it were subject to laws governing movement, it would not be a case of action at all, at least according to the meaning that concept possesses in ordinary language. This is really Taylor's central claim in *The Explanation of Behaviour*, the so-called 'incompatibility thesis': 'our accounting for behaviour by a law governing movement is incompatible with its being brought about by the intention or purpose concerned, and therefore with its being action in the usual sense of the term'(*EB* 44). If a piece of behaviour is explicable in terms of laws governing movement, it must be subject to different laws – to laws that possess a different form – from those that govern behaviour classifiable as action.

So in Taylor's view, the distinction between action and non-action as drawn in ordinary language is incompatible with the determination of behaviour by mechanistic laws. But it does not follow from this – as the linguistic philosophers were prone to believe – that the mechanist or behaviourist theory could be dismissed as conceptually confused. If the positivists were too quick in ruling out teleological explanation for not meeting the standards implicit in mechanistic science, the linguistic philosophers were just as hasty in ruling out mechanistic explanations for not meeting the standards implicit in the ordinary concept of action. For it was conceivable that the standards implicit in the ordinary use of the concept of action could be rendered invalid by empirical scientific research. As Taylor put it, 'the fact that we make the distinction we do between action and non-action offers no guarantee that the type of explanation it presupposes is the correct one, that the conceptual scheme in which it is embedded is the correct one' (*EB* 48). In other words, the conceptual scheme in which intention provides the criterion for making the distinction may itself turn out to be false. One day, we might see that we have 'mischaracterized' the distinction between action and non-action in ordinary language, just as we now know that the Aristotelian science mischaracterized the distinction between natural and violent motion (*EB* 46). There can be no *a priori* assurance against this possibility.

Having set aside the *a priori* arguments for and against the dissolution of purposive explanation, Taylor turns to the phenomena themselves to see if they support the behaviourist theory. For Taylor, it is an empirical question whether behaviour is to be explained at the most basic level by the form of teleological laws called laws governing action or by non-teleological laws governing movement (*EB* 101). And a detailed examination of the evidence suggests to Taylor that the basic laws are not mechanistic in kind, at least not in the way proposed by behaviourism. Taylor summed up his findings as follows: 'faced with the insightful and innovative behaviour of some mammals in learning situations, behaviourists turned more and more to ad hoc hypotheses . . . which became increasingly difficult to give a clear empirical meaning to' (*HAL* 125).[10] In other words, he claims to find just those signs of degenerate science that Galileo exposed in Aristotelianism. He turns the tables on the behaviourist by arguing that on the very criteria of post-Galilean objective scientific investigation, in the name of which behaviourism justifies itself *a priori* as a science, it should itself be rejected. Taylor concludes with the satisfying irony that by the very criteria of success installed by the Galilean revolution psychological behaviourism is refuted.[11]

The Explanation of Behaviour thus offered an alternative to two fundamentally dogmatic approaches to the study of action – behaviourism and ordinary language philosophy. Against the behaviourists, Taylor argued that mechanism in the explanation of action needs to be earned rather than assumed on the basis of epistemological considerations or success in other domains. Against the linguistic philosophers, he wants to open up debate about the direction a science of behaviour should take. Far from arguing that human behaviour is somehow exempt from scientific laws, he wants to foreground the issue of the form of the laws to be investigated by such a science.

The inability of some of Taylor's contemporaries to see beyond the alternatives of 'pro-science' positivism and 'anti-science' ordinary language philosophy is reflected in the critical responses *The Explanation of Behaviour* received. On the one hand, there were those who read Taylor's book as an attack on scientific progress, as imposing arbitrary restrictions on scientific research. One critic even described Taylor's attitude towards experimental psychology as 'reminiscent of the attitude of the Roman Catholic Church towards physics and genetics at certain stages in history'.[12] Others came to the opposite conclusion, accusing Taylor of conceding too much to science, of leaving intentionality and the validity of purposive concepts hostage to the contingencies of empirical science.[13] But if the former camp had little to stand on, the latter at least had a point. For as Richard Bernstein noted, Taylor's position seemed to imply the highly implausible claim that 'someday we might discover that we never really performed an action, or did anything intentionally'.[14] It suggested that ordinary language explanations might be systematically false. Whether this is the view actually put forward in *The Explanation of Behaviour* is unclear. Certainly, Taylor denies it elsewhere. In 'How is Mechanism Conceivable?' (1971), for instance, he writes that a 'complete mechanistic account of human behaviour' which branded 'as erroneous the whole range of our ordinary explanations' is 'unthinkable' (*HAL* 169). But by comparing the distinction between action and non-action with the *hypothetical* distinction between natural and violent motion, in *The Explanation of Behaviour* Taylor does seem committed to the untenable view Bernstein attributes to him. For if our characterization of the distinction between action and non-action was just as falsifiable as the Aristotelian distinction between violent and natural motion, then surely we could one day discover that our 'actions' were really something else, namely complex movements. If there is something unintelligible here – and this is where the ordinary language philosophers have their point – it is because the distinction between action and non-action does not function as a hypothesis at all.[15]

Another criticism commonly made of Taylor's book was that it smuggles in an unwanted dualism. By allowing an ontology of the human to be determined on the basis of teleology, it isolates humans metaphysically from the rest of nature, which is subject to laws of a mechanistic form. But, in defence of Taylor, it could be argued that the whole thrust of *The Explanation of Behaviour* is to expose the continuity that exists between humans and other sentient life forms. Taylor himself wrote that he was investigating 'that aspect in which human and animal behaviour is alike', or commonly thought to be alike (*EB* 70). Taylor objects strongly to the thesis, sometimes put forward by the linguistic philosophers, that the linguistic ability to ascribe mental states to oneself is criterial for agency. This view excludes the agency of animals by stipulation, but it goes against substantial empirical evidence, including the experimental results of behaviourist scientists. These results indicate that explanations by purpose are apt for the behaviour of at least the higher animals. They suggest that animals do display intentionality. On the other hand, it is also true that linguistic ability raises intentionality to a qualitatively higher level. As non-language users, animals clearly cannot act upon desires described or interpreted in one way or another. While animals can be ascribed consciousness, it is a consciousness of a 'reduced' or diminished sort, one which is only of immediate relevance to behaviour. In later work, Taylor will attend to those aspects of agency that are unique to human beings. The capacity to act on interpreted and evaluated desires is indeed crucial for human agency. But here, the point Taylor stresses is that agency as such is not uniquely human, and certainly not the basis for introducing a metaphysical distinction between the natural world and some supernatural space occupied by human beings.

Let me now try to relate these conclusions back to Taylor's understanding of the tasks facing philosophical anthropology, as originally inspired by Merleau-Ponty. We can read *The Explanation of Behaviour* as a systematic study in 'retrieving the phenomena' of embodied subjectivity. The perceptual experience of an embodied subject, we have seen, places the subject in a field of meanings. The perceived object refers beyond itself; it 'announces more than it contains'; it has a meaning that is never fully self-present or made explicit without remainder. The significance of objects depends on their appearing against a never fully enclosed or explicited background. The embodied subject is also essentially at grips with this world. Its perceptions are bound up with possible actions, and its actions are bound up with desires and purposes. An embodied subject is an agent, a being capable of action, whose capacities for action structure its world. But in the behaviourist's universe there are no embodied subjects. There are no fields of meaning, only correlations of stimuli and responses; no actions, only movements. It is important to see that Taylor has no *a priori* objection to this as a scientific hypothesis. It is an empirical matter whether, at the ultimate level of explanation, we need anything more than notions like stimuli, responses and movement to explain behaviour. If we do not, then there is a sense in which there are indeed no embodied subjects. Taylor scrutinizes the evidence and finds that it does not support the hypothesis. The mechanisms invoked by behaviourism do not do their explaining well, they are inadequate as explananda – a judgement borne out by the subsequent decline of behaviourism as a research programme in psychology. But a more fundamental flaw with behaviourism, according to Taylor, is that it does not even *begin* with embodied subjects. The phenomena of embodied subjectivity are excluded from the start because they do not meet the requirements of the data language of the science. So the phenomena of embodiment are not just ruled out as explanatory. They are overlooked as something *needing* explaining. Behaviourism begins with a conception of what we are entitled to speak of from a scientific point of view. But if we begin there, it will never occur to us that there are embodied subjects to account for at all. We need to be reminded, in the face of behaviourism and its epistemological foundation, that there are such subjects.

However, it should also be said that the conclusions reached by *The Explanation of Behaviour* are quite limited in view of the broader ambitions of Taylor's project. First, with its emphasis on the critique of the behaviourist version of mechanism, its implications for a constructive philosophical anthropology, in which the category of meaning or intentionality is secured, are left undeveloped. One might think that 'teleological laws' would have a place in such an anthropology. But besides invoking psychoanalysis as a general exemplar of teleological and intentional theory (*EB* 271), at no point does Taylor specify what the laws might be. And in the absence of any such determination, one is entitled to ask what relevance conceptual analysis has for the theory of subjectivity in its constructive aspect.[16] Second, as Taylor himself conceded, even the critical or therapeutic force of his analysis is weakened by its exclusive focus on peripheralist rather than centralist functionalisms. Centralist functionalisms account for intentional states not by the condition of the environment but by neurophysiological laws. Taylor's conclusion, that the peripheralist account of learning needs notions like 'the way the animal sees the situation', the 'general capacity to get around', 'know-how' and 'the notion of a natural tendency to engage in a certain type of activity or pursue certain goals' (*EB* 269), has little impact on more recent centralist theories. They do not impinge on the doctrine that succeeded behaviourism as the dominant research programme of mechanistic psychology – cognitive science. We shall look at Taylor's position in relation to cognitive science's approach to human subjectivity below.

The Reification of Mind

Taylor expresses two basic reservations about cognitive science. The first concerns its underlying concept of the 'mental'. This concept, in Taylor's view, misconstrues the nature of human experience. The misconstrual is also present in psychological behaviourism, indeed it manifests itself in all sorts of contemporary theories of the mind. The concept Taylor targets is formulated most clearly not in cognitive science itself – which, he thinks, often just takes it for granted – but in classical Cartesianism and empiricism, the philosophical precursors not just of cognitive science but of a spectrum of positions in the philosophy of mind. While Taylor's strategy here is partly reminiscent of Ryle's attack on Descartes' concept of mind, it in fact shows more affinity to Merleau-Ponty's critique of the classical doctrines of perception. Taylor's second concern is actually not with cognitive science as such, but with certain 'hegemonic' claims

made on its behalf. There can be no questioning the great explanatory power of cognitive science within a certain domain. But Taylor
has serious doubts about its explanatory competence as a more
comprehensive theory.

The fundamental feature of the concept of mind or the mental
which causes havoc, according to Taylor, is that it is arrived at by
what he calls the 'inner/outer' sorting.[17] Descartes' formulation of
this taxonomic principle has been the most influential, but it is by
no means the only one. Descartes, as we know, saw a clear distinction between mental states and physical events. The class of mental
states consisted of whatever is an object of conscious awareness.
A wide range of phenomena – Taylor mentions 'tickles and pains,
feelings of nausea and discomfort, emotional experiences like love
or anger, perceptions of the world around us, and thoughts of
the most abstract and exalted character'[18] – seemed to Descartes to
have one thing in common: they are *present* to the subject who
thinks them. They are intelligible in their own terms, without
reference to anything in the other sorting box, the 'outer' world.
The characteristic of self-presence demarcates the inner world of
experience – the mind – from the external world, however that is
conceived. The two worlds, the mental and the non-mental, are
intelligible independent of each other. Classical empiricism gave
a different formulation to essentially the same contrast. On the
empiricist model, the mind is furnished by 'ideas' acquired chiefly
through perception. But the ideas themselves are like Cartesian
thoughts in being the self-present content of an independently intelligible inner world. Once the mind is conceived in this way the
question of its relation to the outer world naturally arises. Arguably,
this is the central question of the 'philosophy of mind'. For dualists,
the inner world is grounded in something real – a mental substance
– existing independently of the physical world. For materialists,
there is no such ground. But in both kinds of theory, we have experience construed in a way that makes it *contingently* connected to
its embodied locus. That is to say, both theories construe experience
as intelligible without referring to the meanings disclosed to an
embodied subject.

It should come as no surprise that it is this construal of experience, rather than a particular position *within* the philosophy of
mind, that Taylor finds objectionable.[19] His response is to try to
show how we so readily find ourselves in the grip of the mentalist
picture. What, he asks, makes the inner/outer sorting so compelling
when it delivers a conception of the mind that is so alien to our pre-

reflective experience? As we saw in the last chapter, Ryle posed a similar question in response to the 'ghost in the machine' doctrine of the mind. How is it that we end up believing in such an absurdity? For Ryle, the diagnosis lay in category-mistakes. The 'mind–body problem', according to Ryle, calls less for solution than 'dissolution'. And the way to do this is by tidying up our logical geography. Taylor's tactics, however, are different. In Taylor's view, we need to do more than identify conceptual confusions if we are to liberate ourselves from the mentalist picture. We require a better account of the motivation behind the inner/outer sorting, of why it seems so natural despite its manifest shortcomings.

To get to the bottom of this, Taylor suggests, we have to appreciate the power that *epistemology* – or the modern theory of knowledge – has over our thinking. Epistemological considerations were particularly important for Descartes, and they shaped his concept of mind, Taylor suggests, in an exemplary way. Genuine knowledge, Descartes thought, had to have a basis in certainty. Certainty in turn could only be achieved by a rigorous examination and rational ordering of the knower's thoughts. In Descartes' view, in order to possess certainty, thoughts had to be focused on in their own right, that is, independently of any further reality they may or may not point to. And the mere fact of having a thought, of having something immediately present, seemed to Descartes as firm a basis for certainty as could be imagined. As Taylor puts it, this ideal of 'self-given' certainty thus provided Descartes with 'a strong incentive to construe knowledge in such a way that our thought about the real can be distinguished from its objects and examined on its own' (*PA* 3). In his pursuit of certainty and hence knowledge, Descartes is thus led to a notion of experience as something that can be examined on its own in isolation from the world. But this is not what an embodied subject experiences: it is an abstraction from that experience, not its essence.

Descartes is by no means the only culprit in Taylor's account. For classical empiricism the primary means by which we acquire ideas, and hence knowledge, is perception. Perception, it is presumed, is a causal process; or rather, that is what a science of perception must suppose. Classical empiricism then assumes that experience can be made fully intelligible within a causal account, that is, an account that has the same form as mechanistic theories of nature. The notion of a sense-impression plays the role of a thing-like entity that enters into causal relations with other entities, and ultimately with things in the outside world. Again, a requirement of what we are entitled to say we *know* about experience shapes, or rather misshapes, the description we then give to experience. The question of how experience is to be mechanistically explained, of how it arises from the operational processing of an 'input', overrides and makes invisible the question of the intelligibility of experience. In this way too an epistemological requirement leads to distortion. Furthermore, for perception to deliver certain knowledge, the empiricists argued, it had to supply a foundation of directly apprehended sense-data. As 'bare input', sense-data introduced the crucial ingredient of 'givenness' to our representations. Without something 'given', the empiricists and indeed Descartes thought, our knowledge would be 'foundationless' and so subject to doubt. Here again, an epistemological requirement presses the concept of experience into an alien mould.

But Taylor discerns something even more troubling going on. The method advanced by Descartes and other epistemologists of the early modern period required a breaking down of beliefs into their separate components. This epistemological requirement, which Taylor takes to have some validity in its own right, is then transposed into the very nature of the human subject. That is, the mind is regarded as *itself* structured and furnished by atomic bits of neutral informational input and processing capacity. The empiricist notion of simple ideas thus arises from a 'reification' of scientific procedure. The idea that the mind consists of neutrally describable, atomically decomposable mental events, like the notion that it consists of 'thing-like' objects, arises from 'ontologizing' the procedure by which modern science makes sense of the happenings of disenchanted nature. The disengaged, 'absolute' perspective adopted by modern natural science is read into the 'very constitution of the mind' (*PA* 64).[20]

The point of Taylor's reflections here is therapeutic: his aim is to dispel an illusion by tracing back its genealogy. If we do not find ourselves bewitched by this concept of mind, his argument will not address us. Taylor is convinced that a concept of mind determined by the same inner/outer sorting continues to hold sway in contemporary culture, not least in computational models of the psyche. But even if such models avoid mentalism, he thinks other problems beset them. According to cognitive science, the mind is defined by functions which can also be performed by computing machines. The mind is essentially a mechanism for processing neutrally and atomically registered input. Like a computer, the mind processes bits of information in a neutral way, according to some specified, in-built, rational procedure. But this model, Taylor insists, is inconsistent with the phenomena of embodied subjectivity. We have seen that an embodied subject is essentially a being at grips with the world. It perceives a world that is non-indifferent to it and acts in the world on the basis of its desires and purposes. As Taylor puts it in his 1983 essay 'The Significance of Significance: The Case of Cognitive Psychology', this is what makes human beings 'subjects of significance'.[21] He concedes that cognitive science goes some way towards accounting for action in terms of the programming of the complex mechanisms that make up the neural system. But he also insists that the actions of human beings, and other animals, have a meaning or significance not covered by this cognitive model. For the 'significant' performances of a machine are relative to something outside it: the designer of the program, the user of the machine, or an observer of its use. By contrast, the significance we attribute to the actions of embodied subjects *matters* to them: 'the crucial thing that divides us from machines is also what separates our lesser cousins the dumb brutes from them, that things have significance for us non-relatively' (*HAL* 201). In Taylor's view, to be an embodied subject is not essentially a matter of possessing consciousness. It is not to be the subject of 'mental' predicates as well as physical ones. And it is not to have privileged access to an 'inner' world of conscious states. It is a matter of possessing the 'significance feature' non-relatively.

In denying that consciousness is an essential attribute of embodied subjects, Taylor of course is not saying that human beings are only contingently subjects of experience. His point is rather to distinguish full-blooded human experience from mere conscious awareness. The notion of consciousness suggests that experience is, on the one hand, fully present to itself, and, on the other, simply given to us, so that we are passive in relation to it. But the former characteristic is not a typical feature of experience and the latter is not a necessary feature. Rather than being fully open to view, the content of experience is often implicit. Or more precisely, whatever is explicit in experience occurs against an implicitly apprehended background. And rather than being passive in relation to experience, human beings typically find themselves actively – if not consciously or reflectively – engaged in the world experience reveals. Following Merleau-Ponty, Taylor emphasizes the qualities of implicitness and activity in perceptual experience. It is crucial that we do not overlook these qualities because if we do we are liable to forget that the quality of perceptual experience is in a sense contingent on what we do with it. Perception is a skill. Some perceivers are able to see more than others. We are able to express or bring our percepts to language in more or less insightful ways. But if this is true of perception, it holds all the more so in other modes of experience, such as emotion. Taylor stresses how the content of human emotions is bound up with the ways in which we understand them. The experience of many emotions is neither fully transparent nor fixed once and for all, but open to various possibilities of interpretation, explicitation and hence transformation. To articulate an emotion, the very act of putting it into words, can change its nature, how it feels and what it means. Again, this possibility is hard to keep in view if we think of experience as a conscious event. With the distinctions between the implicit and the explicit, and between observer-relative and non-observer-relative significance in place, the idea that emotions may be constituted and transformable by modes of articulation is more readily intelligible.

To the extent that computational models of the mind are inconsistent with the 'significance feature' they are incompatible with the reality of embodied subjects. But again, Taylor does not argue on that account that such models are false. They become false, he argues, only in conjunction with a certain construal of their relation to non-mechanistic modes of explanation. Their validity depends on the explanatory level at which they work. It would be incorrect to suppose, say, that the 'deep-level' explanation of an action, offered by a cognitive scientist, shows that a 'higher-level' explanation invoking the situation of the agent is mistaken or confused. For the meaning the situation has for the agent is essential to its being a case of action at all. The applicability of the higher-level explanation is a condition of there being actions to explain. So it is not as if explanations invoking meaning are falsified in the way that Aristotelian cosmology was refuted by mechanistic physics. It remains conceivable that the meaning-invoking explanation is dispensable. There can be no metaphysical guarantee against this possibility. Whether such explanations are dispensable or not is an empirical matter: it just depends on the availability of better explanations of the phenomena at the lower level. But the crucial ingredient of actions – the significance feature – has not, in fact, been explained by cognitivist models. The correct way of viewing the science, according to Taylor, is to see it as supplementing the meaning-invoking accounts. It can give us 'a theory of the underlying structures which help explain how things happen as they do', as well as 'some of the conditions of the higher level events occurring as they do' (*HAL* 205). But the higher-level descriptions for their part remain indispensable for answering why the higher-level events happen. The reductive mistake is to suppose that all the explanatory factors can be identified at the lower level. So long as this mistake is not made, and so long as it does not reintroduce the mentalist picture, Taylor has no objections to cognitive science.

The idea that cognitive science has its rightful place alongside higher-level explanatory discourses suggests a pluralistic perspective in psychology. And such pluralism is what Taylor expressly commends. There is room in psychology for both 'correlators' – who aspire to transform psychology into an exact mechanistic science – and 'interpreters', for whom meaning retains an indispensable role in the explanation of behaviour.[22] If we want to understand the infrastructural conditions of behavioural capacities, we need 'to discover correlations between physically defined dimensions and certain psychic states or capacities which are unambiguously present or absent' (*HAL* 129). If we want to understand the structure and development of rational competencies such as speech, the genetic approach of Piaget and Chomsky, which rejects many of the assumptions of mechanism, is appropriate.[23] But for the explanation of 'fully motivated behaviour', where formal competencies are applied in the course of a life to a variety of desired ends, an 'interpretative' psychology is required. Different methods are appropriate for the different areas of psychological investigation. Psychological pluralism means giving up 'the myth of the omni-competence of the classical model'. It means bringing to an end, as Taylor puts it, 'the limitless imperialism of the correlators' (*HAL* 129, 132).

3

The Romantic Legacy

In Taylor's view, human experience has a content which could only be that of an embodied agent. This content is given by the world in which the embodied agent is placed, a world which possesses meaning or significance. Drawing on existential phenomenology, Taylor puts forward this thesis in opposition to constructions of experience as something 'mental', that is, as a property of 'the mind' that can be understood independent of human embodiment and therefore of human practical concerns. But phenomenology is not the only philosophy to challenge the mentalist concept of experience. The challenge was given its first and in many ways paradigmatic formulation in the late eighteenth and early nineteenth centuries by the philosophers of the German Romantic movement. Of these philosophers, no one was more systematic in his reflections on experience, subjectivity and their place in nature than Hegel.[1] As Taylor put it soon after the publication of *The Explanation of Behaviour* and ten years before the appearance of his book on Hegel: 'The ambition to overcome the dualism of mind and nature, the attempt to achieve this by a conception of the mind which is inseparable from its incarnation in matter, the resultant preoccupation with problems of genesis, these are all Hegelian ideas. Indeed, we might consider them as *the* Hegelian bequest to philosophy.'[2] Taylor's interest in the philosophy of Hegel and the German Idealist tradition, which provided the focus of his research in the early to mid-1970s, is thus a natural development of his concern, inspired in the first instance by Merleau-Ponty, with 'putting the mind back into nature'.[3] This is not the only issue which drove Taylor to Hegel, nor,

perhaps, is it the decisive one: as a political thinker and active socialist, Taylor had to come to terms with Marxism, and that required a
thorough engagement with Hegel's theory of modernity.[4] I will consider Taylor's treatment of the Hegelian bequest to social and political philosophy in later chapters. In this chapter, my focus will first
be on how Taylor interprets and critically appropriates *the kind of*
argument Hegel used to realize his ambition of overcoming the
dualism of mind and nature. In order to exhibit the unity of mind
and nature, Hegel and the other German Romantics had to develop
new modes of philosophical reasoning. Indeed, they had to develop
new conceptions of reason itself. This went hand in hand with a
transformed understanding of what it means to say that a human
being is a rational animal. Taylor calls this new understanding
of human subjectivity 'expressivism' and it was to supply a crucial resource for his own philosophical anthropology. However, in
Taylor's view expressivist theories enjoyed various degrees of
success. As we shall see, Taylor rejects what he takes to be Hegel's
overly rationalistic articulation of the link between subjectivity and
expression. At the same time, Taylor wholeheartedly embraces the
expressivist theory of human linguistic powers developed by contemporaries of Hegel such as Herder and Humboldt, a theory he
believes to be superior to the mainstream philosophies of language
of our day.

Transcendental Arguments

Let us begin by reminding ourselves of an ambivalence Taylor felt
towards both linguistic analysis and phenomenology as methods
of philosophical enquiry. His misgivings rested on their failure to
address adequately the question of validity. Both methods are
essentially descriptive. In the case of linguistic analysis, the descriptions serve to make explicit the conceptual scheme embedded in
ordinary language. This scheme is not, as the linguistic philosophers often presumed, metaphysically neutral or self-validating. It
can be challenged, and when it is – for instance by mechanistic theories of mind and behaviour – arguments that go beyond linguistic
analysis need to be mounted in its defence. Phenomenology, which
aims at a retrieval of lived experience, can likewise never come up
with pure, presuppositionless and self-authenticating descriptions.
One descriptive vocabulary can always be challenged by another;
any given description must 'prove itself' when challenged by a

rival. But the phenomenological method does not tell us what is involved in such 'proof'. Once the notion of purity or presuppositionlessness in the way of description is dropped – as Taylor thinks it must be – it is not clear, from what we have seen so far, how descriptions can be endowed with validity at all.

So the question arises: what, if anything, lends validity to philosophical accounts of human subjectivity? It is important to see here that philosophical anthropology is not interested in offering just any description of the human subject. It claims to say something *essential* about it. In Taylor's case, he wants to show that human existence is in some sense essentially structured, even constituted, by layers of meaning or significance. The name Taylor gives to the kind of reasoning he thinks can perform this task is 'transcendental argument'. For the purpose of clarifying the nature and validity of transcendental arguments, Taylor turns first to their great pioneer, the eighteenth-century philosopher Immanuel Kant.

What interests Taylor, and us, is not so much the details of Kant's argumentation as the model it provides for philosophical anthropology. A philosophical anthropology, as Taylor envisages it, attempts to capture something essential about its subject-matter: it proposes substantive, non-trivial and *necessarily true* claims about human subjectivity. How is it possible to vindicate such claims? According to Kant's model, as Taylor interprets it, a transcendental argument begins with some platitude or truism about human subjectivity. The truism states something about human subjectivity which is necessarily true but which needs no vindication. The self-evident feature of subjectivity that serves as the point of departure for Kant's transcendental arguments in the *Critique of Pure Reason* is mere conscious awareness. Not even the most hard-bitten sceptics need to be convinced that they appear to themselves as consciously aware. With this certainty in place, Kant then aims to show that the undeniable feature is only possible given some other, non-platitudinous feature of human subjectivity: in Kant's case, the necessary applicability to experience of categories such as 'cause and effect'. The latter provides the 'condition of possibility' or 'transcendental condition' of the former. As Taylor puts it: 'the condition stated in the conclusion is indispensable to the feature identified at the start' (*PA* 27).[5] But while the conclusion of the argument makes an informative, substantive claim, while it tells us more about subjectivity than the platitude we began with, it nevertheless also has, at least for Kant, the status of a self-evident, *a priori* truth. In order for this to be the case, the indispensability claims of a valid transcendental argument must themselves be 'apodeictic'. That is to say, they must convince merely by the fact of being properly understood.

But what is involved in establishing an apodeictic indispensability claim? According to Taylor, the argument works by formulating the 'boundary conditions' of the self-evident phenomenon it begins with. Taylor reads Kant's critique of Hume's empiricism as resting on an intuition Kant thinks we all implicitly share about the minimal conditions of coherent experience. If Hume were right, Kant argued, and experience were really pieced together contingently from atoms of sensory input, it would not possess the coherence we encounter whenever we have an experience of an object: it would be 'merely a blind play of representations, less even than a dream'.[6] Hume's depiction of experience depends on, yet is inconsistent with, an ability we have and which we are all capable of recognizing in ourselves once explicitly pointed out. Roughly, it is the ability to distinguish between the objective world and subjective states of mind. The argument appeals to something implicit in an agent's knowledge: a sense of what it is like for the agent's subjectivity to fall apart. The 'boundary conditions' without which subjectivity collapses or disintegrates are not initially evident; they require formulation. To show that some feature is indispensable for another is thus to show that without it, the point of the 'activity' would be missing, and the standard implicit in it would not be met. Once the boundary conditions of success and failure have been established, it becomes self-evident that the indispensability condition is true.

If Kant was the pioneer of transcendental argumentation, its greatest genius, according to Taylor, was Hegel.[7] By way of his 'dialectical' method, as Taylor interprets it, Hegel systematized this mode of reasoning more than anyone else. The aim of dialectics, at least as set out by Hegel in his 'Introduction' to the *Phenomenology of Spirit*, is to retrace the steps by which consciousness reaches an adequate conception of itself.[8] An adequate conception of consciousness is one free of dogmatic suppositions and internal contradictions. How do such contradictions arise? They arise, Taylor notes, when the idea consciousness has of itself fails to match up with the 'effective experience' shaped by that idea. The result is not just a contradictory conception *of* consciousness, but a contradiction *in* it, since the idea consciousness has of itself, together with the effective experience it yields, actually makes up that consciousness. Given that *there is* consciousness, the contradiction between 'model and reality' must be resolved, and resolved in a way that is satisfactory to the reflecting consciousness. A dialectical movement is thus triggered whereby the model, and so the consciousness itself, is transformed in a rational or 'determinate' negation of its contradictory form. The new idea of consciousness arising from the self-negation then provides the starting point for a fresh dialectical movement, and so on until all contradictions are resolved.

According to Taylor's exegesis in 'The Opening Arguments of the *Phenomenology*', the position reached at the end of the first dialectical progression of Hegel's *Phenomenology of Spirit* is one that by now should strike us as familiar: it is an indispensable feature of the experience we have that it belongs to an embodied agent, a being essentially at grips with the world. Using the techniques of transcendental argument, Hegel reinforces Kant's critique of the empiricist concept of mind. But Hegel also turns this critique against Kant by linking phenomenal causality necessarily to the embodied experience of the perceiving subject. This conclusion runs against Kant's doctrine that we have distinct faculties of sensibility (delivering intuitions) and understanding (delivering *a priori* concepts, like cause and effect). Hegel's arguments thus anchor experience in the body more solidly than Kant's theory. They lay the foundation for a 'genetic view of consciousness, in which our way of conceiving the world alters and progresses through the transformations that our ways of dealing with it undergo'.[9] In this way they resonate with the critique of empiricist and Kantian doctrines of perception that Taylor draws from Merleau-Ponty in his earlier works.

Indeed, Taylor's study of Hegelian dialectics enabled him to formulate more clearly the claim to *validity* of Merleau-Ponty's phenomenological description of embodied subjectivity. Merleau-Ponty began with certain truisms about the quality of our experience. His point of departure was a minimal description of an undeniable activity. We experience objects in a 'field of meanings', as nearby or distant, as up or down, as a means to fulfilling purposes or as an obstacle. It is undeniable that our perceptual field, at least when it is functioning properly, 'has an orientational structure, a foreground and a background, an up and down' (*PA* 23). The argument then appeals to our implicit sense that when we lose our orientation 'we lose the thread of the world, and our perceptual experience is no longer our access to the world, but rather the confused debris into which our normal grasp on things crumbles' (*PA* 23). This is a description of a boundary condition. At the boundary, experience as we normally have it begins to fall apart. It is similar to Kant's description of intuitions without concepts: such experience would be 'even less than a dream'. We have here, then, a transcendental condition of experience which has been revealed as such through an explicited contrast between functioning experience and experience on the point of breakdown. The description of the boundary state is what *entitles* us to say that our experience is essentially that of embodied subjects. Without embodiment, our experience could not conceivably be the way it is. And the inconceivability has been shown by bringing the 'limits of experience to clarity' in a progression from 'sketchier to richer descriptions'. In Hegelian terms, the dialectical transition from sketchier to richer descriptions involves a determinate negation of contradictory characterizations of experience, that is, characterizations that fail to match up with the 'effective experience' they yield.

The nature and extent of a philosophical anthropology based on transcendental argument becomes clearer in view of a distinction Taylor draws between two kinds of dialectical movement. On the one hand, there are 'strict' or 'ontological' dialectics. The starting point in a chain of transcendental arguments that make up a strict dialectics is undeniable. It begins with something that is intrinsically characterized by a standard or purpose that is already indisputably realized. And it concludes with a redescription of the standard that shows its indispensability for the phenomenon at hand. Now the arguments Taylor has produced so far have ontological force in this sense. They start with a standard that is already met – the possession of experience – and they serve to deepen our conception both of the standard and of the reality which meets it. So far little has been achieved by way of a *constructive* philosophical anthropology by this means. We have been reminded of something we knew all along: that human beings are embodied agents. To be sure, we now know that our embodiment is not accidental to our experience. But we have not learnt anything about how things are 'in themselves', that is, how things are independent of our experience. We have not arrived at any metaphysical truths. Furthermore, our knowledge claim is conditioned by formulations that may be challenged. While strict dialectics aspires to self-evidence, its conclusions are always open to dispute. The philosophical anthropology secured by transcendental arguments as strict dialectics is thus minimal (restricted to standards we already know are met) and weak (subject to possible revision). In their *therapeutic* capacity, however, much more has been gained by the transcendental arguments we have considered so far. The strict dialectics that open

Hegel's *Phenomenology of Spirit*, as well as Merleau-Ponty's and Kant's arguments, serve a critical function by releasing us from the 'contemplative' or 'representationalist' misconstrual of the knowing subject. They help cure us of a tendency to slip back into the mentalist model of what it is like to be a subject with the capacity to know.[10]

In the case of what Taylor calls 'interpretative dialectics', on the other hand, the starting point in the chain is not undeniable. Interpretative dialectics begin with an *interpretation* of an activity as aimed at a certain purpose or as directed by a particular standard. But it does not irrefutably establish that the activity in question does possess the purposive feature. In Taylor's view, interpretative dialectics does not entitle us to ontological claims. It does not inform us about the essence of human subjectivity. But it is a useful tool for understanding changes in the way human subjectivity is conceived and actualized. It helps us understand transitions in forms of life. Indeed, Taylor is of the firm conviction that changes in forms of life can *only* be understood by characterizing them as bent towards the realization of certain standards and purposes. Explanations of historical change convince, in Taylor's view, by offering the best interpretation both of the standards that guide human activity and of the reality that either meets or fails to meet them. Interpretative dialectics thus have a role to play in the constructive or historical aspect of Taylor's project. But in taking this position Taylor departs significantly from what he takes to be the Hegelian view. On Taylor's reading, Hegel illegitimately raised interpretative dialectics to the level of an ontological vision.

Hegel's Vision

A conception of subjectivity that takes the subject's interaction with the world as prior to its contemplative representations of objects in an important sense overcomes the dualism of mind and world, for it dispels the Cartesian illusion that human experience is contingently related to the world. So far, this is as much as Taylor has been able to countenance by way of philosophical reason. But Hegel goes much further in his efforts to bring mind and world together: he wants to show not just that subjectivity is *embodied in nature*, but also that nature is *embodied subjectivity*. At this point we enter what Taylor calls Hegel's 'ontological vision' and the speculative metaphysics Hegel elaborated to support it.

The vision Taylor attributes to Hegel provides an account of how things must be if subjectivity is to be self-defining or free; without, on account of that fact, experiencing itself as alienated from nature. The notion of self-defining subjectivity, for Taylor, is central to modern understandings of the self. It first emerges in conjunction with the mechanistic cosmology of the scientific revolution. As we saw in the last chapter, modern mechanism displaced a teleological and 'enchanted' view of the world according to which nature instantiates a pre-given order of divine purposes or 'Ideas'. Within the pre-modern framework, human self-realization is defined in relation to the Ideas, that is to say, as fixed in advance by patterns of significance already realized within the cosmic order. But with the demise of the enchanted world view, new conceptions of the self emerged which dispensed with this dependence on an external, pre-given ground. On the modern conception, the subject defines its principle of self-realization for itself, from its own resources, so to speak, and not from a ready-made order of being. According to Taylor, there are two basic models of self-defining subjectivity at play in modern culture. One of them construes self-definition *instrumentally*. The other, which arose historically as a reaction to the first model, conceives self-definition *expressively*. The aim of Hegel's ontological vision, on Taylor's reading, is to provide an account of how things must be if human beings are to be self-defining subjects in the latter sense – that is, as expressive freedom.

On the expressivist model – which Taylor, following Isaiah Berlin, traces back to Herder – human beings are rational animals in the sense that they strive to realize goals and purposes which provide a standard or measure for what it is to be a fully realized human being. But it is up to each particular subject to define for itself what this measure is by bringing it to 'expression', and thereby completion, through its own life activity. The measure only means something to the extent that a subject strives to realize it, and more to the point, the meaning only comes to light in the manner of its expression in the life of the subject. Conversely, the subject is able to complete itself – or realize itself as a unity, and not be divided within itself – only in being guided by the measure. The freedom of the self-defining subject, on the expressivist model, is thus a question of authentic self-expression, of being true to its own measure as clarified through its own expressive activity. Now according to Taylor's reading, Hegel develops his vision in order to save the expressive model from a potentially fatal contradiction. For as Hegel believed Kant had shown, freedom required not just

authentic self-expression but radical self-determination understood
as rational autonomy. The activity of an autonomous being is
guided by its own principles or norms, by principles or norms it
can will as its own. A subject who is not free in this radical sense
suffers from a certain alienation, or lack of self-completion, for it is
then dependent on norms or principles that are foreign or external
to it. Yet as we have already seen, human subjectivity is essentially
embodied, and that means embodied in nature. If the subject is to
reach integral self-expression, it must therefore strive to realize a
standard or measure which is implicit or nascent in nature itself.
Nature must be conceived as a locus of meaning if subjectivity is
not to be alienated from itself as embodied in the world, that is, if
it is not to experience its embodiment in nature as an 'exile'. Integral self-expression is thus only possible if the natural order in
which the subject is set is itself an expression of subjectivity.

But if harmonious integration with nature is not to be achieved
at the cost of freedom, this order cannot be imposed as a given from
the outside, as it was on the pre-modern view. What Hegel required,
then, according to Taylor, is an 'enchanted' conception of nature, a
conception of nature as embodied subjectivity, where that subjectivity realizes itself in the freedom of the human subject. Since
freedom is rational autonomy, the enchantment of nature must be
the work of *reason*. It must be reason itself that gives meaning to
nature *at the same time* as it makes for the self-definition of the finite
human subject. In Taylor's view, this was the decisive point at
which Hegel departed from Schelling and the Romantic philosophers. According to Taylor, the contradiction between freedom as
self-defining, autonomous subjectivity and nature as a locus of
meaning is resolved for Hegel in their unity in a universal, infinite
or 'cosmic' subject – Hegel's *Geist* or Spirit – which brings itself to
self-completion through, and only through, the vehicle of rational
finite subjectivity. Only in this way is it possible for a subject to be
both free and in genuine expressive unity with nature.

At the heart of the ontological vision Taylor ascribes to Hegel,
then, is an idea of body and mind, culture and nature, the finite and
the infinite, reconciled by necessity as vehicles for the self-positing
or self-realization of Spirit – without annulling their difference. The
finite requires the infinite and the infinite must be embodied in
the finite. While indebted to Romanticism, Hegelian reconciliation
is achieved through reason, not intuition or imagination. And while
allied to pantheism, particularity and finitude are not subsumed

under universality and infinity, but preserved, as Hegel famously put it, in 'the identity of identity and non-identity'.

Clearly, however, the thesis that mind and nature, or the finite and the infinite, are reconciled 'by reason itself', as a matter of rational necessity, is empty unless reason can actually establish how the reconciliation works. As Taylor says, the truth of Hegel's vision – presuming he has it – requires that it can be presented as a *demonstration*. The system stands or falls, as Taylor puts it, on its validity as 'strict dialectics'. Taylor then distinguishes two kinds of strict dialectics in Hegel. The more fundamental is the 'ascending dialectic' of Hegel's *Logic*. Here the focus is on the categories through which we think the world rather than the various levels of reality. Hegel's strict ascending dialectic identifies contradictions in these categories when taken in isolation, contradictions that lead us to posit more self-sustaining categories until we ultimately reach the Hegelian 'Idea'. Such is a demonstration, Taylor writes, 'which starts with the poorest, most empty category, with "being", and which shows internal contradiction, and hence passes on to other categories which are in turn shown to be contradictory . . . until we come to the Idea' (*H* 123). But Hegel also deploys what Taylor calls a 'descending dialectic' to support his vision. This shows the hierarchy of beings as 'the embodiment and manifestation of a formula of rational necessity in which each level has its necessary place' (*H* 122). According to Taylor, this is what Hegel tries to do in his philosophy of nature and spirit. The two then form a circle, with Hegel's *Logic* showing that certain categories are necessarily embodied in the world, and with his philosophies of nature and spirit showing how they are manifest there. 'At the culmination of this', Taylor writes, 'we reach the vision of absolute spirit, of the life of God as the perfect self-knowledge of the whole' (*H* 123).

Having looked at the expressivist ontology Taylor ascribes to Hegel, let us now turn to his assessment of it. As we have seen, the truth of Hegel's ontology and the mode of its demonstration are so indivisible that anything short of strict proof in the chain of transcendental arguments that make up Hegel's dialectic will be enough to undermine the ontology. And Taylor finds such shortcomings in both the ascending and descending dialectics. Taylor's examination of the ascending dialectic focuses on the first transitions in the *Logic*, especially the transition from being to determinate being, and from finite to infinite being (*H* 233–44). In Taylor's view, these transitions in categories are not demonstrated in the strong sense required, and he suggests that Hegel's dialectic progresses *in conjunction with* the ontological vision of self-positing spirit. The ontological vision itself is not yielded by strict argument. The arguments presuppose the soundness of the vision as much as they establish it. But no such presupposition is legitimate for strict dialectics. The ascending dialectic thus fails as strict – or, as Taylor also says, 'self-authenticating' – dialectics. We could try to save Hegel's arguments by taking them as interpretative dialectics, that is, as interpretations of the ontological vision. But this move, Taylor points out, is fatal to the vision itself, which is only valid to the extent that it is demonstrable through reason alone: the ontology of self-positing *Geist* as rational necessity must be reflected in the argument establishing it. In Taylor's view, Hegel's ascending dialectic has 'the force of a more or less plausible interpretation of the facts of finitude, the levels of being, the existence of life and conscious beings, the history of man, as "hints and traces" of the life of an absolute subject, deployed in the world' (*H* 348). It does not have the force of a demonstration or strict conceptual proof. This undermines the whole systematic ontology because it means that *Geist* does not fully return to itself in a concept.

The main thrust of Taylor's critique of Hegel's ontology is that Hegel does not prove it in the rigorous manner required. It is primarily the status of Hegel's arguments that Taylor questions, that is, their validity as strict dialectics. However, Taylor also has reservations about the content of the ontology irrespective of the status of its purported demonstration. In other words, even if Hegel's ontology is considered at the level of interpretative dialectics, Taylor has misgivings about it. These misgivings apply to a whole series of claims Hegel makes in his philosophy of nature and philosophy of spirit. But I would like to draw attention to two in particular.

In the first place, Taylor takes issue with Hegel's understanding of religion – and especially Christianity – as a stage in the development of absolute knowledge. Taylor agrees with Kierkegaard that Hegel's system both misunderstands and is incompatible with Christian faith. By identifying (however ingeniously) God, man and rational necessity, it rules out 'the kind of radical freedom of God to which faith relates' (*H* 493). If Hegel's ontology were true, Taylor speculates, it would be impossible for God truly to *give* to man. Creation, revelation and salvation are, for Hegel, properly understood as the 'emanations of a necessity' rather than the deliverances of a love. With an understanding of God like this, Taylor wonders

how a Hegelian Christian manages to pray, at least prayers of petition, gratitude and praise. 'The creaturely response of gratitude and
praise of God', Taylor writes, 'takes on a radically different sense in
the rarefied altitudes of the Idea. Both these responses transmute
into a recognition of my identity with cosmic necessity and hence
must cease to be gratitude in any meaningful sense' (*H* 493). In
short, the problem with Hegel's ontology, at least from a Christian
point of view, is that it has no room for God's *grace* or *agapē*. In
Sources of the Self, Taylor was to suggest that *any* ontology of the
human that fails to make room for something like grace is problematic, at least in the modern world. But whatever might be made
of that claim (we will consider it in chapter 8), it is clear that as an
interpretation of the meaning of Christianity, Taylor finds Hegel's
rationalist expressivism seriously wanting.[11]

Taylor's second source of dissatisfaction with the so-called
descending dialectic is Hegel's understanding of art. Art, for Hegel,
is also a stage in the unfolding of absolute knowledge, but one
which falls short both of religious understanding and of conceptual
thought. As such it is Spirit aware of itself, as Taylor puts it, 'in
default of concepts' (*H* 467). Hegel's view, on Taylor's reading,
borrows from Herder's expressivist model of art, but takes Herder's
expressivism in a distinctively rationalist direction. The expressivist
model construes a work of art as a vehicle for 'a higher awareness
of reality'. But the reality, which the work heightens our awareness
of, is not presentable separately from the work. The work of art
helps constitute that which it makes manifest. We will look at this
idea a bit more closely later. The point for the moment is that, in
Taylor's view, the ideal of total clarity, which Hegel thinks is
achieved when Spirit returns to itself in the concept, ultimately
spoils his expressivism. For such an ideal runs against the idea that
the truths disclosed by art are not expressible in another medium.
For Hegel, as Taylor understands him, the truth of art is taken up
at a higher and more satisfactory level in philosophy: 'the obscure
and the inarticulate is ultimately captured in the net of clear conceptual description', such that 'in the end description is totally vic-
torious and swallows up the conditions of its own impure birth' (*H*
476). Taylor is clearly unhappy with this subordination of art to philosophy. Not only does it question art's role as an irreplaceable
vehicle of truth-disclosure, according to Taylor it also mislocates
the spiritual significance of art in the modern world. With the
emergence of Idealist philosophy, Hegel thinks, art ceases to be 'the
highest need of spirit'. But as Taylor sees it, art is not of secondary

spiritual significance in the culture of modernity: 'far from taking a
second place in the spiritual life of modern man, art has taken over
from religion in the lives of many of our contemporaries, in the
sense that it is for them the highest expression of what is of ultimate importance' (*H* 479). And it is clear that Taylor considers this
to be a positive development. He finds the prospect of a culture
in which art assumes a secondary role, merely 'illustrating truths
more clearly known in other media', a 'depressing' one. Hegel
himself, Taylor acknowledges, often writes as if he would share this
sentiment. But regrettably, Taylor suggests, the systematic metaphysician in Hegel ultimately won over the Romantic in him.[12]

Taylor's evaluation of Hegel's system is also based on the
system's continuing ability to 'capture its time in thought'. Taylor
is sure that in this respect Hegel's fortunes are in terminal decline.
To his great credit, Hegel identified a central dilemma of modern
civilization: how to reconcile the apparently conflicting ideals of
radical freedom and expressive unity; or in other words, how to
understand and realize self-defining expressive subjectivity. This
problem, Taylor thinks, remains with us. It stands behind much of
the alienation, or 'diremption of spirit', that continues to characterize modernity. However, the ontological vision meant to solve this
problem, Taylor thinks, can no longer carry conviction. In part this
is due to its failure as strict dialectics: the comprehensive ontology
is not demonstrated in the manner required; it does not exhibit strict
necessity. But much more significantly, it has been rendered obsolete by developments within modern civilization itself. All sorts of
factors are relevant here. Taylor mentions the 'ever expanding
frontier of modern science' and 'the growing control over nature of
modern technology'. Such developments have destroyed for good
the credibility of an ontology of nature as the manifestation of a
divine principle (*HMS* 138). The entrenchment of Romantic ideals
in mainstream modern civilization by way of their incorporation
into the 'private sphere', and the rise of post-Romantic moral and
aesthetic sensibilities, have also contributed to its demise. These are
just a few of the historical changes that undermine the plausibility
of the great 'synthesis' Taylor's Hegel envisaged. But more important still, the *critical* edge of Hegel's synthesis has been worn away
by time. It is crucial to Hegel's philosophy, according to Taylor, that
it serves to articulate a widely sensed feeling of unease – a 'malaise',
as Taylor puts it – with the false, reifying anthropology of the
Enlightenment. But while this unease still grips us, and while
protest against the expressive impoverishment of modern life

still thrives, Hegel's system, Taylor thinks, can no longer give it adequate philosophical expression. Furthermore, Hegel presents a vision of a world which, seen aright, is *already* reconciled. But this is not how things seem to the many critics of modernity. Taylor concludes his study of Hegel with the suggestion that it is not Hegel, but his contemporary Hölderlin and philosophers like Herder and Heidegger, who formulated the expressivist ideals of the Romantic generation in a manner that continues to be of relevance today.

The Non-metaphysical Hegel

Before turning to this other lineage, I want briefly to consider the validity of Taylor's interpretation of Hegel. For some time now, the whole framework of Taylor's reading has been out of favour amongst Hegel scholars. The trend has been to read Hegel first and foremost as an *anti*-metaphysical philosopher, that is, as a philosopher whose primary concern was to take up and bring to completion the *critique* of metaphysics initiated by Kant.[13] The central point of Hegel's 'Absolute Idealism', on this reading, is that it strengthens the anti-metaphysical stance announced by Kant under the banner of 'transcendental idealism'. Once Hegel is read in this way – the 'post-metaphysical' interpretation of Hegel goes – it becomes ludicrous to ascribe to him, as Taylor does, the ontological thesis that 'the universe is posited by a Spirit whose essence is rational necessity' (*H* 538). The non-metaphysical Hegelians point out that the claim that the universe is self-positing spirit is both wildly implausible and 'metaphysical' in just the sense criticized by Kant: two good reasons for supposing that Hegel never so much as entertained it. The idea that Hegel was committed to such a view, according to this interpretation, is simply a myth. While Taylor may not have created the myth – it has always had a place in the popular imagination about Hegel – he more than most is responsible for perpetuating it today. The charge against Taylor is thus a serious one. Has he got Hegel completely wrong?

Let us look a little more closely at the agenda ascribed to the non-metaphysical Hegel. As elaborated by Robert Pippin, Hegel's chief concern is to offset sceptical doubts about the objectivity of our (or any) conceptual scheme. Such doubts inevitably emerge, Kant thought, whenever we reflect on our cognitive predicament from the metaphysical (or realist) standpoint. Roughly speaking, the realist assumes that objects taken in themselves can endow concepts

with objectivity. But reflection shows that the norms determinate of objectivity cannot be found there. Human knowledge is only intelligible, Kant thought, if it is supposed to be grounded in structures of subjectivity, and in particular the reflexive capacity of consciousness, the capacity for self-awareness. This is the key insight of Kant's 'idealism', and Hegel's idealism, Pippin maintains, should be read in a similar light. Like Kant, Hegel has to elaborate a theory of concepts consistent with the idealist principle, and it is his engagement in this enterprise, according to Pippin, that is decisive for his turn away from Kant. The crucial move here is Hegel's rejection of Kant's idea that concepts need to be anchored by intuitions. As Pippin puts it, Hegel's abandonment of Kant's doctrine of pure intuition leads to his account of 'the content of concepts as fixed by their possible relations to other concepts' and 'his rejection of the claim that we do not know things in themselves'.[14] For Pippin, this, and not 'pre-critical claims about cosmic mind', is the central thesis of Hegel's idealism. It deserves the title 'Absolute Idealism' not because it posits a super-entity – the 'Absolute' or the 'Idea' – as the highest reality. Such a doctrine would in any case be a version of metaphysical realism, albeit an idealist one. The expression 'Absolute Idealism' refers instead to the achievement of a certain perspective on knowledge, one that conforms, more fully even than Kant's philosophy, to the idealist, anti-metaphysical principle that thought is self-determining. Likewise, Hegel's term 'Absolute knowledge' refers to 'an absolute or final account of what it is to know, and not a knowledge of a divine Absolute'.[15] Absolute Idealism is thus a felicitous name for the claim that 'there is literally *nothing* "beyond" or "behind" or responsible for the human experience of the world of appearances', least of all the Absolute Spirit Taylor conjures from traditional metaphysics and theology.[16]

Pippin concedes that there is something 'bowdlerized' in this reconstruction of Hegel's project. It puts to one side Hegel's application of speculative philosophy to art, religion and nature. And it does not tackle from the outset the practical questions, the problems of freedom and morality, that mattered so much to Hegel. But in defence of his approach, Pippin can at least claim that it reconstructs something plausible in Hegel's *Logic* and *Phenomenology*, whatever its rightful applications may be. And he also proposes that Hegel's alternative to Kant's doctrine of freedom and morality is 'clearly intended by Hegel to be the *result* of his original argument with Kant about pure concepts, the nature of their objectivity, and the status of sceptical doubts about such objectivity'.[17] One needs to grasp these issues first to appreciate Absolute Idealism's power as a practical philosophy.

At first sight, the non-metaphysical Hegel cuts a completely different figure to Taylor's Hegel. But it may be that the rhetoric of the non-metaphysical interpreters – the rhetoric of debunking a myth – exaggerates the difference. First, it should not be forgotten that Taylor too emphasizes Hegel's Kantian roots. For Taylor, after all, Hegelian dialectics simply draw out a potential opened up by Kant's innovative use of transcendental arguments. It could also be argued that the very fact that Hegel does proceed by way of transcendental argumentation protects him from the charge of metaphysical realism, even on Taylor's reading. For if the procedure by which an ontology is established is transcendental argument – and it is clear this is the way Taylor thinks Hegel does proceed – then the metaphysics issuing from it cannot but be refracted through an awareness of its basis in subjectivity. But to grant this, as Taylor insists we must, is to see Hegel in a non-realist or non-dogmatic light. It is a mistake, then, to call Taylor's Hegel a pre-critical metaphysician. Taylor's Hegel is very much aware that he is thinking after Kant, in the sense that the constraints of transcendental argument prevent him (or ought to prevent him) from making arbitrary or dogmatic suppositions about the nature of reality or the grounding of thought in something outside it. Furthermore, Taylor's Hegel also crucially departs from Kant in rejecting the idea of pure intuition and the separability of intuitions and concepts. Admittedly, the account Taylor gives of the reasons behind Hegel's objection is different – referring as it does to the phenomenology of embodiment. But it is still the case that Taylor's Hegel is intended to be more robustly Kantian or 'critical' than Kant's view itself.[18]

So the first point to make is that Taylor's Hegel does not ignore the problem of epistemic grounding in the way that a pre-critical metaphysician does. But if that is the case, how could Hegel possibly end up espousing anything like the 'cosmic subject' thesis, unless it were mistakenly attributed to him? Two points need to be made here. The first is that Taylor does not suppose Hegel reaches his ontological vision *directly* through the *Logic*. Hegel's *Logic*, Taylor is perfectly aware, concerns categories, not things.[19] And the 'ascending dialectic' as Taylor outlines it represents the transitions in *thought* that are necessary for thought's or consciousness's adequate conception of itself, an enterprise that culminates in the Idea. Its purpose is not to inform us about what there is, and Taylor's criticisms of it do not rely on the supposition that it does have that purpose. It is the necessity of the transitions that Taylor questions. Second, the non-metaphysical Hegelian's claim that there is nothing 'beyond' or 'behind' or responsible for the human experience of the world is not incompatible with the so-called metaphysical Hegel's thesis that the world is the self-positing of Spirit. It is the rhetoric of the non-metaphysical Hegelians, rather than Taylor's Hegel, that makes self-positing spirit a non-human super-entity. In fact, as we have seen, one of the major problems Taylor has with his Hegel is his anthropocentrism: *there is* nothing but human spirit in Hegel's vision, and that is precisely what is so troubling about it.

This is not to say that Taylor's treatment of Hegel's *Logic* is satisfactory. Too often he invokes the vision of self-positing spirit to explain the moves Hegel makes, without considering them seriously enough in their own terms. We do not need to resort to the comprehensive ontology to grasp the theoretical motivation behind Hegel's transition from one category to another. And, as Pinkard observes, the theoretical integrity of the *Logic* stands independent of the plausibility of the broader vision.[20] This is the central lesson of the post-metaphysical reading of Hegel. But if this is a weakness in Taylor's approach – and we must concede that it is – the post-metaphysical interpretation raises questions of its own. First, it is either silent or unconvincing on the issue of Aristotle's influence on Hegel. Where Pippin, for instance, dismisses Hegel's Aristotelian talk of the 'organically growing life of the Notion' as merely 'metaphorical',[21] Taylor at least takes seriously Hegel's high estimation of and avowed indebtedness to Aristotle's thought. For Aristotle, an important if not the first task of philosophy is to formulate the categories that are best suited for understanding nature, including human nature. After all, human beings are rational *animals*. But this is just the sort of issue that the post-metaphysical Hegel allegedly wants to avoid. He thinks he can circumvent it, supposedly, because he has taken the 'critical turn', and realizes that the idea of nature is secondary (indeed otiose) from an epistemic point of view.[22] But this will not make the problem of understanding human subjectivity as a *natural* phenomenon disappear. And nor should it, for surely this is an absolutely fundamental problem for philosophy, especially where nature is conceived, as it is so frequently in the modern world, as deeply inhospitable to subjectivity. Rather than defusing the problem of nature by epistemic fiat, as the non-metaphysical Hegel is wont to do, it would be better to ask how it is intelligible (rather than causally explicable) that nature can be said to exhibit subjectivity at all. If one takes Hegel's philosophical orientation to be shaped significantly by Aristotle and the Romantics, as Taylor does, one should not be surprised to find Hegel seriously engaging with this problem.[23]

The fact that Hegel does engage with it so seriously is one of the reasons why Taylor thinks Hegel still commands interest today. Of course, it is not the only reason: for Taylor, Hegel's social and political philosophy provides a crucial reference point for understanding the nature of modern society and diagnosing its ills. It gets things wrong to say, as Paul Redding does, that Taylor attempts 'to separate the "good" Hegel, the social philosopher, from the "bad", the metaphysician and systematic philosopher'.[24] In Taylor's view, there are good and bad parts in both the expressivist ontology and the theory of modernity. It is also false to suggest, as Kolb does, that Taylor wants to put Hegel's mode of argumentation to one side in order to focus on what really counts in Hegel, the social philosophy.[25] As we shall see, dialectics, or the structure of self-negation, is, for Taylor, a crucial tool for an understanding of modernity, as well as subjectivity. But it is true that Taylor approaches Hegel looking for answers to questions posed by the agenda of philosophical anthropology, an agenda that is ultimately practical in orientation. This clearly diverges from the approach favoured by Pippin, who turns to Hegel's practical philosophy only after and strictly in the light of the theoretical philosophy. Thanks to the work of Pippin and other non-metaphysical interpreters of Hegel, some of Hegel's profound theoretical insights are now being recovered. But it should be said that when Taylor casts his downbeat judgement on the prospects facing Hegel's system today, he does not have its reputation amongst professional philosophers in mind. It is rather Hegel's philosophy as a cultural presence that Taylor considers to be over. It is Hegelianism as living critique, as a practically orienting form of self-understanding, that is a spent force. Whether or not this is something Hegel expected from his philosophy himself, it is something Taylor thinks we are entitled to expect from it.

The Expressivist Theory of Language

If Hegel fails in his attempt at unifying mind and nature by construing both as necessary moments in the self-expression of a cosmic subject, it is not because the expressive conception of subjectivity is flawed. The problem arises from Hegel's grounding of human expressive powers in the unfolding of 'Spirit' as rational necessity. Once this move is made, only speculative metaphysics can seem up to the task of articulating the conditions of human self-realization. But the expressive model of subjectivity need not take this path. A more fruitful line of development suggests itself to Taylor in the philosophies of language pioneered by Herder, Humboldt and later Heidegger. Taylor's debt to Romantic thought is in fact nowhere more evident than in the philosophy of language he extracts from these thinkers. This in turn carries much weight for his own philosophical anthropology. Let us consider then the basic features of the theory of language Taylor creatively appropriates from this tradition and his reasons for preferring it to more mainstream approaches in the philosophy of language.

According to Taylor, Herder begins his reflections on language more or less where the thesis of embodied agency leaves off. Rejecting the division between mind and body, he takes our primary access to the world to be practical, that is, shaped by the desires and purposes that come with embodiment. Before anything else, the human being is 'at grips' with things as an organic unity. Now what is it for such a being to have language? The first point to make is that just as humans are not the only species of embodied agent, they are not alone in using language. Language features in the natural history of many species, in at least two ways. First, it functions as a mechanism for coordinating behaviour. Non-human animals are just as capable as humans of communicating, in the sense of conveying useful information to each other by emitting and responding to signals. To use Taylor's example, when a bird in a flock emits a shriek upon perceiving a predator, it alerts the rest of the flock to the danger, eliciting a response from the other birds which leads them from the danger (*PA* 85).[26] Clearly, the ability to communicate in this rudimentary way has evolutionary advantages. Higher animals, such as chimpanzees, can also elicit responses by combining signals, and this capacity for combination enables them to build up a potentially indefinite repertoire of signs. Furthermore, higher animals are capable of emitting and responding to signals in ways that are not directly related to self-preservation through action-coordination. This happens in the playful use of signals, an activity which seems crucial to the bonding process between creatures. So even as a mechanism of primitive socialization, language is also cross-specific.[27]

The point Taylor makes about both these uses of language is that the purposes they realize can be defined non-linguistically. To think of language as a mode of adaptation to the pressures of an environment, for instance, is to think of it as serving a function which could in principle be served some other way. One could conceive of non-linguistic ways, for instance, of securing the survival of an individual, a species, or the continuation of genes. We do not need to be inside the language that helps bring about these ends to understand the purposes met by it. Language at this level is intelligible as a mechanism of natural selection. But we can imagine other mechanisms taking its place, that is, we can imagine the purpose served without language. Again, the end of social bonding is something we can conceive being realized by some non-linguistic means. In both cases, then, language is explained by its role in furthering some non-linguistically defined purpose or task.

Following Herder, Taylor does not deny that such functions are crucial to language. The question is rather whether language can be explained solely in such terms; whether it is exhausted by these biologically defined functions. It is this that Taylor denies. Moreover, he thinks that functional accounts that reduce language to some non-linguistic mechanism miss the essence of language, or what is distinctive about language for us, where language realizes a potential dormant in non-human uses. Taylor calls the potential language has that is realized only in human language the 'linguistic dimension' (he also calls it the 'semantic dimension') (*PA* 103). The distinctiveness of the linguistic or semantic dimension lies in the fact that it is only here that the issue of *meaning* or significance arises. The issue of meaning refers to the possibility of talking about the 'rightness' of whatever is expressed in language. At this point Taylor draws on some distinctions made famous by his teacher at Oxford, J. L. Austin, to clarify the issue. Austin distinguished between a locution and its force, and between the illocutionary and perlocutionary forces of utterances. Language is an activity of an embodied being; through it we do things with words (or with non-verbal expressions) which bring about certain effects. The human act of locution conveys a meaning. But *in* performing it (say as a promise, a confession or a warning) an illocutionary force appends to the words. And *by* saying it in a particular context, certain consequences follow: the action has effects, a perlocutionary force, on the interlocutor and maybe elsewhere. The fact that we are able to make such distinctions in the case of human linguistic activity but not of the communication systems of other animals – the distinctions have no application to the cry of the bird, for instance – suggests a qualitative difference between the two kinds of language use. So while it is important to see that before we reach the semantic dimension language is *causally* efficacious in coordinating behaviour, it is even more important to see that language, at least human language, does not *just* succeed (or fail) in that way. The 'rightness' of a locution, the kind of rightness that gives it meaning in the linguistic dimension, is quite distinct from the causal efficacy of a bird's shriek. It has a different and irreducible kind of intelligibility. Once we are in the semantic dimension, what concerns us is not success in serving this or that non-linguistic end, or in meeting an independently definable function, but a relationship of 'fit' between the expression and what is expressed. We have to be *in* language to grasp the way in which rightness works. Rightness is normative and normativity is *sui generis*.

Having located the meaning-dimension of language, the next step is to identify the basic ways in which meaning can emerge in it. Drawing on Herder, but more as a point of departure for his own thinking, Taylor mentions three: language *expresses* meaning, it *constitutes* meaning, and it *produces* meaning. Each overlaps with the others. The idea that meaning is *expressed* in language follows from the fact that language is in the first instance situated. Language arises from an engaged stance in the world, from bodily stances and actions. Human actions are always in some manner expressive of thoughts, feelings, desires and purposes, and speech is a natural development of this expressive potential of action. As Taylor writes: 'Our power to function in the linguistic dimension is tied for its everyday uses, as well as its origins, to expressive speech, as the range of actions in which it is not only communicated but realized' (*PA* 92). Our original condition, then, is not that of minds with private thoughts and feelings which are subsequently communicated in speech (though this is an ability we later acquire as a refinement of our capacity for linguistic expression). Rather, the thoughts and feelings we recognize in ourselves and others come to be as we recognize them through the way we express and articulate them. To say that language expresses meaning, then, is to say that the meaning language conveys is – at least in the original and typical cases – essentially bound to the medium of its conveyance. In this way, meaning is realized and not just communicated in the linguistic dimension. The primary function of language is not to *describe* something already there, something that would be there even without language; though again this is not to deny that language is often descriptive. Rather, language originally expresses things, things that can only be made manifest through the expression, that is, internal to the semantic dimension.

But if meanings do not pre-exist expression, in an important sense the expression *constitutes* the meaning. As we express something, so we constitute it. Taylor identifies three main ways in which meanings are constituted internally to language. First, there are certain interpersonal relations that only come about in so far as they issue from an expressive act. All sorts of social relations are only possible on account of the right word being said, at the right time, in the right way. Just by saying 'sorry', for instance, a whole new social space can be opened up. Second, there is a range of feelings and emotions whose very content depends on the words used to express them. By finding just the right expression, for example, a confusing, troubling emotion can become clear, and with the clarity a new feeling manifests itself. And third, Taylor draws attention to moral standards whose ability to convince and move us is conditioned by the expression we give to them. In all three cases, linguistic expression brings about something which cannot exist without language or outside the linguistic dimension. But this is just another way of saying that language has an internal and intrinsic capacity for meaning *creation*. In Taylor's words, language makes possible 'new purposes, new levels of behaviour, new meanings, and hence is not explicable within a framework of human life conceived without language' (*PA* 101).[28] By expressing thoughts, feelings, desires and purposes in language we can transform them. By giving them a reflective dimension, we can, in effect, create new ones. Taylor mentions the reflective transformation of anger into indignation, of desire into love and admiration. While the outcome of the transformation need not be as morally improving as these examples suggest, the essential point is that language is *productive* of meaning. The semantic dimension makes possible new feelings or emotions, new kinds of interpersonal relations, and new kinds of value – possibilities that do not exist for non-linguistic beings.

In the light of these Herder-inspired reflections on the semantic dimension, Taylor sets out some constraints on an acceptable theory of meaning. Obviously, the theory first has to accept that the semantic dimension is no realm of illusion. Reductive theories of rightness, theories that attempt to analyse rightness in non-normative, causal terms, are non-starters in Taylor's view. But once rightness is recognized as irreducible or intrinsic, it is then important to build into the theory recognition of the *diverse* ways in which 'getting it right' can happen in language. Many critics of the reductive approach have stopped short of this next move. For they have focused their attention too narrowly on one particular mode of rightness, one kind of fit between the expression and what is expressed: namely, truth as the fit between a representation or description and its object. But truth-as-correspondence, or rightness understood as the alignment of a word and an object, is not the only norm holding sway in the semantic dimension. As Taylor writes, 'a creature is operating in the linguistic dimension when it can use and respond to signs in terms of their truth or descriptive rightness, or power to evoke some mood, or recreate a scene, or express some emotion, or carry some nuance of feeling, or in some such way to be *le mot juste*' (*PA* 84). Rightness is not just descriptive; a word or expression can be 'right', 'true' or 'valid' in other ways. To return to Taylor's three ways in which expressions constitute meaning, a word can be the proper one for establishing a desired interpersonal relation ('sorry' bringing about reconciliation); it can be right for clarifying an indeterminate feeling (as 'indignation' rather than 'anger'); and it can articulate a strong value (guide me in my morally significant action) in just the way called for by a situation. So as well as recognizing the *sui generis* normativity of language – that is, the very fact of semantic autonomy – an acceptable theory of meaning must also recognize the plurality of the norms prevailing in it.

For Taylor, then, an important requirement for the theory of meaning is that it acknowledges 'rightness' constraints on non-representative or non-designative modes of language use. In many cases, 'getting it right' does not involve talking *about* something: 'in light of the constitutive nature of speech', Taylor writes, 'talking *about* is only one of the provinces it constitutes' (*PA* 98). We often find ourselves looking for the right word or sequence of words, say, for a deep feeling we have or an unfamiliar relationship we are entering into. When reflecting on our emotions, interpersonal relations and deepest ideals, ordinary descriptive language often lets us down. In order to be *true* to them, we have to *invent* the right words, or perhaps express them in a non-verbal form like music or dance. That is to say, linguistic innovation, or the creation of meanings, is crucial to the constitution of meaning in these provinces. Not just descriptive prose, but broadly speaking 'poetic' modes of expression, are needed for getting at the truth. The capacity of language to get things right without talking about something – the capacity, for instance, to evoke the right mood or express a feeling with the right nuance – should therefore be as central an issue in the theory of meaning as its designative capacity. Prose then loses its status as the paradigmatic mode of getting things right in language. Indeed, not only should the 'poietic powers' of language be considered as essential to it, as a development of a capacity intrinsic to language itself, but they should now be seen as *more* fundamental to language than its capacity for description. Aligning a word with an object is after all contingent on the expressive/ constitutive power available within a language. And if this is so, then the key feature of language that needs to be addressed by a theory of meaning is the *creation* of meaning. As Taylor puts it, 'the constitutive theory turns our attention toward the creative dimension of expression' in which it 'makes possible its own content' (*PA* 107). This orientation, Taylor notes, provided the point of departure for the Romantic theorists. The work of art was not paradigmatic for the Romantic theories of meaning by chance. It is the consequence of a deep insight into the essence of language, namely its capacity to generate meaning from its own resources, spontaneously, as it were, from within. The Romantics rightly saw that the capacity for world-creation and the capacity for world-description have the same origin.

So a theory of meaning has to accommodate the rightness dimension, the plurality of ways in which rightness can come about, and it must not subordinate the world-disclosive power of language to its ability to represent objects. A fourth requirement is that it take seriously what might be called the trans-subjectivity of language. Language is trans-subjective in two important senses. First, language exceeds the powers any subject has to control it. This is partly due to its intrinsic capacity to create meaning, which entails that it is never fully encompassable. The thematization and analysis of any part of language is only possible against an unthematizable, unanalysable 'background'. This is one of the points that 'holist' theories of meaning try to formulate. Holists emphasize that the meaning of an expression is intrinsically bound to the role it plays in the larger language, and this implies that a subject's understanding of an expression involves her in the language as a whole. But language as a whole must not be reified. It is not some static, fixed entity, and no acceptable theory of meaning can make it seem that way. Live, shifting, unpredictable patterns of speech activity are essential to language. And this suggests a second sense in which language is trans-subjective: it situates any particular subject in a language community. As Taylor puts it, the language I speak 'can never be just *my* language; it is always *our* language' (*PA* 99). The grammatically regulated framework of meanings which a subject needs to draw upon to express herself in speech is always already there.[29]

If we let our thinking about language be guided by the constraints just adumbrated, Taylor contends, we are bound to feel dissatisfied with the canonical theories of meaning in the analytic tradition. In Taylor's view, mainstream philosophy of language has entrenched what he calls 'designative' theories, theories that are fundamentally at odds with the 'expressive/constitutive' theories of Herder and the Romantics.[30] As Taylor stages them, designative theories of language originate in the seventeenth century with Hobbes, Locke and Condillac. But they flourish today in the more refined theories of Quine and Davidson. The key idea of designative theory is that the designative power of language is the most 'fundamental in the order of explanation' of language: 'the meaning of words or sentences is explained by their relation to things or states of affairs in the world' (*HAL* 220). These theories acknowledge that language also has an 'expressive' function. But the expressive function of language is made contingent upon its designative or representational powers. Accordingly, the basic unit of meaning – be it the word or the sentence – is in some sense already contained in the object it represents, and the rightness of the word or sentence is determined by the accuracy of its depiction. Some theories of this kind – behaviourist theories, for instance – go so far as to reject any intrinsic difference between words and objects, as if meaning is intelligible in just the way that causal relations between objects are. But most contemporary theories accept that the designative relation is not reducible to a causal one. In this way, they at least acknowledge the linguistic dimension. Yet within their construction of the linguistic dimension, the designative relation is basic. This is the case, Taylor maintains, with the 'neo-designative' truth-conditional theories inspired by the work of Davidson. For such theories, understanding a language is a matter of grasping the truth-conditions that obtain for utterances in the language.

Taylor objects to this kind of theory on a number of grounds, but I can only briefly state the main ones here.[31] First, the theory owes what persuasiveness it has, Taylor thinks, to its artificial focus on a narrow range of descriptive expressions. It arbitrarily takes the use of words that designate the medium-sized material objects of our environment as paradigmatic. Second, it illicitly privileges the perspective of a 'monological observer', that is, the perspective of someone trying to make sense of a language from the outside. Like its narrow focus, this blinds it to the problem of making intelligible constitutive expressions, or expressions which are partly responsible for their own content. And while Taylor acknowledges that truth-conditional theories go some way towards explaining the intrinsic capacity of language to create meaning, he doubts if they do so fully or properly. For in order for the truth-theories that explain meaning to get going, they need to have in place a questionably rigid and hierarchically conceived distinction between strict literal meaning and metaphorical meaning. It makes strict or literal meaning first in the order of explanation, but this clashes with the primordiality of the capacity for world-disclosure. And world-disclosure in turn requires porosity between the two levels of meaning. Furthermore, in Taylor's view the distinction embroils the neo-designative theories in ethnocentrism. For while a hard distinction between literal or strict meaning and metaphorical meaning, and the priority of the former in the determination of 'rightness', has become entrenched in the culture of western modernity, it is not so fixed in other cultures. To read other cultures, or to interpret their languages, *through* this distinction is to blind oneself to the possibilities of cultural variation.

In fact, in Taylor's view designative theories reinforce the dominant philosophical anthropology of modernity in a number of ways. And it is ultimately this feature of them, he conjects, that explains their appeal. By making the designative function paradigmatic, the theory lends credence to a notion of subjectivity as disengaged from the world. It encourages us to think of language as a neutral medium or instrument of representation, one which in a deep sense is at our disposal. It presents language as material for the subject's instrumental freedom. Taylor has no difficulty in showing how the original seventeenth-century formulations of the designative theory at least were informed by such an anthropology of instrumentally self-defining subjectivity. By regarding language as 'an assemblage of separable instruments, which lie as it were transparently to hand', the instrumentally self-defining subject is able to marshal his ideas and put them to his own chosen use (*HAL* 226). By contrast, the theory depicts the engaged, pre-reflective subject as prone to bewitchment by language. Subjects must rid themselves of its control over them to be free. Language must be made maximally transparent if self-defining subjects are to flourish. And this transparency is secured through the designative relation. In designating objects, language is purged of mystery, for objects purely and undistortively represented, represented as they are in the disenchanted world, have no intrinsic significance for us. The alternative to having access to such a neutral instrument of representation is 'to lose control, to slip into a kind of slavery', an 'alienation of my freedom as well as the great source of illusion' (*HAL* 226).

The philosophical anthropology supported by the expressive theory, however, is quite different. If the Romantics were on the right track, then a language being is never fully transparent to herself and is never in full self-possession.[32] Simply by being placed in the semantic dimension – which all but the most primitive language users are – the language being finds herself subject to independently given norms, norms not fully under her control. Her predicament is unavoidably that of a *situated* being, or in Heidegger's expression, of 'thrownness'. The linguistic resources she has for understanding herself and the world are always in some sense borrowed, and the debt, so to speak, is never fully repaid. The dimensions of subjectivity that are constituted by language also militate against transparency. If we consider ourselves to be constituted by our feelings, if the quality of our feelings helps define who we are, then the fact that they can be expressed with more or less clarity, or with more or less intensity, means that we can never fully know ourselves. We have an intrinsic capacity to be surprised by ourselves, and this is in part due to the intrinsically generative (and so never encompassed) world-disclosive power of the language that constitutes us. Similarly, if the interpersonal relations and the standards by which we assess the intrinsic worth of things shape our subjectivity, then the fact that they can be disclosed in unprecedented ways in language also entails limits on our self-possession as subjects. But these limits on self-transparency are not viewed by the Romantics as limits on our freedom. They are not seen as modes of self-alienation. On the contrary, they are the ways in which an expressive subject properly realizes itself, and it is the delusion of a potentially self-transparent subject relating instrumentally to language that confines us and alienates us from ourselves.

The expressive/constitutive theory departs from instrumental and neo-designative theories in taking the power of expression to be the essence of language. But the idea that language is distinguished by its expressive power can itself be taken in different directions. The direction one takes, Taylor suggests, depends on the stance one adopts on three basic issues. First, there is an issue about the nature of the expressive power. What brings it about? Taylor runs through a number of proposals found in the expressivist tradition. For Hegel it was the unfolding of Spirit, for Schopenhauer it was the cosmic Will, for Nietzsche it was the Will-to-Power. But the tradition took a decisive step forward, Taylor suggests, with Heidegger's so-called 'ontological difference': the differentiation of 'Being' (*Sein*) and 'beings' or entities (*Seiende*).[33] This move, as Taylor reconstructs it, enabled Heidegger to talk about the expressive power of language – its power to show things up in a 'clearing' – without bringing into play considerations of its *ontic* foundation (be it self-positing Spirit, the Will, the Will-to-Power, or whatever). This is an important move not just because ontically grounded theories have lost credibility in the modern world: just as damagingly, ontic theories underplay the personally indexed manner in which the creative imagination makes meanings manifest. A second area of controversy within the expressivist paradigm concerns the nature of the reality which manifests itself through the expressive power, if indeed anything real is made manifest there at all. And third, there is the question of the agent of expression, of 'who' is responsible for it. The agency of the clearing can be construed as an individual, as a community of conversing individuals, or as an anonymous structure.

It is important to separate these issues, Taylor argues, because each of them prompts 'subjectivist' and 'anti-subjectivist' responses. One can take an anti-subjectivist stance on the issue of the agent of expression, for instance, but a subjectivist position on the question of manifestation or reality. According to Taylor's interpretation, this is the combination of views held by the influential French philosopher Jacques Derrida. Derrida is often presented as an anti-subjectivist theorist of language. But while, as Taylor sees it, this is true with qualification *vis-à-vis* his stance on the issue of agency – there is no 'subject' responsible for the expression, only structures of 'difference' – it is a misrepresentation of Derrida's position on the issue of reality, which is firmly subjectivist. By contrast, Heidegger is robustly anti-subjectivist on all three issues. He thinks that something makes itself manifest in the clearing, that this reality is beyond the self, and that the agent primarily responsible for disclosure is the speech community. Here again, Taylor commends the direction Heidegger takes.[34]

For Taylor, the anti-subjectivist orientation of Heidegger's thinking about language makes it a suitable successor to Hegel's ontological vision. Hegel, at least according to Taylor's interpretation, tried to show that human subjectivity, properly conceived, is not alienated from nature, for nature itself is the manifestation of spirit. Heidegger, too, wants to keep hold of the idea that the order in which human beings are set is a locus of significance. He shares the aspiration of the Romantic generation to move beyond the separation of meaning and being. But unlike Hegel, and rightly in Taylor's view, Heidegger does not do this by re-enchanting nature at the ontic level. He does it rather by reflecting on the nature of the expressive power. According to Taylor, Heidegger in his later work reasons that if language is able to make things manifest or 'show things up', it must also be able to show up its power to show things up. Language has the potential of bringing to light its own capacity to bring things to light. How a thing looks when it is disclosed in a manner that co-discloses this power or capacity is not a matter of subjective choice. It is something subjects are responsible for – after all it is only human beings who inhabit the linguistic dimension – but in exercising this responsibility we are responding to a norm that is given to us by language itself. And by attending to what the perspicuous expression of the expressive power requires, we alert ourselves to the non-instrumental, intrinsic significance things disclosed that way possess. Not all uses of language, of course, are equally well-suited to this task. In our everyday language we can even forget that language has a world-disclosive power at all. But in the language of 'authentic thinking and poetry', to use Heidegger's terms, we can retrieve a sense of the non-instrumental meaning of the non-human world. Taylor suggests that with this insight, Heidegger points, more surely than Hegel and others in the Romantic tradition, to a place beyond the modern alienation of mind and nature.

4

The Self and the Good

Up to this point we have examined two elements of Taylor's philosophical anthropology. The first, borrowed from existential phenomenology, is that human beings are essentially embodied agents. Experience is in the first instance not a disinterested contemplation or representation of objects but an encounter with things that concern us. The second element, adopted from the German Romantic tradition, is that among the things that concern us, there are some – the quality of our feelings, for example – which owe their existence to the way we express them. Human subjectivity is in important ways constituted by the language in which it is expressed. Entry into the linguistic dimension, as Taylor called it, enables us to express and so realize emotions that are beyond the range of non-human experience. The fact that we are able to 'get things right' about our feelings and emotions in the very course of creatively exploring and articulating them gives us a sense of possessing a 'self' with 'inner depths'. But there is another sense in which humans possess a self, another way of distinguishing human agency from that of non-human animals, that Taylor wants to build into his philosophical anthropology. This has to do with the fact that human beings lead their lives and assess themselves in the light of broadly speaking *moral* standards. As we shall see, this feature of subjectivity is not, in Taylor's view, ultimately separable from the expressive element. They are two aspects of the one anthropological reality. But Taylor's idea that the self has an intrinsic moral dimension has its own justification and can be treated as the third key element of his theory of subjectivity. It can also be considered

as the gateway through which his thinking moves from philosophical psychology and the philosophy of language to ethics.

In the first section of this chapter, we shall examine the meaning
and justification of Taylor's thesis that the self is constituted by
broadly speaking 'moral' concerns. Taylor presented a thesis of
this kind in his well-known 1977 essay 'What is Human Agency?'.[1]
In this piece, Taylor introduced a distinction between 'strong' and
'weak' evaluation. Human beings, Taylor argued, are 'strong evaluators' in the sense that they possess a self, or as Taylor also puts
it an 'identity', constituted by moral concerns (broadly understood).
Taylor proposes this as an ontological thesis: he claims to be identifying something essential to human agency, something without
which an agent would not be recognizably human. At first sight,
Taylor's claim that human agency necessarily has a moral dimension looks implausible, and it has attracted formidable criticism.
However, it becomes less counter-intuitive, though by no means
uncontroversial, if one pays more attention than some of Taylor's
critics do to the expansive meaning Taylor gives to the expression
'a "moral" concern'. This meaning becomes clearer in the opening
chapters of *Sources of the Self*, where Taylor's account of the inseparable connection 'between our sense of good and our sense of self'
(*SS* 41) is elaborated in greater detail. For Taylor, to say that the self
necessarily has a moral dimension is in the first place to say that it
cannot but be 'oriented to the good'. Taylor's defence of this thesis
is certainly forceful, if attenuated by the rather limited scope of his
approach to the self. Taylor then argues that the moral meaning of
subjectivity is also displayed in the 'narrative identity' that the self
possesses. Narrative identity provides the key for thinking about
the meaning of our lives as a whole. While Taylor's account of
narrative identity is extremely suggestive, I will argue that it falls
short by the standards of philosophical anthropology. It is not clear
that narrative identity is an *essential* structure of subjectivity as an
orientation to the good is.

In the third section of the chapter, we turn to Taylor's account of
practical reason. The question of *how* we orient ourselves in relation
to the good, of how we move in the 'moral space' we unavoidably
find ourselves in as agents, is for Taylor the proper subject-matter
of a theory of practical reason. For Taylor, practical reason is primarily a matter of interpreting our often colliding moral concerns
in the best way. It is a matter of articulating and integrating the
substantive demands strong values make on us. As we shall see,
Taylor's approach brings him into dispute with those who think

that morality, strictly or narrowly understood, has its *own* demands irrespective of the strong values an individual or group recognizes. This leads us to Taylor's critique of proceduralist theories of practical reason. Modern proceduralist ethics, according to Taylor, fails to give due consideration of the fundamental issue of moral motivation – a shortcoming reflected in its blindness to the role of what Taylor calls 'moral sources' in human life.

Strong Value

Taylor's point of departure in 'What is Human Agency?' is Harry Frankfurt's famous distinction between first- and second-order desires.[2] First-order desires are desires that human beings share with other animals. Animals desire food, a mate, to avert danger and so forth, and their behaviour can be explained in terms of whatever is required to satisfy such desires. Human beings have similar 'first-order' desires or appetites, but their behaviour is also motivated by positive or negative feelings about the desires themselves. Human beings have the capacity to evaluate their desires accordingly, and they are often motivated to act on the basis of such evaluations. 'Second-order' desires, then, are desires about desires, desires which enable us to arbitrate between motives and so to act in a way that is distinctive of human agency. Taylor is happy with Frankfurt's distinction up to a point. But we have to go on to ask what we do when we evaluate different desires, Taylor thinks, to see an even more important feature of human agency. He identifies two distinct ways of going about it. On the one hand, we can weigh up which of the desires will, as a matter of fact, provide the most satisfaction. Faced with the choice, say, between two desirable flavours of ice cream, I can compare the strength of the desires I happen to have and I can choose on the basis of my stronger desire. The decisive issue in my evaluation is just what I happen to feel like. Taylor calls this a 'weak evaluation'. But a quite different issue is at stake, Taylor remarks, when we find ourselves evaluating desires in terms of their *worth*. So, for instance, petty feelings of spite might incline me one way, but I am also aware that I can be moved by a more generous spirit. What counts now is the way I locate or interpret the feelings, that is, how I characterize them as something base and petty, or as something higher and more admirable. To take another example, I might want to evaluate the love I have for a person in terms of its depth or superficiality. Faced with a choice between this love and another, the quality of it, the way I locate its worth (as deep or superficial, consummate or fatuous), is a crucial consideration. Here too, something is in play that has no equivalent in the case of weak evaluation: namely, some articulation of a standard of worth, or in a phrase Taylor borrows from Elizabeth Anscombe, some 'desirability-characterization'. When we strongly evaluate something, then, we 'classify it in such categories as higher and lower, virtuous and vicious, more and less fulfilling, more and less refined, profound and superficial, noble and base' (*HAL* 16).

With the distinction between strong and weak evaluation in place, Taylor's next move is to show its relevance for our understanding of identity or the self. He first notes that the strong evaluator has a depth and articulacy lacking in the weak evaluator. This is obviously true for the quality of their practical reflection. Faced with a choice, the weak evaluator has a sense of which outcome he would prefer – a sense that he would rather have one of his desires satisfied than another – and he can reflect on the likelihood of satisfying his desires through the course of action he adopts. But he only has an inarticulate, inchoate sense of what it is that makes one desire 'superior', or more worth going for, than another. All he can say is that there is a certain 'feel' to it which appeals to him. The strong evaluator, on the other hand, can articulate his sense that one desire is more worth satisfying than another by locating the desires in a qualitative contrast. His access to a language of qualitative contrasts – such as the contrast between a mean and generous spirit, or between a consummate and fatuous love – enables him to reach a more nuanced and refined understanding of the options available to him. Taylor is not just claiming that the strong evaluator is more articulate *about* his options. His claim is not just that the strong evaluator is capable of a deeper kind of self-*reflection*, important though that is. For he is also claiming that there can only be said to *be* a range of options on account of their 'desirability-characterizations'. The range of possibilities facing the strong evaluator does not pre-exist the articulation of his desires and purposes, as if the weak evaluator had simply overlooked them. The nuance and depth with which the strong evaluator reflects upon his desires and purposes finds its way into the desires and purposes themselves. As the desires and purposes we have constitute us, the life or being of the strong evaluator has a different character to the life or being of the weak evaluator. For Taylor, then, strong evaluation is not just 'a condition of articulacy about preferences, but also about the quality of life, the kind of being we are or want to be' (*HAL* 26).

In a strong evaluation, we give reflective expression to our sense of the contrasting worth of things. But it is important to see that strong evaluations do not create this sense on their own. Rather, they make explicit the sense of worth the evaluator has in his pre-reflective life. The distinction Taylor makes between strong and weak evaluation is a distinction between two kinds of deliberation. And the contrast between the strong and weak evaluator is a contrast between two kinds of agent engaged in deliberation. But we do not have to be engaged in deliberation to have a sense that things differ in quality or worth and to desire them on account of their quality and worth. For this reason the notion of strong value, the notion of whatever is desired for the worth it possesses, is more fundamental than the notion of strong evaluation. Strong values provide us with standards by which we assess the quality of human life. But they also provide us with motivations to live in ways that meet these standards. Strong values are 'goods' in the meaning Aristotle gave to the term: desirable things which are worthy of desire. And it is the relation we have to goods – or, taken together, 'the good' – which, for Taylor, defines our identity as human agents. Taylor's thesis is that human beings owe their identity to the role played by strong value in their lives.

Before we consider the argument Taylor gives in support of this thesis, we must note the full range of things that count as strong values or 'moral' concerns. Taylor distinguishes three 'axes' or 'dimensions' of the good or moral life, dimensions he suspects are found in one form or another in all cultures (*SS* 16). In every culture we find practices that express some conception of concern, love or respect for the 'other human being'. This class of life goods includes the duties, obligations and responsibilities human beings owe to each other. People fall short of the standard set up by this class of life goods when they are cruel to others, betray them, humiliate them, wrong them and so forth. As Taylor suggests, it is hard to imagine any conception of the good, any interpretation of an admirable form of human life, which finds no place for this class of goods. But it is by no means the only class. For there is also the human aspiration to enjoy a fulfilled, meaningful life, rather than one which is empty, shallow or lacking purpose. Of course, there is enormous variation amongst cultures in the content given to this aspiration, even more than is the case with the previous dimension of goods. But it is not unreasonable to suppose that some contrast between the fulfilled and the misspent life has to be drawn in any form of life, and as this contrast articulates something crucial to any understanding of what it is to lead a fully human life, it properly belongs to a conception of the good. The third class of goods Taylor identifies concerns dignity. Dignity elicits the respect of others, a respect born not so much from the duty of care or responsibility for the other as from the recognition of something like nobility. The dignity of another, be it an individual person, group or form of life, is what we acknowledge when we find ourselves 'looking up' to the person, group or life form. Not to measure up to goods in this class, especially in the eyes of dominant or significant others, correlates with a collapse in self-esteem on the part of the individual or group.

Taylor tries to bring out the necessary nature of the connection between strong value and the self by reference to the existential orientation strong values furnish us with. While this idea can be found in Taylor's earlier works, it is elaborated most clearly in *Sources of the Self*. Taylor begins by noting how our sense of self is connected to the 'stand' we take on issues that matter to us. It matters to us that we lead lives that are fulfilling rather than empty, noble rather than base, admirable rather than contemptible, and the like. And we are able to tell the difference between a worthwhile and a wasted life, or between noble and base modes of existence, by being placed in what Taylor calls 'frameworks' of qualitative contrast. We need the frameworks to know where we stand on issues of significance. They provide us with an orientation not for *mere* life but for living well, for leading a fully human life. Taylor also uses the metaphors of 'moral space' and 'space of questions' to describe this predicament. We lead our lives in moral space in the sense that we aspire to live well, but to find our way about the space we need to be oriented correctly in it, and for this we require the frameworks. We lead our lives in a space of questions in the sense that we can always be asked, or ask ourselves, where we stand in relation to the good. We can always be asked who we are in a way that requires us to articulate the purposes we find worth pursuing. An orientation to the good enables us to grasp the meaning of the question of our identity, even if we may not be able to settle on an answer.

Now Taylor claims that it is impossible to sustain a human life without such an ethically oriented self. That there is a moral dimension to subjectivity, that the subject must appear to itself against a background of strong value, is not just a 'contingently true psychological fact about human beings, which could perhaps turn out one day not to hold for some exceptional individual or new type' (*SS* 27). Rather, Taylor's claim is 'that living within such strongly qualified horizons is constitutive of human agency, that stepping outside these limits would be tantamount to stepping outside what we would recognize as integral, that is, undamaged personhood' (*SS* 27). But why *must* we think of ourselves as oriented to the good in this way? Taylor responds with a transcendental argument that tries to show that an orientation to the good is an indispensable feature of actual agency. The argument has the same form as the 'proof' Taylor gave of the thesis that human beings are essentially embodied agents. As we saw, the proof of our embodiment proceeded by way of a formulation of how experience would be if it were not organized around some point of embodied practical orientation. The formulation made explicit our intuitive sense of the boundary at which experience as we normally have it falls apart. The description of the boundary state entitled us to say that our experience is essentially that of embodied subjects, for there can be no doubt that normal experience does match up to a certain standard of coherence. Taylor argues in a similar manner about our orientation to the good. He presents a description of how our lives would be if they were not organized by some sense of moral orientation or strong value. To be without any sense of strong value, as Taylor depicts it, is to suffer a painful and frightening emptiness. It is to be in the grip of something like an 'identity crisis' in the sense described by the psychologist Eric Erikson. Once we make explicit that this is how life without strong value would look, it becomes clear that an orientation to the good, or possession of an identity defined in relation to the good, is indispensable to healthily functioning agency. For this reason we are entitled to say that an orientation to the good is an essential feature of human subjectivity. The contrary ontological thesis, that the self's connection to the good is contingent, merely a matter of choice, 'defines as normal or possible a human life which we would find incomprehensible and pathological' (*SS* 32). If Taylor has formulated the boundary condition of agency here correctly – and he acknowledges that such formulations are always subject to dispute – then we have moral concerns, in an expansive sense, as a matter of anthropological necessity.

One way of disputing Taylor's claim is to question whether Erikson's descriptions of identity crises are descriptions of people who have lost their sense of strong value. Owen Flanagan objects to Taylor's argument on this score.[3] Flanagan accepts that the people described by Erikson as suffering identity crises experience a loss of self. But he denies that the self which is lost is constituted by *ethical* aims and purposes. The problem faced by a person in an identity crisis, Flanagan contends, is that she cannot identify with *any* desire or purpose. It is not that the person has lost her power of moral reflection or sense of what is noble and base or right and wrong. This is evident in the fact that weak evaluators as well as strong evaluators suffer identity crises. Flanagan gives the example of an athlete who at the end of her career finds nothing worthwhile. Though she is a weak evaluator in the sense that her life has been built around 'non-ethical aims', she nevertheless suffers the frightening emptiness of an Eriksonian identity crisis. This objection, however, betrays the misunderstanding I flagged before: it construes 'moral' or 'ethical' concerns – that is, strong values – too narrowly. Taylor is certainly not suggesting that only people who dedicate their lives to the reduction of suffering, say, have selves that can be plunged into crisis. The athlete who has devoted herself to sporting excellence may well value that activity strongly, even if she never explicitly reflected on it as such. If at the end of her career she finds that her life and purposes lack meaning, perhaps it is because she has lost something that previously conferred dignity on her life. And dignity, we have seen, is one of the three axes of the good or the moral life as Taylor construes it. When Taylor argues that there is an inescapably 'moral' dimension to human subjectivity, he is not saying that all human agents must be concerned with the welfare of others. His claim is that recognizable human agency involves some grasp, however inchoate or inarticulate, of the contrast between mere life and good life. It is the loss of *this* sense that Taylor relates to an identity crisis.

A brief look at some of the other criticisms Flanagan makes of Taylor will serve to reinforce the importance of interpreting 'moral' concerns in an expansive way. Flanagan reads Taylor as proposing an empirical claim: namely, that only strong evaluators have a healthily functioning identity. This claim must be false, Flanagan argues, because there are plenty of people with rich and effective identities who do not strongly evaluate. First, there is a large class of indisputably moral agents who simply do not reflect on their moral standards. The uneducated but dignified peasants of Tolstoy's novels, for instance, are inarticulate, they do not strongly evaluate, but no one would doubt they have morally effective selves. This objection is weak because while one can be inarticulate about the qualitative contrasts or strong values one lives by or aspires to, one must be *capable* of recognizing them in an explicit formulation (though any one formulation may of course be contested). In any case, as I noted above, strong value is logically and ontologically prior to strong evaluation. It is strong values rather than strong evaluations that are constitutive of identity. But in Flanagan's view, not even inarticulate awareness of qualitative contrasts is necessary for identity. To be aware of a qualitative contrast is to have some comprehension of an alternative to the life one leads. But there may be people, Flanagan suggests, for whom no other possibilities are conceivable. We would not on that account judge them as lacking selves. However, it is not clear what it would really be like to be 'unaware of contrastive possibilities' in the relevant sense. It cannot simply be to lack awareness of other cultures, whether actual or imaginary: that would beg the question, for the very notion of a culture seems to involve the idea of a framework of qualitative distinctions, which is, *ex hypothesi*, precisely what such people find it impossible to grasp. Nor can it be that within a culture there may only be one conceivable standard of living well: even that would require a background qualitative contrast. Moreover, the inherent generativity of language ensures that there are *always* new contrastive possibilities immanent to a culture, so the thought that contrastive alternatives may be inconceivable is incoherent. Flanagan's third objection is that Taylor's criterion of identity excludes all those people for whom morality is not a central concern. There are many people, for instance, who value pleasure more than anything else. Strong evaluation plays little if any role in their lives, without it depriving them of a sense of self. But once again, the objection rests on a too narrow construal of a moral concern. Like Tolstoy's inarticulate but upright peasant, the contemporary hedonist has a sense of the worth of things. He has a sense of the contrast between a wasted or misspent life and a fulfilled one, and this is enough to place him in 'moral' space in the expansive meaning Taylor gives to the term.

In Flanagan's view, Taylor's account of identity has two basic flaws. It is 'intellectualist' on account of its lending too much importance to reflection and articulacy. And it is 'moralist' on account of its exaggerating the role played by moral principles in constituting identity. In Taylor's defence, we can say that the crucial feature is strong value, not the narrower intellectual category of strong evaluation. On the moralism charge, we can say that moral principles are only one way of characterizing one of the dimensions of strong value. The link Taylor makes between identity and the good is premised on a non-moralistic, expansive understanding of the good. However, it may still be that Taylor's concept of the good is not broad enough to connect it with identity in the manner proposed. As Taylor often says, the most fundamental feature of a self is that things matter to it. The self is first and foremost a being with concerns. If my desires and purposes mean nothing to me, I suffer a loss of self in this sense. Such is the unfortunate predicament of the person in an identity crisis. Nothing matters to him. But the person without a horizon of qualitative contrasts is in a slightly different predicament: she is at a loss to say what is *worth* mattering. There does seem to be an equivocation in Taylor's use of the concept 'mattering' here. On the one hand, there are things that matter to us just on account of our embodiment in the world. On the other, there are things that matter to us on account of their worth. Even if we understand 'worthiness' of desire and purpose in Taylor's expanded, non-moralistic sense, it may simply be the sheer insignificance of embodied life that cripples the person in the identity crisis. Her affliction may be the non-mattering of 'mere life' rather than the invisibility of anything worth mattering, that is, the invisibility of a 'good life' compared with it. The real force of Flanagan's objections is that Taylor does not do enough to accommodate this possibility within his own account of identity. It is important that Taylor is able to do this to back up his claim that disorientation *vis-à-vis* the good has the same phenomenological characteristics as the pathological dislocation of the person in an identity crisis.

Furthermore, even if one's sense of self is intrinsically linked to one's orientation to the good, it does not follow that the self is *only* constituted that way. To suppose that identity is exclusively a matter of strong values, as Amelie O. Rorty and David Wong have observed, is to have an implausible 'top-down view' of the self.[4] It is to ignore the crucial role played by factors at the bottom end of identity, so to speak, such as temperament, psychological habits and emotional dispositions. My temperament and emotional dispositions, at least as much as the ideals I identify with, determine who I am. There is a somatic dimension to identity as well as an ideal dimension, and a theory of the self must take both into account. It is also important to take both dimensions (and others too) into account when engaged in practical deliberation. An agent whose self-reflection focuses exclusively on her ideal identifications, without any reflective awareness of her temperament and emotional dispositions, is unlikely to reach sound judgements about the course of life best suited to her. The suitability of this or that ideal for any given agent is crucially conditioned by the agent's somatic constitution. In virtue of my temperament, I will be drawn to or repelled by this or that purpose without strongly evaluating them. But nor is the attraction or repulsion merely a matter of pro- or con attitudes to be weighed up in the manner of a weak evaluation. I have to take into account the non-strongly valued desires and purposes I have in virtue of my temperament in a more complex way than weighing them up as preferences. Such desires and purposes are neither merely '*de facto*' nor strongly evaluated ones. One of the key issues practical reason must address is the match between temperament and ideal, or as Rorty and Wong put it, the practical reasoner seeks 'an equilibrium in the relative importance that should be accorded to different identity aspects'.[5] While, as we shall see in a moment, Taylor's model of practical reason is more sophisticated than the one attributed to him by Rorty, Wong and Flanagan, it is not unfair to describe it as being 'top-down' in character.

Narrative Identity

In Taylor's view, a life without strong value would not be recognizably human. The self cannot but be oriented to some conception of the good in the sense that human beings cannot but live with some comprehension of the distinction between mere life and a properly human life. The argument Taylor gives in support of this thesis says nothing about the indispensability of moral principles in a narrow sense, though Taylor does think that, as a matter of fact, respect for others is strongly valued everywhere. But for Taylor, the indispensability of strong value is not the only reason for supposing that human subjectivity has an inescapable 'moral' dimension. There is also something about the *unity* of a self that necessarily lends it a moral meaning. Taylor introduces this idea by way of extending the metaphor of a life led in moral space. Our sense of who we are is linked to the stand we take on issues of concern, and for that we need points of orientation, the reference points provided by frameworks of qualitative contrast. But we are not fixed in this space once and for all. Our lives and concerns change. No one is frozen in time, and it follows from the sheer temporality of life, Taylor thinks, that 'the issue of the direction of our lives must arise for us' (*SS* 47). On account of the fact that self-understanding inescapably occurs in time, it requires some synthesis of the present, past and future. Narratives provide the vehicle of such synthesis. So for Taylor, just as the self is and must be oriented by a framework which maps a moral space, it must also be located in a narrative which tracks its unfolding in time. As Taylor puts it, 'making sense of one's life as a story is also, like orientation to the good, not an optional extra' (*SS* 47). In order to be able to answer the question of who-identity, the question 'who am I?', one must have recourse not only to strong evaluation but also to narrative.

Taylor is not saying here that the self has a *substantive* unity, as if the self were some kind of entity that endures through time. And he is not offering a criterion of 'personal identity' as that notion is commonly understood amongst philosophers. On the contrary, he is highly critical of the philosophical discourse that takes its departure from the question: 'in virtue of what property am I the *same* person now as I was before or will be in the future?'. For that discourse puts in play a highly stylized and truncated conception of the self – what Taylor calls the 'punctual self' (*SS* 49). The punctual self is set up as an object to be known through its transparent presence to a consciousness reflecting on itself. If no such presence comes to mind, it is discounted as an illusion (roughly Hume's view), and where something is deemed present (as in Locke's theory), it is abstracted from the concerns that characterize real embodied selves. In both cases we find the kind of reification Taylor earlier diagnosed in empiricist theories of the 'mental'. The unity or 'narrative identity' of a self, as Taylor envisages it, is better described in terms introduced by Heidegger, as a synthesis of 'thrownness' and 'projection'.[6] This brings us closer to the crucial idea, in Taylor's view, that the various moments of a life, in relation to which we understand who we are, have a *direction*. It only makes sense to ascribe direction to a life if we can distinguish between more or less significant moments, events or experiences. But in doing this we are articulating a changing relation to the good. The fact that the story I am living projects me into a future, to a self I am not yet but which must be of concern, gives my life, indeed all human life, the character of a 'quest'.

The full force of the idea of a life quest – which Taylor borrows from Alasdair MacIntyre[7] – only comes to light when one considers the temporal scope of the concerns that frame answers to the question of who-identity. We have seen that in answering the question of identity we have to place ourselves in a time sequence. It is only by placing one's concerns in a sequence that the relatively fixed and stable parts of one's character stand out from the variable and the changing. Only by placing my self-understanding in a story of 'maturations and regressions, overcomings and defeats' – that is to say, in a narrative which articulates direction – can I make sense of myself as 'a being who grows and becomes' (*SS* 50). But in Taylor's view, the narratively connected sequence of events I need to answer the question of who-identity must be a sequence that extends over a *whole* life. Taylor appeals here to a general human aspiration for meaning and substance covering the whole of one's life. Human beings live in the hope that the future will in some sense 'redeem' the past. This is illustrated by projects of imaginative temporal recovery where, as in Proust, 'a formerly irretrievable past is recovered in its unity with the life yet to live, and all the "wasted time" now has a meaning, as the time of preparation for the work of the writer who will give shape to this unity' (*SS* 51). In view of this aspiration, which can be articulated in many ways, any restriction of the temporal sequence of one's life in either the past or future must appear as a 'mutilation'. One cannot make sense of one's life, nor experience it as truly meaningful, while repudiating one's childhood, for instance, or limiting its directionality to some arbitrarily chosen point in the future. In this sense, 'it is *not* up for arbitrary determination what the temporal limits of my personhood are', so that 'there is something like an a priori unity of a life through its whole extent' (*SS* 51). Taylor concedes that other cultures may experience time differently. Decisive ruptures in the flow of a life, understood as the death and birth of completely different selves, are conceivable. But they can be so conceived only by stepping outside the horizon of western modernity. Within this culture at least, 'the supposition that I could be two temporally succeeding selves is either an overdramatized image, or quite false. It runs against the structural features of a self as a being who exists in a space of concerns' (*SS* 51).

Let us reflect for a moment on just what Taylor is claiming when he says that narrative identity is essential to human beings. For on first hearing, the thesis that narrative self-understanding is an inescapable, structural requirement of human agency does not ring true. We consider story-telling to be a special art, a skill only some people possess. Surely, to be incapable of telling a convincing story about oneself does not thereby forfeit one's claim to agency. Even the capacity to care deeply about one's narrative identity, we might think, is hardly a requirement of having identity at all. Compare at this point Taylor's thesis about the inescapability of frameworks of strong value. One objection that could be made against this thesis is that if strong values are so essential, how is it that many people – hedonists for instance – seem to manage without them? Taylor's reply, we saw, was that strong value seeps more deeply into our understanding of the worth of human life than we might initially suppose. Once we make explicit what would really be involved in a life without moral horizons – understood broadly as an orientation to the good – it cannot but strike us as pathological. No one could conceivably choose to live a 'care-free' life in the sense of a life led without background distinctions of worth. Taylor thus provides us with a good reason for accepting his claim that strong values are necessary. But can the same argumentative strategy be applied to the alleged inescapability of narrative identity? It is not clear that it can. Taylor does not show that the loss of narrative identity would have devastating consequences for the subject. And without such an argument, we are not forced to the conclusion that narrative identity is necessary in the requisite sense. Failing some demonstration that narrative self-understanding is indispensable to the well-being of an individual, we need not accept Taylor's thesis that narrative identity is 'inescapable'.

This is not to deny, however, that a narrative identity may be desirable. The central point about narratives, for Taylor's purposes, is their 'capacity to confer meaning and substance on people's lives' (*SS* 97). In Taylor's view, the desire for such meaning is shared by all human beings. It is, in a phrase he sometimes invokes, an 'anthropological constant'. Now we could interpret Taylor as arguing that narrative identity is a capacity human beings have for meaning in this desirable sense, even if the realization of the capacity is not necessary for recognizable, functioning human agency. The argument would then be not so much that we *must* be able to make sense of our lives as having a direction, but that narrative self-understanding helps us lead *more* fully human lives, precisely by realizing the capacity we have for meaning and substance. Failure to realize this capacity may not be *as* self-destructive as the absence of an orientation to the good. But it is still self-mutilation of sorts. If we are committed to the good of a meaningful life – and who in their right minds would not be? – then we should develop our capacity for narrative identity. Only people with such a developed capacity have access to this crucial human good.

While this line of argument is more persuasive, it is still not clear why a meaningful life must be one which, as a whole, has direction. We have seen that the narrativity of identity, in Taylor's view, is only fully captured in the idea that one's life as a whole has the character of a quest. But even if we accept that the meaning of a life requires some narrative figuring, why must it be as a quest-type story, a story of self-discovery in relation to the good? In the first place, one might simply be sceptical that the meaningful moments of one's life can be encompassed in a single unifying narrative. One might just think that this kind of approach tends to falsify things. On the other hand, over and above the question of its truth, one might feel unduly restricted, strait-jacketed perhaps, by the thought that one's life can be so encompassed. And Taylor himself sometimes distances himself from the idea that a life can be properly articulated in a single story. In the later chapters of *Sources of the Self* Taylor applauds many of the ways in which the modernist literary imagination departs from traditional notions of a unified self. The modernist turn inward, as Taylor puts it, 'may take us beyond the self as usually understood, to a fragmentation of experience which calls our ordinary notions of identity into question' (*SS* 462). Again, the modernists 'carry us quite outside the modes of narration which endorse a life of continuity or growth with one biography or across generations' (*SS* 464). But if we really *can* do without narratives that present our lives in terms of continuity and growth, and do so, moreover, in a manner truer to our experience, then what are we to make of the thesis expressed earlier in *Sources of the Self* that we are essentially beings of 'maturation and regression', of 'growth and becoming', beings essentially on a quest? These two ways of narrating the self – and there may well be others – seem to contradict each other.

The problem we see here reflects in a particularly vivid fashion a more general tension in Taylor's project. On the one hand, the aim of philosophical anthropology as Taylor understands it is to identify certain human constants, that is, more or less universal features of human subjectivity. The basic model is Aristotelian in inspiration, though with important expressivist accruements. Human beings are creatures with distinctive natural capacities, capacities that are realized, or 'expressed', in different forms through history and across cultures. Taylor has to be able to specify what these are without naturalizing or falsely universalizing any of their contingent cultural manifestations. This mode of reflection is unlikely to countenance anything but a thin or minimal ontology of the human. Though minimal, the ontology will have normative force to the extent that we find it desirable to realize these capacities in a mature rather than stunted form. But the thinness of the ontology is unlikely to yield much of normative substance. To get beyond a minimal description of who we are simply *qua* human, to bring a richer portrait of *ourselves* into view, Taylor has to interpret the historically specific ways in which these capacities are realized in modern civilization. He has to interpret the specifically modern ways in which meaning is created, recovered and indeed destroyed. This side of the project has 'thicker' or more substantive normative implications. For we have to be able to recognize ourselves in the account he offers, and that involves seeing ourselves as meeting or falling short of specific cultural ideals. But it is not going to be easy to keep the two tasks separate. There is a danger that one will slide into the other. One possible outcome of such a slide is the presentation of a general human capacity in a more substantive form than the minimal ontology warrants. Another is the presentation of norms derived from such culturally embellished capacities as if they were universal. We find both outcomes, I suggest, in Taylor's thesis that self-understanding through a quest-type narrative is an 'a priori structure of human agency'.

Practical Reason

If strong value and narrative identity are to earn their place in an ontology of the human, Taylor has to show that the lives we lead and aspire to would be impossible without them. They must feature as 'indispensability conditions' for something undeniable: the leading of life. Now whether or not the transcendental arguments Taylor marshals in support of this ontology are successful, there is one question that surely does press itself on human beings everywhere: faced with a choice between courses of action, what is the right thing to do? In many circumstances, the answer to this question – to the extent that it can be determined – will have little or nothing to do with strong values or one's sense of self. If I want to save up enough money for a new car, for instance, I must act prudently. The 'right' thing to do here has no moral meaning; it is just a matter of choosing the most effective option, the one that is most likely to lead to success. Practical reason, in the sense of calculating the most efficient means to an end, clearly has a role in determining the right course of action in such circumstances. But there are also occasions where the question 'what is the right thing to do?' can only be answered by bringing strong values and a sense of identity into play. If I am faced with a choice, say, between embarking on a career in industry or the teaching profession, what is the right thing for me to do? I take into account the money I will earn, promotion prospects and so forth. But I also have to reckon with the kind of person I am and aspire to be. I have to consider which option will better serve the things I take to be intrinsically worthwhile, fulfilling and admirable. I want to act in a way that is in some sense 'true' to myself. Or if I find myself at a turning point in a relationship, I might need to reflect on who I am, on what really matters to me and gives me fulfilment, before I reach a judgement on the right thing to do. To take one more example, there are options people face as collective agents, decisions that have to be made concerning what is right for *us* to do. Faced with a choice between becoming a republic or remaining a monarchy, for instance, or between becoming a sovereign state and remaining within a federation, the question 'who are we?' will feature significantly in a nation's deliberations. There are circumstances, then, when we address practical problems by reflecting on our strong values or sense of identity. And like the prudential reasoning we engage in when we think instrumentally about realizing an end, it is something we can do well or badly.

For the most part, we think and act in ways that express our strong values without making them explicit in reflection. Frameworks of qualitative contrast form the 'background' of our moral thought and action. When we express disapproval of someone's cowardly act, for instance, we do not (usually) need to reflect on the matter first: we just take it for granted that disapproval is the right response. Likewise, the gratitude we acknowledge for an act of generosity is not (usually) the product of some reasoning process on our part. It is not the conclusion of an argument. Typically, we have cause for reflection, and so recourse to practical reason, when our moral assumptions become problematic, when the moral space we move in, to use Taylor's metaphor, presents us with a challenge. This can happen at any time, but certain circumstances tend to precipitate it.

First, practical reason becomes necessary when we are faced with incommensurable goods. We face incommensurable goods when we encounter competing demands on our conduct. On such occasions, we recognize that two (or more) goods have a claim on us. We recognize the validity of each of the goods, but we seem unable, at least at first sight, to meet them both. To take a familiar example, people often have to choose between continuing a long-term, strongly valued relationship and exploring dimensions of their identity they believe they can only realize outside the relationship. We have two goods that seem to require different and incompatible courses of action. Generally, we resort to practical reason to help us cope with incommensurability in the ends we pursue. At least in some cases, this can lead us to reflect on the strong values that mean *most* to us. It can involve a ranking of the goods we recognize. Taylor calls the goods that feature at the top of such ranking, the goods that matter most to us, 'hypergoods'. Hypergoods are goods 'which not only are incomparably more important than others but provide the standpoint from which these must be weighed, judged, decided about' (*SS* 63). Hypergoods are 'second-order' goods because they enable us to discriminate between goods or strong values. The task of choosing between goods, in Taylor's view, is often a matter of interpreting the requirements of a hypergood. But hypergoods themselves, as Taylor stresses, are sources of conflict. On the one hand, one might recognize several higher-order goods, that is, different standpoints from which to evaluate or rank first-order goods. On the other hand, the single-minded pursuit of a hypergood has its own costs. Those who aim at the highest good must sacrifice other goods. There are occasions when those who do have such an aim find themselves asking whether the sacrifice required by the hypergood is really worth it, and such moments also precipitate practical reason.

There are circumstances, then, when we have to try to reconcile incommensurable values in our own lives. But practical reason also occurs where different people have incommensurable ends; that is, where there is disagreement or conflict between people over hypergoods. The problem here is not so much integrating incommensurable values within a life as criticizing standards which contradict one's own, or defending one's values from the criticism of others. Such conflict can arise between individuals within societies, that is to say, between individuals who nevertheless share much of a common culture. Or it can arise between cultures, where the dominant values of one are offensive to the broadly agreed standards of another. A third circumstance of practical reason worth mentioning occurs when, in the course of changes in our individual lives or the culture that surrounds us, we come to question the strong values or hypergoods with which we have customarily identified. In conditions of change, traditional values may come to seem inappropriate and new values emerge to challenge them. While this is related to the previous two occasions of practical reason, the outcome here is not so obviously predetermined by our initial strong values or hypergoods. The challenge is not to accommodate recognized but incommensurable goods, nor to criticize practices in the light of accepted standards. Rather, the challenge is to the dominant standards or hypergoods themselves.

While the circumstances that call for practical reason vary, they do have an important feature in common: they are always situations in which agents are *addressed* in concrete situations. In Taylor's view, this gives practical reason an *ad hominem* structure that the mainstream theories of practical reason neglect.[8] The two standard approaches to practical reason in modern moral philosophy are utilitarianism and Kantianism. Both can take naïve and sophisticated forms, and it should be said that the versions Taylor considers lie distinctly in the former category. Still, Taylor is interested in the basic models utilitarianism and Kantianism deploy. For utilitarianism, practical reason is essentially a matter of calculating the measurable consequences of actions. Faced with a choice between courses of action, we should try to figure out which option would have the optimal outcome, that is, bring about the greatest happiness for the greatest number. We should do this if we are interested in doing the right thing, or more accurately, if we are committed to performing the action that is *morally* required of us in a narrow sense. Taylor rehearses many of the familiar arguments against the utilitarian model: the unwieldiness of the calculation involved, the fact that people value diverse goods that cannot be commensurated or converted, so to speak, into the single currency of 'happiness', and the inadequacy of its account of moral motivation. Taylor's underlying objection is the sheer *impracticality* of the utilitarian model – hardly a minor drawback for a theory of practical reason. The basic Kantian model fares no better. Practical reason, on the Kantian account, is a question of submitting the maxims on which one acts to the universalization test. The maxim on which one acts is favoured by reason if I can consistently universalize it, that is, will that everyone else do as I do in similar circumstances. Again, Taylor expresses some widely held reservations about this approach, such as the abstract, indeterminate nature of the norms it generates, its homogenization of moral standards to a single principle, and its roundabout way of addressing the moral motivations of the agent. It thus shares with utilitarianism a certain impracticality. With its focus set primarily on the abstract justification of norms, it does not address itself to the living agent, the agent who must in the end act in accordance with the deliverances of practical reason.

As Taylor sets them up, both utilitarianism and Kantianism work with a 'procedural' conception of practical reason. A procedural conception, as the name suggests, defines the rationality of an agent or an action in terms of the procedure the agent follows. 'Getting it right' is *by definition* a matter of following the proper method in one's thinking. If I reach my decision by following the prescribed method – say by calculating the consequences of the options before me or considering their generalizability – it *must* be the right decision, because that is how 'right' is defined. We can say it is right without having to take into account the content or substance of the decision itself. Taylor also calls such theories 'criterial'. They are criterial in the sense that the requirements of reason are determined in advance by some fixed criterion, the maximization of happiness for utilitarians or the universalizability of maxims for Kantians. The theories construe these criteria as if they were applicable to *any* practical deliberation, that is, as holding independently of subject-matter or context. But by doing this, Taylor objects, the standard theories fetishize practical reason: they endow some formula – which is not without use as a guiding principle in certain circumstances – with a life and validity of its own. By insisting on determinacy, they also give an overly *rationalistic* account of practical reason.

In place of proceduralism, Taylor proposes what he calls a 'substantive' model of practical reason. The central point about a substantive theory is that the rightness practical reason aims at is intrinsically linked to the content of its deliverances and only indirectly to the procedure which generates them. The order of priority in the explanation of rightness is thus reversed. How are we to tell when something is favoured by reason, so understood? We can do it, according to Taylor, by thinking of practical reasoners as engaged in 'rival interpretations of possible transitions' (*SS* 72). The practical reasoner does not abstract from the substance of the options before her; rather, she considers how they compare. She wants to know whether the move or transition from one standpoint to another, from one interpretation of a strong value to another, constitutes improvement. We are able to say that a practical deliberation 'gets it right' to the extent that we can project or reconstruct the transition from one interpretative standpoint to another as an 'error-reducing' one. The crucial point is that the rightness is revealed by the content, not the procedure, by a content clarified through a contrast. So, for example, the person confronted with a choice between staying in the relationship and moving on has two concrete possibilities before him, and he has to interpret the transition from one course of life to another as a loss or gain, as a move towards or away from self-realization. Or, faced with someone whose understanding of what it means to be a patriot is very different to and incommensurable with my own, I can engage in practical reason with the person by comparing interpretations. For the matter to be decided by practical reason is for an 'error-reduced' interpretation to emerge from the encounter. This happens when we arrive at a perspective that identifies and resolves contradictions in the initial interpretation, or removes confusions it relied on, or acknowledges the importance of some factor the initial interpretation screened out. Taylor acknowledges that the substantive model is more modest than proceduralism in only ever telling us which of two alternatives is favoured by reason. It is also 'weaker' in the sense that the rationality of an interpretative position is not fixed once and for all. As the rationality of an interpretation is determined by the improvement it represents *vis-à-vis* a rival, it is always vulnerable to succession by other, more perspicuous interpretations. But the key advantage of the substantive theory, in Taylor's view, is that it gives a more plausible account of the *order of explanation* of practical validity than proceduralism. And while the *ad hominem* structure of practical reason limits the scope of the validity obtained, by the same token it locates validity where it matters – in the experience of agents facing concrete options. The substantive model does not divorce practical reason from the agent's set of moral motivations in the manner of the proceduralist theory.

The Right and the Good

Admittedly, defenders of proceduralism do not necessarily see the separation of justification from motivation as a problem, at least not an insurmountable one. A view like this is expressed by the neo-Kantian philosopher Jürgen Habermas.[9] Habermas is impressed by Taylor's insight that identity-shaping values are not arbitrary.[10] He draws on Taylor's concept of strong evaluation to explain the 'ethical' use of practical reason. In the ethical use of practical reason, we strive to clarify the strong values that define our identity. Its goal, in Habermas's phrase, is 'hermeneutic self-clarification', the clarification of our conception of the good. It is to be distinguished from the 'pragmatic' or 'prudential' use of practical reason whereby we seek to realize some outcome by the most effective means. But for Habermas there is a third use of practical reason, irreducible to these, which following Kant he calls the 'moral' use. We turn to the moral use of practical reason specifically to determine whether the

norms that affect us are just or 'right'. Participants in the moral use
of practical reason are concerned with justice; their purpose is to
test the validity of some socially prevailing norm from a specifically
'moral' point of view. In Habermas's theory, a norm has validity
from a moral point of view, it can be said to be just, if it meets with
the agreement of all those affected by it in a practical discourse.
Agreement in a practical discourse is reached on the basis of arguments rather than coercion. Habermas's theory is procedural, then,
because it construes the justness of a norm as determined by the
procedure through which it is tested. It is the procedure of reaching consensus on the basis of arguments, rather than the content or
substance of the norm on which agreement is reached, that is first
in the order of explanation of 'rightness'.

Now Habermas accepts that, from a certain perspective, his
theory has drawbacks of a kind identified by Taylor.[11] It says little,
for instance, about an agent's motivations to participate in practical discourse or to engage in the moral use of practical reason. And
Habermas concedes that only the most abstract normative principles can emerge from the testing procedure intact. But Habermas's
reply is that these restrictions are necessary if we are to capture an
essential feature of justice: its autonomy *vis-à-vis* the particular ends
people pursue and the strong values they identify with. We can only
come to see things from the moral point of view by abstracting from
our strong values. Only by abstracting from them and assessing
their claim to universality can we determine their moral rightness
– their claim to affect *everybody* as a matter of right. And the validity or lack of validity of this claim holds irrespective of whether
people are, as a matter of empirical fact, motivated to adopt the
moral point of view or to act in accordance with its deliverances.
The justice of a norm is one thing, the ability of people to abide by
it another.

Like his fellow Kantian John Rawls, Habermas deems it an important requisite of a theory of practical reason to display, and indeed
justify, the autonomy of the moral point of view. It is important not
just because it preserves the distinct character of our intuitions
about justice, intuitions that suggest the demands of justice are of
a different order to the demands arising from conceptions of the
good. Over and above that, a rationally secured moral point of view
can be invoked to bring oppressive or violently imposed conceptions of the good to account. The procedural theory enjoins us to
think of the right as prior to the good, as having a uniquely binding
rational claim on us. For both Rawls and Habermas, the political

dividend of the priority of right lies in the space it opens for rationally grounded social criticism.[12] The theory invites us to ask: from a moral point of view, are the dominant norms of a given society justified? As we shall see later, Taylor doubts this is a useful point of departure for the social critic, and it certainly is not his own. But leaving that issue aside, Habermas's theory invites us to ask whether Taylor's 'substantive' model either fails to address a key dimension of practical reason – its moral use – or, if it is meant to address it, whether it does so adequately. At first sight, it does not seem that Taylor's model is well-suited for understanding the moral use of practical reason. It is not set up to test the universalizability of norms. It does not of itself incorporate a mechanism for including the point of view of all others, a mechanism which seems to be necessary if the outcome of practical reason is to reflect the general and not just an individual's or a group's interest. And it is not geared towards establishing the impartiality of norms, a feature we expect of justice. If we want our model of practical reason to show how claims to impartiality can be justified, if we want it to supply a rationally grounded means of testing the 'moral' status of normative claims – with all that implies for their obligatory force – we will have to look elsewhere. Taylor's model simply does not seriously address the issue of the rational foundation of morality construed this way.

But in Taylor's defence two points can be made. First, even if there is a range of norms that can meet with universal agreement, how often do we have to reckon with them? In most cases, the troubling feature of the norms we practically reason about is not their claim to universality: it is rather the ability of the norm to merit the allegiance of people with this or that particular identity. If we find ourselves in *unwanted* conflict over a norm, the relevant topic for deliberation may be: 'what is it about our identities that brings us into conflict?'. If the aim of practical reason is conflict resolution, the participants have to ask themselves how they might change in the interests of peace. They must reflect on whether living in peace with others and resolving conflicts by agreement is itself something they strongly value, and if so, how they might change to accommodate it. It is not clear why such questions raise claims about universality, but they clearly are the kind of questions that practical reasoners ask themselves in Taylor's model. So even in the terrain where the 'moral point of view' is supposed to hold sway – the resolution of conflict by fair rather than violent means – the 'ethical' use of practical reason is of relevance. It could also be said in

Taylor's defence that the demands of justice can themselves be integrated into the ethical use of practical reason. One can reflect, for instance, on whether one's form of life really meets taken-for-granted standards of justice; or one can question the taken-for-granted interpretations of the standards themselves. While such reflection may not be too informative about the ultimate justification of justice claims, it can help clarify what justice demands in particular contexts.

For Kantian philosophers like Habermas and Rawls, beings capable of practical reason have a peculiar dignity. They are unique in being able to determine for themselves their own maxims of action and forms of life. But self-determination or autonomy in turn brings distinct duties and responsibilities. It is our right as autonomous beings to give the rule to our lives; but by the same token, as rational beings we are bound to recognize the same right in others. The very thing that makes it possible for us to be free – practical reason – obliges us to respect the freedom and dignity of others. Kantian practical reason thus secures a special place for autonomy and respect for others in the scheme of human values. Only these values, in the Kantian view, have necessary and universal validity. Furthermore, their unique basis in practical reason helps explain the peculiarly strong commitment people have to them. We do not accord them a special status in our reasoning *because* we strongly value them. Rather, their central role in our reasoning is reflected in the general attachment we have to them as goods. For Kantians, the *feelings* we have about these values, like their institutionalization in society, are contingent matters. Not all individuals strongly value them. And not all societies – perhaps not any – properly embody the values of autonomy and equal dignity in their culture and institutions. But if the actuality of these norms is contingent, their *validity* is necessary. Consequently, all individuals and all societies are bound by them, like it or not. This thought lies behind two characteristic features of Kantian theory. First, the theory insists that questions of moral justification be separated from questions of moral motivation. Models of practical reason that fuse the two issues, as Taylor's model does, are then rejected for robbing moral reason of its singular binding force. Second, Kantianism asserts the so-called priority of 'the right' over 'the good'. The right is logically prior to the good in the sense that it is the proper subject-matter of a theory of practical reason, treatable in its own terms without reference to a theory of the good. And the right enjoys normative priority, in the sense that the claims of right trump the claims of the good. Where the demands of morality clash with the fulfilment of someone's conception of the good the former ought to prevail. The priority of the right means that without moral rightness, goodness lacks worth; but not necessarily vice versa.

While the autonomy of the moral point of view and the priority of right over the good are of long-standing philosophical pedigree, Taylor finds it hard to credit either idea. The wedge proceduralism places between justification and motivation leaves it an open question why anyone, on reflection, should in his particular case choose to act in a way sanctioned by moral reason. And reasons that lack motivating power, in Taylor's view, are not much good as *practical* reasons. To acknowledge the cognitive force of some claim is one thing, to be *moved* by it another. While exclusive attention to the former might be appropriate for theoretical reason – at least in its modern, scientific form – in the case of practical reason, where the leading of a life is at stake, it seems strangely beside the point. Effective practical reason, Taylor wants to say, empowers us to live the way we see fit or to act as the situation demands. He makes a similar point about the priority of the right over the good. The logical priority of the right falsely assumes that the right can be specified independently of frameworks of qualitative contrast – the frameworks of strong value that form the background of moral judgement. As the language of theory is embroiled in these frameworks, the theorist is always at least implicitly dependent on some background conception of the good. Likewise, justice has to *matter* to practical reasoners, it has to engage their hearts and minds if reason is to deliver anything more than empty truths to them. People have to *be* a certain way – they have to have some orientation to the good – *before* they can respond to the claims of right. This is not to deny that the right, or more precisely the principles of autonomy and equal respect for others, will sometimes, in certain contexts perhaps always, trump the claims other goods make on us. It is not necessarily to deny the normative priority of 'moral' values over others. But we are now talking about something that has to be established in the *course* of practical reason. It is not something to stipulate *a priori*. And even if we do want to stipulate some *a priori* constraints in this domain, we misdescribe them as the requirements of right as *opposed* to the good. According to Taylor, what we are doing by laying down such constraints is expressing our commitment to the *hypergood* of autonomy. We are giving acknowledgement to the overriding importance respect for others has for us. But if it were not for the status that 'morality' in the narrow sense enjoys as a hypergood, the demands of 'right' would be *merely* constraints, rather than something to be moved positively by in our practical deliberations. If we think of morality as a hypergood, Taylor suggests, we can make sense of the idea that the demands of right trump other strong values or goods people identify with, without divorcing the moral point of view from an orientation to the good as such. The intuition that the equal dignity of persons should have a privileged place in practical reasoning is preserved by construing it as a hypergood, but it is done without abstracting morality from the horizon of historically situated concerns.

The idea that the fulfilment of our duties and responsibilities to others is the matter of a hypergood could be used to fend off another potential objection to Taylor's theory. Taylor's conception of practical reason takes its departure from the question that initiated much ancient thinking about ethics: namely, 'what is it good to be?'. To this extent, Taylor elaborates a 'eudaimonic' theory. It is a theory that takes the aim of practical reason to be the realization of the good for human beings or 'self-realization'. Now the objection is sometimes put against eudaimonic theories that they prioritize not so much the good over the right as the 'Self' over the 'Other'. The problem with the classical eudaimonic approach, the objection runs, is that the claims of the other person disrupt the project of self-realization. The Other to whom one is responsible is the source of self-negation rather than self-fulfilment. A thought like this lies behind Levinas's insistence that ethics is prior to ontology.[13] In Levinas's view, responsibility to and for the other person takes us 'beyond' the self; even, as he dramatically puts it, 'beyond being'. In the ethical relation, as Levinas presents it, the self is 'substituted' by the Other. Now in depicting concern for the other person as a hypergood, Taylor has his own way of articulating Levinas's basic intuition. A hypergood has its own demands and these may indeed require self-sacrifice. There are life goods that the hypergood overrides. To be fully responsible to the other person, or to apprehend the Other as prior to the self, is in Taylor's terms to be under the sway of the Other as a hypergood. For Taylor as for Levinas, responsibility for the Other transports the self beyond the sphere of self-interest. But for Taylor, other-responsibility *qua* hypergood is also the highest form of self-realization. To the extent to which responsibility for the other person features as the highest vocation of human subjectivity – and Levinas himself sometimes describes it in such terms – other-responsibility plays the role of the hypergood. Thus although Taylor's ethical theory is Aristotelian in form, it does

not subordinate the Other to the self. It does not aggrandize subjectivity at the expense of otherness. As a hypergood, responsibility for the Other is integrated into the structure of selfhood without
compromising the exteriority of the claims of the Other. Taylor's
theory shows that we do not need to step outside ontology to articulate the exteriority of ethics.[14]

Moral Sources

For Taylor, the self has a moral dimension in the broad sense of
having an orientation to the good. According to Taylor's view, one's
identity is defined by one's concerns, and one cannot but be concerned by the worth of one's desires, purposes and life as a whole.
We saw that a theory which focuses exclusively on ideals, aspirations and strong values is unlikely to suffice as a general account of
the self. There are after all other aspects of identity besides ideal
identity – temperament and emotional dispositions, for instance –
that we would expect a full-blown theory of the self to be informative about. Taylor has little to say about the somatic dimension of
selfhood and this makes his approach 'top-down' in a pejorative
sense. It may be a price worth paying, however, for by defining the
self in terms of strong values and hypergoods, Taylor makes room
for one of his most distinctive theoretical moves: it allows him to
talk of 'sources' of the self.

The notion of a source of the self combines two ideas. First, there
is the idea of a constituting ground of the things we strongly value.
Taylor sometimes calls the things we strongly value, or rather a
large class of them, 'life goods'.[15] Life goods are features of human
life that possess intrinsic worth. They are things whose desirability
shows up in a qualitative contrast. Taylor calls the feature that
makes life goods worthy of desire a 'constitutive good'. The constitutive good provides the constituting ground of their worth or
goodness. Constitutive goods are features 'of the way things are, in
virtue of which . . . life goods are goods' (SS 93). A moral source, as
Taylor defines it, is a constitutive good. But it is a 'source' and not
just a 'ground' – this is the second idea – in so far as it energizes the
self into realizing the goods it strongly values. A moral source has
generative power: moral life, in the broad sense of life goods,
springs from it. As Taylor puts it in one formulation, moral sources
are 'goods reflection on which morally empowers us' (SS 264). In
fact, this formulation is not wholly satisfactory, as the empowering

quality of a moral source need not and typically does not arise from reflection.[16] We will return to the issue of access to moral sources later. For the moment, we just need to grasp that when Taylor talks of a source of the self, he is speaking of something that constitutes the goods in relation to which he has defined the self. This makes a source of the self a *moral* source. At the same time, he is speaking of it in its capacity to empower the self to live well, that is, to realize itself fully as a self. This makes it a *source* of the self.

The connected ideas of a constitutive good and moral source are probably best approached through the examples Taylor gives of them. In *Sources of the Self* he looks at three predominant ways of thinking about constitutive goods and moral sources in modern culture. First, we can consider the 'making good' of life goods to be the work of God. According to the theistic option, goodness or worth has a divine source: it is by partaking in this source that life goods – the things we strongly value – are made good. So, for instance, we might consider the good of family life to derive from God's sacrament of marriage, that is, as made good by God's blessing. Second, we can consider the source of the goodness of things to inhere in nature. We can take nature – conceived independently of any divine Authorship – as the constituting force behind the good. To stick with the case of family life, we might consider the good of sexual relations to consist in the fulfilment of natural desires. The third possibility is that autonomous human beings make things good: strong values and life goods are constituted by the human powers of freedom and responsibility. Again, we can consider family life to be good in virtue of being freely chosen, as arising from the autonomy of the individuals engaged in the relations. God, nature and human freedom are ways of interpreting the features of goods that make them good. To function as a moral source, these features must also empower the realization of the good in us. So if we stay with the good of family life, reflection on God's grace, or the gift of the sacraments, can empower people to realize this good more fully. The contemplation of nature, or awareness of one's place in the great current of life, can energize or intensify one's desires, and this in turn can heighten the quality of one's sexual relations. Deeply felt respect for the autonomy of another person, if that is the feature considered to be constitutive of the good, can also empower people who have this strong value to realize it more concretely in their lives. In Taylor's view, wherever there is a life good, we can reflect on the good that constitutes it, and this in turn can motivate us to live or act in the way the life good requires.

This is a particularly important point to bear in mind, Taylor thinks, when it comes to the hypergood of 'morality' in the narrow sense: namely, universal justice and the minimization of suffering. Respect and care for others without discrimination is a life good – it is an admirable feature of human life. And for many people it is also the top-ranking good; it is the good which trumps all others, or to use Taylor's term, it is a hypergood. The constitutive good in this domain tells us what it is about human beings that makes them worthy of non-discriminating care and respect. It is distinct from the features that elicit our many partial loves and concerns; for instance, for family members, friends, co-nationals and so forth. The care and respect enjoined by morality extend to everyone. So what is it simply about being human, rather than being this or that particular person, that elicits the narrowly speaking 'moral' concern? Again there are three basic options. One is to relate human beings to some higher, non-human, divine power. According to this option, human beings are constituted as good through their relationship to God. To the extent that contemplation or love of the divine affirmation of human beings empowers one to realize the life goods of universal justice and benevolence, the constitutive good functions too as a moral source. The constitutive good could also be construed as nature; it is owing to the inherent goodness of the natural order that human beings are worthy of respect. Or one can consider human beings to possess an intrinsic, non-divine and yet non-natural dignity, and it is in virtue of possessing this feature that they are owed an unconditional love and respect. The fact that human beings are able to shape their own lives, to live according to principles they give to themselves, can inspire a certain awe and reverence. If this motivates us to act morally, in the narrow sense of promoting the life goods of universal justice and taking responsibility for other people irrespective of their particular identity, it is also a moral source.

Now Taylor seems to think that moral sources have as much a role to play in an ontology of the human as strong value and narrative identity. He presents the category of a moral source as an indispensable one for making sense of human life. There are two considerations that earn it a place in Taylor's philosophical anthropology. First, it seems to be a general truth about human beings that, across civilizations, they express some desire to be in 'contact' with moral sources. It is a more or less universal human need, Taylor supposes, to be in touch with the feature of things that lends them spiritual meaning or significance, and to gather moral strength from that contact. This is a general truth that Taylor takes to be borne out by the history of civilizations. But even if this were true, it would not of course prove that there is anything in *reality* corresponding to the desire. It may be that the desire exists solely at the phenomenological level, that is, as a truth of subjectivity without foundation in non-human reality. Taylor's second consideration, however, is that the lives of at least certain people – namely, those lives led in accordance with hypergoods – are inexplicable without taking into account their moral sources. That is, if it were not for the potency of moral sources, human beings would be incapable of being who they are or of becoming whom they aspire to be. In Taylor's view, moral sources feature in the best account we have at least of lives directed towards the realization of a hypergood, and in virtue of this, moral sources have ontological significance. According to Taylor, this is as much true of the non-human moral sources (both theistic and non-theistic) as it is of the solely human ones.

I will consider Taylor's reconstruction of the debate between exclusively humanistic moral sources and sources that go beyond the human in chapter 8. If for the moment we leave to one side the issue of the relative validity of particular moral sources, and we just stick to the justification of the very category, Taylor can hardly be said to have demonstrated its ontological stature. If moral sources were indispensable to human agency in the way that strong values are, we would expect a life led without some contact with moral sources to be unbearable. And while this may be true for some people – people who lead their lives in accordance with a hypergood, for instance – it surely does not hold for everyone. It is quite conceivable that a person can live a recognizable human life, a life informed by some conception of the good, without reflecting on constitutive goods or contacting them in some other way. Contact with moral sources may be desirable for living a fully human life. It may heighten our experience or strengthen our motivation to meet certain standards. But it does not follow that moral sources are necessary for moral life. It does not entail that they are an essential component of moral motivation. A point like this has been made by Paul Ricoeur.[17] Ricoeur observes that while life goods stand in an internal relation to constitutive goods and so cannot be conceived wholly independently of them, it is not clear why constitutive goods cannot be conceived independently of moral sources. Moral sources may be *enabling* conditions for the realization of strong values; but an enabling condition is quite distinct from an *indispensability* condition.

We noted an analogous problem with Taylor's claims about narrative identity. It may be a universal human capacity to lead one's life as a 'quest', and the development of this capacity may bestow meaning on life. But we can imagine a worthwhile life led without it being understood as a series of 'victories' and 'defeats'. I suggested then that the problem with Taylor's thesis arose from his depiction of a certain state of cultivation of this capacity as the bare capacity itself: the universal is illegitimately embellished with the particular. Something similar may be going on with Taylor's introduction of the category of moral sources. While there is little reason to suppose that moral sources are necessary for a good life as such, they might have a crucial role to play in the realization of the 'highest' goods, the so-called hypergoods. And this is the issue that really concerns Taylor. More specifically, his concern is with the conditions under which it is realistic to aim for one of the chief modern hypergoods – universal justice and benevolence. Taylor's basic thought is that this ideal is both partly definitive of the modern identity and yet extremely demanding to meet. One needs a particularly strong set of moral motivations to live by this hypergood. If, as Taylor puts it, 'high standards need strong sources' (*SS* 516), a question arises about the capacity of modern moral sources to empower the realization of the modern 'moral' hypergood. Are our sources up to our standards? We shall consider Taylor's answer to this question in chapter 8. The point to be made for the moment is that without a problem like this to solve, it is not clear why moral sources must feature in an *ontology* of the human. It is as if a category Taylor needs for his diagnosis of a peculiarly modern moral predicament is being illegitimately credited with a universal anthropological currency. Even if our best interpretation of this predicament does make use of the category of a moral source – by no means an uncontroversial claim in itself – it would not entitle us to say that human subjectivity is *essentially* constituted by moral sources; a claim that must be warranted if it is to have the status of an ontological truth.

Fortunately, we do not have to take on board the idea that moral sources are indispensability conditions of human subjectivity to accept their relevance for moral philosophy. The mere thought that reflection on constitutive goods *can* be motivationally significant in realizing the good is interesting enough in its own right. We would expect moral philosophy to have something to say about it. For Taylor, one of the great merits of ancient ethics, especially Plato's, is the direct way in which it tackles the issue of sources and the related question of qualitatively distinct kinds of will. Plato's reflections lead him naturally to the question of constitutive goods, of what it is in virtue of which goods like justice, piety and wisdom are good. Plato's answer to the question is that life goods are constituted by the Form of the Good, by an order of being apprehensible by philosophical reason. For Plato, contemplation of the Form of the Good empowers one to be good; one cannot grasp the Form without being moved by feelings of love, awe and reverence. Plato's *solution* to the problem of sources, Taylor concedes, cannot carry conviction today. It leans heavily on the idea of an ontic logos, a meaningful order pervading through the cosmos and accessible to reason, which is no longer credible. But if modern moral philosophies, specifically utilitarianism and Kantianism, take a step forwards in rejecting Platonic doctrine on this account, they take two steps backwards in pushing the issue of constitutive goods and moral sources off the theoretical agenda altogether. Their neglect of this issue lends false credibility to their procedural theories of practical reason and reinforces the dubious distinction between motivation and justification.

But the modern forgetfulness of moral sources, according to Taylor, is not just a theoretical oversight. It has practical consequences for agents, especially those who lead their lives in view of some hypergood. For if we do not reflect on moral sources, or articulate them in whatever manner is appropriate, we are in danger of losing contact with them altogether. And if we do lose contact with them, or if we simply do not bother with this level of reflection or articulation at all, we put the life goods themselves in jeopardy. There is thus a practical as well as a theoretical imperative behind Taylor's project of putting the issue of moral sources back on the philosophical agenda. To pose the *question* of moral sources is the first step towards *reawakening* them. It can contribute towards an enrichment of moral life by reactivating the sources underneath the frosty rationalistic surface of modern proceduralist ethics. Articulation can also bring to life other sources that proceduralism serves to suppress. Moral philosophy should set its sights on the work of 'recovery' and 'retrieval' through *rational* articulation. A major task of philosophy, as Taylor understands it, is to 'uncover buried goods through rearticulation – and thereby to make these sources again empower' (*SS* 520). No doubt such talk of awakening, reactivation and retrieval makes some philosophers – particularly those in the analytic tradition – feel nervous. Philosophy, in their view, is circumscribed by the task of producing and assessing valid arguments, where validity is determined by strictly logical criteria rather than anything like 'potency', 'proximity' or 'empowerment'. Such philosophers are liable to see Taylor's understanding of the tasks of philosophy as a regressive attempt 'to combine the universalistic tradition of philosophical analysis with an older philosophical tradition that also tries to be rhetorically and normatively persuasive'.[18] The recovery of moral sources, on this view, may be an appropriate goal for rhetoric, literature or evangelism, but it is unworthy of philosophy. On the other hand, there are philosophers – particularly in the Continental tradition – who agree that something like the recovery of moral sources is their true vocation, but who turn away from traditional modes of philosophical analysis in pursuit of this goal. It is naïve, they think, to suppose that 'rational' articulations are capable of uncovering modernity's buried goods. Taylor certainly has some sympathy for this view, as we saw in the favourable way in which he reconstructs Heidegger's later work. This creates a certain tension in Taylor's understanding of the tasks of philosophy, as by his own admission perspicuously ordered sequences of rational argumentation, of the type Taylor strives for in his own philosophical prose, may not be well-suited for exploring or 'recovering' moral sources. Perhaps, by striving for an ideal of clarity, Taylor even contributes to the suppression of sources by philosophical reason. He would of course reject the latter charge: no articulation, he would insist, is ever too perspicuous. And in response to the former point, he can concede that philosophical prose has its limits as a vehicle of retrieval, without forfeiting the self-orienting capacity of reason as such. There is a lot of 'uncovering' and 'recovering' for the philosopher, as well as the poet and the rhetorician, still to do.

5

Interpretation and the Social Sciences

It is conventional to distinguish two broad tendencies within the philosophy of social science. According to one tendency – sometimes referred to as 'naturalism' – the social sciences, in their mature form, are accountable to the same standards as prevail in the modern sciences of nature. For naturalists, the social sciences earn their right to be called 'scientific' by producing explanatory theories, ideally with precise predictive power, which admit of exact and unambiguous verification. According to the second tendency – pioneered by the German philosopher Wilhelm Dilthey – the social sciences possess a logic which departs from the natural sciences in fundamental ways. For Dilthey, the discontinuity between natural and social science arises from the fact that the social sciences have to interpret or reach an *understanding* of their subject-matter. This tendency in the philosophy of social science is sometimes called the *Verstehen* school. But if Dilthey was the founder of the *Verstehen* approach to social science, it was modified first by Heidegger, and later by Hans-Georg Gadamer, in a way that refined and radicalized Dilthey's notion of 'reaching an understanding'. In recognition of this advance, it is now common to use an expression made famous by Gadamer, 'hermeneutics', to denominate a way of thinking about the social sciences as essentially interpretative. It is no exaggeration to say that Taylor has been the most eloquent and influential advocate of the hermeneutic model of social science in the English-speaking world.[1]

In fact, Taylor's defence of hermeneutic social science is a natural extension of his philosophical anthropology. For the central claim of philosophical hermeneutics is that human beings, as Taylor puts it, are 'self-interpreting animals'. Their self-interpretation – the meaning they have for themselves – is integral to who they are. The first question for the philosophy of social science, then, is 'how is a science of self-interpreting animals possible?'. What is its structure and what kind of validity does it have? We shall take up Taylor's treatment of these issues in the first part of the chapter. In the second part, we turn to a cluster of related questions concerning the critical potential of social science. In Taylor's view, social science is essentially a critical enterprise, whose whole point is to improve upon naïve self-interpretations, to offer justified critical judgements on them. Taylor is thus a vociferous critic of relativism in social science. At the same time, social science must be vigilant to avoid ethnocentrism in its attempt to reach a critical understanding of the self-interpretations of others. In fact, Taylor does not see these two requirements – criticism and the avoidance of ethnocentrism – as incompatible. On the contrary, he tries to show that only critical hermeneutics makes sense of the possibility of a non-ethnocentric science of other cultures and societies. Social scientists – and anyone else for that matter – are able to avoid ethnocentrism just by virtue of their ability to make valid or rational cross-cultural judgements. The chapter concludes with a discussion of this claim.

Interpretation and Validity

Let us begin by considering the interpretative or hermeneutic conception of social science Taylor defends in his now classic essay, 'Interpretation and the Sciences of Man'.[2] The point of departure for interpretative social science, as Taylor defends it, is the thought that the social enquirer typically faces a predicament analogous to that facing the interpreter of a text. The interpreter of a text has something before her which possesses meaning. But it is a meaning which, for one reason or another, is problematic: it requires further laying out in order to be understood. The meaning of the text may be unclear, fragmentary or incoherent, and because of this, the text stands in need of interpretation. The aim of the interpretation is to bring out a meaning which would otherwise remain hidden in the text itself. If the interpretation is successful, the meaning of the text becomes clearer – sense is made of it. But the activity of interpretation presupposes that the meaning and the text are separable. If they were not, the question of how to interpret it could not arise. We

could say that in an interpretation, the field of signifiers which constitutes the text is 'reconfigured' in a way that exhibits the meaning more perspicuously. The predicament of the interpreter, or in
Gadamer's expression the 'hermeneutic situation', thus involves an
'object' which is a bearer of meaning or sense (a text), a clarifying
reconfiguration of the field of signifiers in which that meaning is
expressed (the interpretation), and a 'subject' for whom the sense is
made (the interpreter).

How does this relate to the predicament facing the social sciences? Taylor begins by noting that the subject-matter of the social
sciences – human activity – itself foreshadows or anticipates the
hermeneutic situation. Human beings are 'always already' interpreting themselves. In the first place, the intentional structure of
human action, the mere fact that action is directed by desires and
purposes, implies that actions have meaning. We act 'for the sake
of' things – to realize a purpose, to satisfy a desire, to meet some
practical demand – and prior to any systematic or scientific reflection, we identify our own and others' actions by reference to that
'for the sake of' which they are done. So there is meaning *in* human
activity – namely, the experiential meaning it has for the agent. In
the second place, we find it natural, prior to adopting a reflective stance, to distinguish between actions and the meanings they
express. The meaning of an action is not always obvious. We often
have to *make* sense of our actions and the ends which shape them
(though of course we do not always succeed in this endeavour).
That is why human activity admits of interpretation. We can recon-
figure the meaning it expresses or 'for the sake of' which it is done.
Thirdly, it is clear that the meanings expressed in actions are for a
subject. Hence there is something like a hermeneutic situation built
into the structure of agency as such. As Taylor puts it, 'already to
be a living agent is to experience one's situation in terms of meanings; and this in a sense can be thought of as a sort of "proto-
interpretation". This is in turn interpreted and shaped by the
language in which the agent lives these meanings. This whole is
then at a third level interpreted by the explanation we proffer of
his actions' (*PHS* 27).

So prior to adopting a theoretical perspective on their activity,
human agents have an understanding of it which is shaped by their
practical experience and the language that articulates their experience. Moreover, as we saw in chapter 3, human agents are partly
constituted by the interpretative or explanatory language they
use. There is a range of experiences, desires, purposes and there-

fore actions that only come into being in the course of a specific interpretation. In 'Interpretation and the Sciences of Man', Taylor invokes 'shame' as an example (*PHS* 23). The experience of shame, and its presence as a motivating factor, must refer the subject to a situation that occasioned it, something that can be described as 'shameful'. But we can only identify 'shameful' situations – and other objects to which complex emotions refer – with concepts embedded in a whole language. And whole languages are embedded within specific cultures; a language is expressive of a particular form of life. For this reason, the vocabulary of self-interpretation is interwoven with the *object* of interpretation, or in other words, the self-understanding of the agent helps constitute or define the agent's identity. A condition of there being feelings like shame, pride or remorse is the availability of a language for understanding them that way. Take away the vocabulary and you lose the object the vocabulary identifies. When we use such talk to explain an action – if we say, for example, that 'she did it out of remorse' – we call upon concepts that also have a self-defining function for the agents involved.

But what is the relevance of this kind of interpretative activity for science? How should the social scientist situate herself *vis-à-vis* the pre-theoretical stance of the self-interpreting agent? In Taylor's view, the goal of social science is to bring about an *advance* in the understanding of a practice relative to the pre-theoretical self-understanding generated spontaneously within the practice itself. The social scientist *qua* interpreter makes the grade by improving upon the 'readings of meanings' embedded in the self-defining vocabulary under investigation. Now one of the main motivations behind naturalism, in Taylor's view, is the idea that no such advances are really demonstrable. And if we are not able to tell when one interpretation rather than another gets it right, then social science should not bother with interpretations at all. Taylor thus has to show how validity in interpretation is possible.

Taylor's first move is to deflate expectations here, expectations that arise in connection with the standards that prevail, or are imagined to prevail, in the natural sciences. In order to test a theory, the physicist might point to 'brute data', that is, experimental evidence the significance of which is beyond interpretative dispute. It thus makes sense to attribute disagreement over the validity of a physicist's hypothesis to insufficient evidence or some failure to understand or apply some formalized language. But these options, Taylor insists, are not available in the social sciences. The social scientist must be able to convince another of the validity of her interpretation without calling upon brute data or formal rules of inference. When disagreement occurs, all the interpreter has to go on are more interpretations. There is something unavoidably circular about the process of giving reasons here. It has often been observed that textual interpretation gets caught up in a 'hermeneutic circle'. The interpreter justifies her reading of parts of the text in relation to her background grasp of the meaning of the whole. But her grasp of the meaning of the whole in turn evolves from her understanding of the parts. Taylor identifies an analogous circular movement in the social sciences. The interpreter of unfamiliar or inadequately understood human activity must draw on her background sense of what is going on – her 'sense of reality', as Taylor calls it – to justify her interpretations. But asked to justify those background intuitions, she has nowhere to turn but to the interpretations themselves. This means that if two interpreters have radically different background senses of reality, they are unlikely ever to get started in an interpretative dispute. And even if there is enough background agreement for a dispute to get going, there may be no ultimate way of settling it rationally. There may be no way of bridging the 'gap in intuitions', as Taylor puts it, between different interpreters once the interpretative argument has run its course.

But Taylor insists that the hermeneutic circularity of the social sciences is not vicious. For within the circle, one interpretation can prove itself superior to another. The validity of an interpretation is shown in the epistemic gain we make when we move to it from another, inferior interpretation. We can say an interpretation has validity when we can look back at the transition to it as a cognitive advance. In this sense interpretative validity has a retrospective as well as a circular character. While the hermeneutic testing procedure may not have the precision of prospective modes of verification such as prediction, this is not something the social sciences should be embarrassed about. For the fact that human beings are self-interpreting animals, combined with the fact that they are intrinsically capable of conceptual and linguistic innovation, means that there is something inherently unpredictable about the subject-matter of the social sciences – the life activity of human beings.

We must be careful not to misunderstand Taylor's argument here. A number of Taylor's critics take him to be espousing a version of epistemological *scepticism*. That is, they take him to be denying that the social sciences are capable of delivering genuine knowledge at all. Terry Pinkard, for instance, reads Taylor's appeal to intuition in resolving interpretative disputes as reflecting his commitment to the 'non-verifiability' of the findings of hermeneutical science.[3] Taylor's view allegedly 'outlaws rationality' by proposing that there are 'no rational procedures for deciding on a given case at all'.[4] As Pinkard reads Taylor, making sense is 'totally a function of one's intuitions such that no rational guidelines can be laid down for it'.[5] Michael Martin also accuses Taylor of 'epistemological subjectivism'. According to Martin, Taylor's position implies that 'there is no objective way of validating interpretations of social phenomena, and hence, interpretations are ultimately based on rationally unsupportable intuitions or value decisions'.[6] On James Bohman's reading, Taylor embraces scepticism when he claims that 'interpretations do not constitute knowledge based on evidence'.[7] While Bohman appreciates that Taylor is not a general sceptic about knowledge, Taylor remains an interpretative sceptic for Bohman on account of his view that interpretations are ultimately based on 'unformalizable insight' rather than 'publicly accessible evidence'. Taylor's social science thus lacks the 'intersubjective' validity of natural science. According to Bohman, for Taylor insight is 'the only possible form of verification', since 'the limits of interpretation mean that evidence must eventually fail to resolve disputes'.[8]

However, all of these criticisms conflate Taylor's description of the *limiting* case of interpretative dispute with the normal case. In the normal case of social scientific enquiry, according to Taylor, interpreters share enough common background for testing to take place on the basis of evidence. The rationality of any particular interpretation will be decidable in terms of its superiority relative to the pre-theoretical understanding of the agents, or relative to the prevailing interpretative paradigm of the science. There is no sceptical thesis here: there are epistemic gains as one interpretation makes more sense of a phenomenon than a rival one, by resolving contradictions in the rival interpretation, for instance, or by bringing otherwise hidden aspects more clearly into view. Admittedly, Taylor doubts that much can be said by way of formal rules for determining validity. But this scepticism is directed at *formalism* in social science rather than *validity* in it. Like Gadamer, Taylor wants to open up the question of truth in social science without identifying truth with the outcome of a procedure or method. We do not need the backing of a canon of rationality to be able to test interpretations. However, Taylor does accept that the normal ways of arbitrating interpretations may fail to produce agreement. At that point interpreters have to resort to intuitions, and these may not be shared. But it by no means follows, in Taylor's view, that private intuitions form the basis of validity. He does not claim that validity rests on intuitions. Rather, his point is that at the moment of breakdown in interpretative argument intuition comes into play. This is the limiting case of argument in social science, not its foundation. Taylor's position is that the recourse to insight is necessary only in certain (not all) cases of interpretative dispute, though he is in no doubt that such dispute is widespread in the social sciences.[9]

Furthermore, even in cases where interpretative dispute cannot be settled by normal means, the appeal to intuition is not the end of the matter. To see why, it will help to consider an argument Taylor mounted against a certain conception of value-freedom in the social sciences in his 1967 essay 'Neutrality in Political Science'.[10] Here, Taylor concedes that in an extremely minimal sense the social sciences can be value-free. Political science, for instance, can document voting patterns, it can carry out demographic and ethnographic observations, and so forth. In short, it can collect information. In this sense neutrality is possible. But mere information-collecting is not desirable even by scientific standards. For the goal of a science is to explain its object-domain. And as soon as the social sciences attempt to explain human behaviour, Taylor claims, neutrality is no longer possible. Taylor's argument has two stages. In the first, he tries to show that explanations only make sense within the context of some 'theoretical framework'. A theoretical framework provides the concepts through which a phenomenon is first identified and then explained according to the dimension of society picked out as the most important causal variable. It may be the economic relations in the society, kinship relations, or, say, the relationship between identity and political power. A framework identifies something to be explained and provides the resources for explaining it. Inevitably, a framework prioritizes certain kinds of functional relation while leaving others aside. The second stage of Taylor's argument is to show that such frameworks, themselves indispensable for explanation, are logically connected to a range of evaluative positions. Taylor's main point here is that the dimension of variation prioritized by any given theoretical framework will reflect a certain conception of the basic human needs. It will reflect an understanding of the desires and purposes that motivate human action. And it will, however implicitly, introduce standards by which to assess the state of health or malfunction of the society. In other words, frameworks inevitably bring into play a conception of human flourishing or the good. The frameworks political science needs to fulfil its explanatory tasks thus have their own 'built-in value slope' (*PHS* 73). They come packaged with a schedule of human needs which in turn 'secretes' evaluative judgements, judgements about the nature of the good society. For a good society is just one which meets the fundamental human needs, and the role of frameworks is to identify the most significant causal variable for their realization. A political science that was value-free or neutral with respect to the human good would have to dispense with frameworks, but a framework-free science would be impoverished as a source of explanation and thus as a science.

For this reason, it turns out that the 'gap in intuitions' between rival interpreters coincides with a conflict in their *practical* orientations. Taylor makes the point allusively at the end of 'Interpretation and the Sciences of Man', where he comments that ultimately 'a study of the science of man is inseparable from an examination of the options between which men must choose' (*PHS* 54). The fact that social theories *themselves* provide us with an orientation for making such choices – the fact that they are 'self-defining', as Taylor puts it – can then be introduced as a criterion for assessing their validity. This is the move Taylor makes in 'Social Theory as Practice' (1981).[11] For Taylor, 'real debate between living theories' typically involves dispute over the ends or purposes practices serve; and the stakes of such dispute, Taylor suggests, are set not so much by rival causal hypotheses as by 'rival maps of the terrain' (*PHS* 110). And just as the proof of a good map lies in its ability to orient us, so the test of a self-defining social theory is how well we are able to realize ourselves through it. The truth of the theory thus lies not so much in the accuracy of its account of practices considered as independently existing entities, but in the way our practices fare when informed by the theory. This kind of testing, testing in practice, must be distinguished from the problem of applying theory to practice, as if there were some 'pure' social theory whose validity could be determined prior to its 'application'. Self-defining social theories cannot be judged by the standard of technical success (their capacity to manipulate objects effectively) as theories in the natural sciences frequently are. But then neither should they be judged simply by the clarification they bring to the meaning of a text (or text-analogue). Rather, the validity claim most relevant to social theory is 'emancipation', that is to say, a fuller or more authentic realization of the goods that define us. In this way, Taylor shows his allegiance to the tradition of *critical* social theory rather than the interpretative or *Verstehen* school narrowly conceived.

Ethnocentrism and Relativism

According to Taylor, the social sciences deepen and enrich our understanding of human activity by making sense of things that are opaque, inadequately comprehended or unexplained at the pre-theoretical, common-sense level of reflection. It is only to be expected, then, that successful social theories will sometimes come into conflict with common sense. Even if social science cannot coherently challenge the very idea that human activity is intelligible on account of the purposes that direct it and therefore the meaning it possesses – interpretative social theory does not challenge common sense as mechanism does – it can still seek to correct or improve upon the ways in which that meaning is naïvely interpreted. Interpretative social theory, as Taylor conceives it, thus has an intrinsically critical bent: it takes the spontaneously generated self-interpretations of a culture as its point of departure, and advances new, more perspicuous and more explanatory interpretations in their place. But while it is hard to gainsay the appropriateness of such a critical attitude in relation to the theorist's 'home' culture, it is less obvious that the endeavour to understand *other* societies can or ought to follow this model. For in the first place, it is not clear why the theorist is entitled to presume she *can* make sense of the meanings expressed in a culture radically different to her own. Why assume that a given cultural practice can be undistortively translated into the theoretical vocabulary of social science? Is not the language of social theory itself the expression of a particular culture, and so restricted in its scope? And even if the practices of an unfamiliar society can be made intelligible by the social theorist, is it not arrogant to suggest that the excellence of theory consists in its reaching a better understanding of the culture than the culture has of itself? Taylor is sensitive to these issues: 'One of the striking faults of transcultural and comparative social science', Taylor writes, 'has been its tendency to ethnocentrism' (*PHS* 124).[12] By inviting 'scientists of a dominant culture to "correct" the self-understanding of the less dominant ones by substituting their own', transcultural study has allowed itself to become 'a field for the exercise of ethnocentric prejudice' (*PHS* 124). If the hermeneutic model of social science is to be defensible, then, Taylor has to show that it is not doomed to ethnocentrism.

Taylor's response is to unpack what it means to reach an understanding of an unfamiliar culture. To reach an understanding, one must first learn how to interpret the agents as the agents interpret themselves. This is crucial because, as we have seen, there are aspects of agency that are constituted by self-interpretations. First, there is a range of human feelings and emotions whose content is essentially bound up with their manner of articulation. Second, there is the range of strong values determined only within a framework of articulated contrasts. And third, there are common meanings that make possible distinctive forms of human interaction. One cannot hope to understand the agents in an unfamiliar culture without taking into account the ways in which their emotions, values, aspirations and common practices are shaped by their language. The agents are who they are in virtue of the language, so one cannot understand them without understanding their self-interpreting vocabulary. As Taylor puts it, 'interpretive social science requires that we master the agent's self-description in order to identify our explananda' (*PHS* 118). This is what Taylor takes to be involved in the process of 'reaching understanding' with another. Reaching understanding is distinct from merely 'empathizing' with the agent, and it is not to be identified with adopting the point of view of the agent, for it remains an open question whether the agent's self-descriptions are the most perspicuous ones available for understanding who they are or what they do.

But it could be argued that by this point the opportunity of avoiding ethnocentrism has already been missed. For it might seem that ethnocentrism is best avoided by adopting a neutral stance to the self-descriptions, particularly their evaluative component. The neutralist or objectivist solution to the problem of ethnocentrism is to translate the agent's self-descriptions into a scientific language that is neutral *vis-à-vis* their evaluative force. Only accounts couched in such language can claim universal, scientific legitimacy, and according to this line of argument, this is the most effective way for social anthropology to guard against ethnocentrism. Taylor illustrates the point in relation to functionalist theories of religion. The functionalist analyses religious belief in terms of the social function it serves – social integration, for instance – and he 'finesses' the self-understanding of the agents to fit the theory. But attempts to finesse understanding are futile, Taylor argues, because they run up against insuperable problems of validation. Such theories need to explain why these *particular* religious practices are in operation, and this requires an adequate understanding in detail of the actions and values as they are understood by the agents. So even here agent-understanding is necessary. But Taylor's point is not just that the neutralist approach cannot in the end be coherently carried through, and so must fail to avoid ethnocentrism. Worse, it actually engenders ethnocentrism. For the scientific language it proposes as neutral and universal is typically lifted from a specific culture where it does seem valid: the western scientist's own. This is especially true, Taylor thinks, of functionalist explanatory models in political science. Rather than being 'neutral' or 'universal', too often they merely express the bargaining culture of North Atlantic societies. By ignoring the cultural specificity of their explanatory schema, they reproduce an ethnocentric prejudice.

A bias like this has been noted in the way in which the Victorian anthropologist Sir James Frazer dealt with magic and witchcraft in primitive societies. Frazer interpreted magic as essentially an error. As Taylor put it, magic was seen as 'an attempt by primitive people to master their environment, to do what we do better by science and technology' (*PHS* 127). In other words, magic was interpreted as a mistaken form of theoretical activity, as misled in a way which can only be seen from the cognitively superior vantage point of modern western science. Taking up Evans-Pritchard's rebuttal of Frazer's thesis, Peter Winch drew attention to the ethnocentrism of this view.[13] The ethnocentrism arose from the assumption that the primitives are engaged in the same kind of activity as that characteristic of modern western societies. The assumption betrays an ethnocentrism in so far as it projects the 'standards of rationality' of the home culture onto the alien culture. The alien culture may be irrational by 'our' standards. But these may be standards the other culture does not recognize. Winch countered the ethnocentrism of such anthropology with an influential formulation of cultural relativism. The essence of relativism, as Taylor understands it, is 'the incorrigibility thesis': the claim that the self-understanding of the agents is not just the first but the *final* word in interpretation. Relativism rebuts ethnocentrism by denying there are any cross-cultural standards of judgement. For relativism, standards are internal to practices. Each 'language game', to use Wittgenstein's expression, has its own standards. The aim of social science, on the relativist model inspired by Wittgenstein, is to describe practices and not to judge or criticize them. We can then avoid ethnocentric talk of 'primitive irrationality' by interpreting rationality as irrelevant to the practice of magic, or by interpreting magic as doing a different kind of thing to science, theory or technology. It is better to say either that magic is indifferent to rationality or that it incorporates alternative standards of rationality to those prevailing in modern western modes of thought and practice. For instance, magic can be interpreted as possessing 'symbolic' significance rather than as serving a 'technical' (or 'rational') interest, as expressing 'spiritual' needs rather than being guided by an interest in predicting and controlling the environment. So, for instance, a rain dance might seem irrational if it is understood as a mechanism for intervening in natural causal processes to bring about rain. But as 'symbolic' activity, as an expression of existential dependence on the awesome powers of nature, it makes sense. If we interpreted the activity in 'its own terms', Taylor's relativist urges, we would see that the standards applying in the primitive society are 'incommensurable' with those of modern societies. And seeing the incommensurability of standards will enable us to avoid ethnocentrism.

But according to Taylor the relativist view, like neutralism, is itself unwittingly ethnocentric. In the particular case of the rationality of magic, the ethnocentrism comes out in the projection of a distinction that only makes sense in western, theoretical culture: namely, the distinction between 'technical' and 'symbolic' interests. The assumption that 'the tribe's practice must be *either* proto-science/technology *or* the integration of meaning through symbolism' (*PHS* 128) is one which only makes sense to a modern point of view, that is, within a civilization that has separated out these two dimensions of human experience. Taylor's point is not that the distinction itself is ethnocentric. Rather, his point is that the distinction is something which has emerged *historically* in a particular culture. But the Winchean relativist, in a well-intentioned but ill-thought-out attempt to save primitive thought from the charge of irrationality, treats the distinction as something 'given', as a fixed and implicitly unchallengeable point of reference. The fact that the distinction between the technical and the symbolic is presupposed as an implicit universal does not of course make it false. But it does make the presupposition ethnocentric. The ethnocentricity arises from a failure to reflect on the peculiarly modern, western provenance of the framework being invoked to account for the self-defining activity of the members of the non-western, traditional culture. This lack of reflection also leads to misunderstanding, for the participants in the magic ritual themselves do not see their practice as divorced from its 'technical' utility.

A better way of avoiding ethnocentrism – indeed, the only way, in Taylor's view – is to strive for a 'third language' in which the 'home' and 'alien' languages are brought into 'perspicuous contrast'. Interpretative social science does not pursue a neutral, context-free language, nor does it rest content with the agent's self-description. Both these options serve to hide the historicity of the observer's self-understanding, which is precisely the vice of ethnocentrism. Understanding the other culture requires a better understanding of ourselves, or of the distinctions that help express the observer's agency; and this, Taylor suggests, is the normal case for the encounter between two cultures. 'The language of perspicuous contrast which is adequate to the case', Taylor writes, 'forces us to redescribe what we are doing' (*PHS* 129). The danger of ethnocentricity is that of 'seeing our ways of acting as the only conceivable ones', a danger which is not averted by refusing to make a judgement. Understanding another culture is successful when it leads to an altered and more perspicuous self-understanding. The great merit of the interpretative view, as Taylor defends it, is that it explains how self-transformation can come about through an encounter with another. The great challenge to comparative social science, the requirement it must meet if it is to be non-ethnocentric and successful, is to recognize two incommensurable classifications of human activity when it sees them.

But it was just the incommensurability of classificatory schemes that led the relativist to deny that there can be any cross-cultural standards of judgement. The relativist position is that in cases where incommensurability holds, there is no rational basis for judging one classificatory scheme superior to another. A classificatory scheme contains standards for judging claims internal to the scheme. Within the scheme, some claims will be more justified than others, some ends or purposes more valued than others, and so forth. It will have internal standards determining meaning, truth and value. The aim of the social anthropologist is to reach as much of an understanding of them as possible. But in doing so, she will see that the internal standards of her own scheme are not applicable to the other one. Who, then, is to say which scheme is right or superior?

The appropriate response, according to the relativist, is either to refrain from making cross-cultural judgements altogether, or if one must make them, to do so in the awareness that such judgements have no rational basis. But Taylor reaches the opposite conclusion. In Taylor's view, it is precisely the incommensurability of classificatory schemes, of modes of identifying and distinguishing activities, that makes them rivals. And where we have rivals we have competing claims over a domain, claims that compete with each other for superiority. Taylor takes up the distinction between the technical and the symbolic as a case in point. Modern science, Taylor reiterates, evolved from its predecessor by separating the task of acquiring useful knowledge of nature from the goal of attaining spiritual harmony with it. The modern scientific standard of rationality is incommensurable with its predecessor to the extent that it rejects as irrational the simultaneous pursuit of knowledge and attunement. But the new classificatory scheme made something possible that the old one cannot but take seriously: enormously effective technological control over nature. The reason a defender of the old scheme cannot but take it seriously is not that he must especially value technology. This may well not be the case. Rather, the reason lies, on the one hand, in the fact that even pre-scientific knowledge enables agents to get around in the world, and the better it enables agents to do it the better it is likely to be as knowledge. And on the other hand, merely in virtue of being embodied in the world the agent cannot but be impressed by a mode of knowledge that enables more effective action. As Taylor puts it, 'given the kind of beings we are, embodied and active in the world, and given the way that scientific knowledge extends and supersedes our ordinary understanding of things, it is impossible to see how it could fail to yield further and more far-reaching recipes for action' (*PHS* 147–8).[14] Such recipes for action are what technology provides. The enormous technological advance yielded by modern scientific knowledge thus presents the defender of pre-modern science with a formidable case to answer. And it gives us very good grounds for judging the modern classificatory scheme as superior, at least in its capacity to generate knowledge of nature.

This rider is crucial. Taylor is not proposing an argument that would establish the *global* superiority of one scheme, and the practice it informs, over another. Indeed, he suggests that the scheme which separates knowledge of nature from attunement with it may be inferior with respect to the goal of attunement than a scheme which unites them. And there will be other goals, only indirectly related to these, that cultures realize in better or worse ways. Now if schemes can be judged as superior or inferior with regard to their understanding of the natural world, there may be *other* dimensions of human agency that are also amenable to cross-cultural judgement. For Taylor, superiority is shown, as we have seen, in a 'language of perspicuous contrast'. He describes this as 'a language in which we could formulate both their way of life and ours as alternative possibilities in relation to some human constant at work in both . . . Such a language of contrast might show their language of understanding to be distorted or inadequate in some respects, or it might show ours to be so . . . or it might show both to be so' (*PHS* 127–8).

But this reference to 'human constants' might seem worrying. Is this not just the idea the relativist is rightly suspicious of? Bohman expresses the worry well when he writes that Taylor's approach 'relies on metaphysical assumptions that there are indeed uninterpreted "human constants" '.[15] While Bohman by no means wants to defend relativism, it is a mistake, he thinks, to criticize it by way of 'strong metaphysical and essentialist notions' such as the ones Taylor invokes. However, we should not be scared off by this talk of 'metaphysics' and 'essentialism'. After all, the 'human constant' at issue in the particular case Taylor considers is hardly controversial: it is simply the embeddedness of human beings in the world and their need to cope with it. Taylor does construe this as an 'essential' feature of human subjectivity. But it is defined in a quite minimal way, and if there should be any doubt about it, one can always consult the arguments rehearsed in the earlier chapters of this book. Furthermore, if we were to doubt that human beings are essentially embodied, what force could *any* anti-relativist argument have for us? Relativism is a much milder form of scepticism than the Cartesian variety that questions our essential embodiment. So essentialist notions need not be as troubling as they first appear, and certainly should not be rejected *a priori*. Are there any other 'human constants' besides embodiment? Of course there are birth, sex and death, though Taylor himself does not explore (or has not yet explored) these inescapable consequences of embodiment in any depth.[16] He seems to see them as a matter of empirical anthropology rather than philosophical anthropology. Whether or not we are satisfied with this restriction, there are other human constants Taylor does claim to identify and bring to a more perspicuous expression: strong value, narrative identity, moral sources and, as we shall see in the next chapter, collective identity. In Taylor's view, these are all dimensions of subjectivity that are 'inescapable'. And at least in the first case, and maybe the last, he is surely right. If he is, then they are 'human constants' and the culturally divergent languages that give expression to them are potential objects of cross-cultural criticism.

Taylor has argued that hermeneutic social science is not just one way of avoiding ethnocentrism but the only way. It is a condition of reaching an understanding of the other culture that the agents' self-descriptions are understood. This rules out neutralism. But it is also a condition of reaching an understanding that the truth of the matter is not pre-empted. This excludes Winchean relativism, or at least the incorrigibility thesis. Avoiding ethnocentrism is a matter of being open to self-criticism, an aim which is secured not by immunizing the other from judgement but by striving for a 'fusion of horizons' or a third language of perspicuous contrast. I have just argued that the adequacy of Taylor's model for avoiding ethnocentrism is not compromised by its appeal to the notion of human constants. But it might be challenged in another way. According to David Couzens Hoy, there is a residual ethnocentrism in Taylor's ideal of a language of perspicuous contrast.[17] In the first place, Hoy contends, Taylor puts the wrong emphasis on Gadamer's notion of a fusion of horizons. For Gadamer, as Hoy reads him, the fusion of horizons serves primarily to awaken the interpreter to 'the strange in the familiar'. But according to Taylor's reformulation, fusion brings about a familiarization of the strange. Taylor's language of perspicuous contrast, as Hoy understands it, is essentially a translation of the strangeness of the other into something more manageable. It makes sense by privileging the language of the observer. After all, Hoy points out, it is 'we', the observers, who speak the language of contrast. It is 'we' who describe 'their' language as 'unperspicuous' as a result of the successful interpretative encounter. And it is hard to see how this gets us past the ethnocentric stance. The underlying problem here, as Hoy sees it, is that the ideal of a perspicuous contrast assumes the possibility of *convergence* between the 'home' and 'alien' languages. Taylor's interpretative social scientists, according to Hoy, expect a *truth* to emerge from the encounter with the other, a truth disclosed in the new language of contrast. Not only is this an unreasonable expectation – one self-interpretation is often just as 'true' as the next – it also lays the ethnocentric trap, because the third truth-disclosing language is invariably spoken by 'us'. If, as Hoy puts it, 'we expect every other self-understanding to converge with ours', we are by that fact ethnocentric. Taylor's model, with its in-built expectation of convergence, serves to ensnare us within ethnocentrism rather than liberate us from it.

In a follow-up essay to his earlier articles on ethnocentrism and the problem of cross-cultural judgement, 'Comparison, History, Truth',[18] Taylor seems to concede that a genuine, non-ethnocentric fusion of horizons may be more difficult to achieve than he had previously let it appear. On the one hand, serious motivational obstacles stand in the way of genuine other-understanding. We should not underestimate, Taylor admits, the considerable subconscious resistance to changing our self-definition. If we are comfortable with the familiar, and disinclined to change the way we understand ourselves, we are not likely to make much progress in our effort to understand others. To be open to the other is at the same time to put oneself in question, it is to make oneself vulnerable to an unflattering contrast, and this is not easy to do. On the other hand, Taylor concedes that the third language of perspicuous contrast is itself a new 'home language', and it is quite possible that it will in turn embody an ethnocentrism. Taylor has 'no answer in principle' against this charge. He has no proposals for *guaranteeing* the avoidance of ethnocentrism. The interpreter encounters the other with a background sense of what is possible and desirable for human beings. He arrives loaded with a framework by reference to which he is able to identify meaningful and acceptable modes of human self-interpretation. A framework is only able to perform this function by setting *limits* on the possible and the acceptable. Such 'limits of intelligibility' are always already in place whenever there is understanding. But when the interpreter reaches an understanding of the other, in the sense of achieving a fusion of horizons, he is forced to redraw these limits. He finds himself having to articulate them in a manner that now includes the other's self-definition as one of a range of recognizable human possibilities. In the contrast with the new, the old way of seeing now seems *unduly* limited. The feature that previously seemed given, fixed and inescapable is disclosed as one option amongst others, options that now *include* the other's self-definition. In Taylor's view, this makes inclusive recognition the key goal in the struggle against ethnocentrism, where inclusiveness is always a relative rather than absolute matter.

These comments certainly go some way to addressing Hoy's objections. It was never in fact Taylor's view that the interpreter *expects* the other's self-understanding to converge with his own. Taylor's view has always been that if the interpreter is to find the other's self-understanding *intelligible* it must fall within certain limits – the 'limits of intelligibility' the interpreter brings to the encounter. But there is nothing ethnocentric, at least nothing malignly ethnocentric, about this starting point. It is a necessary structure of reaching understanding. At the same time, there is nothing necessary about the social scientist's claim to have drawn the limits in the right place, and it is awareness of this, of the contingency of the limits we do draw, that helps counter ethnocentrism.

On this point, there is really little difference between Hoy's and Taylor's hermeneutics. Similarly, Taylor's insistence that inclusiveness is never attained absolutely is congruent with Hoy's understanding of anti-ethnocentrism. The two proposals for overcoming ethnocentrism diverge, however, in their conception of the primary task facing the interpreter. While both models present the goal of interpretation as 'other-understanding', for Taylor but not for Hoy understanding is always guided by the critical norm of truth. Hoy insists that interpretation can have a critical function without concerning itself with the 'truth'. It suffices, in Hoy's view, that the other-understanding *unsettles* the interpreter. And it is surely undeniable that critically effective interpretations have this effect. But in fairness to Taylor, perhaps we are most unsettled by things that bring home an uncomfortable truth. If we are seriously unsettled by the other-understanding, we will not let our understanding rest there. A concern with the truth can inspire as much as impede the process of reaching an understanding of the unfamiliar other.

To conclude, Taylor's hermeneutic model of comparative social science has many attractive features. It offers a plausible account of the process by which one reaches an understanding of another culture. It shows how cross-cultural judgements can have a rational basis. And it has a commendable diagnosis of ethnocentrism. 'Understanding other societies', as Taylor writes, 'ought to alter our self-understanding', and it is indeed 'the merit of the interpretive view that it explains how this comes about, when it does' (*PHS* 129). But when does it, in fact? In what particular cases has an understanding of other societies transformed our self-understanding? It has to be said that it is hard to find an answer from Taylor's own writings. He does little to show how self-transformation through the encounter with non-western cultures happens in specific cases. Sparse in examples of successful cross-cultural understandings, Taylor's model takes on a rather abstract, formal character. In this respect, it is not unlike his model of the natural sciences. Furthermore, the case Taylor most often invokes to illustrate the 'fusion of horizons' does not relate to an encounter between the western 'horizon' and another at all. Rather, it refers to a transition *within* western culture: the transition from a conception of knowledge that amalgamates the purposes of control and attunement to one that separates them. The fact that Taylor draws on an episode in the evolution of modern thought to clarify what goes on in successful cross-cultural understanding fuels the suspicion that his model has not fully escaped the ethnocentric snare. But it also reflects his commitment to the unsettling and self-transformative power of *historical* understanding. If we want detailed examples of how understanding other societies can transform self-understanding, the place to look is Taylor's historical studies of the rise of the modern identity. Here he does more than stipulate in general terms what interpretative social science ought to do. He tries to exhibit or instantiate the standard in his own interpretative practice. It may be Taylor's concrete historical studies, rather than his general analysis of cross-cultural judgement, that provide his best argument on how to avoid ethnocentrism.

6

Individual and Community

Individual human beings are dependent on others at a number of levels. At the most rudimentary level, we are dependent on others for the satisfaction of our biological needs. No individual can survive, for instance, without being fed, protected and nurtured during infancy, and we remain dependent on others for the material basis of our existence throughout our lives. Human beings are thus social animals in the minimal sense that the individual is not biologically self-sufficient. But individuals are dependent on others for more than the conditions of their self-preservation. At a higher level, the individual is dependent on others for things that give meaning to life, that is to say, for things that turn mere life into good life. The other on whom I, as an individual, depend in this way might be familiar to me – a parent, for instance, or a child, a friend, and so forth. To be so dependent is for the significance of one's desires, one's purposes and perhaps one's life as a whole to hinge on the relation one has to the other. In Taylor's terms, it is for one's identity, one's sense of self, to be constituted by the relation. Taylor describes this as the 'dialogical' structure of identity and he takes it to be another transcendental condition of human subjectivity (SS 38). A self, as Taylor puts it, invariably exists in 'webs of interlocution' (SS 36) with significant others, webs we can deny but never entirely escape from. Significant others are others who are essential for the individual's full self-realization. The good of the individual, the definition and realization of strong value in her life, depends on them.

But familiar significant others are not the only others on whom the individual *qua* self depends. In order to have any sense of the good at all, the individual must be able to draw on linguistic and cultural resources that have been passed on across generations. Of course, the socialized individual may reject many of the values that prevail in her culture. She may not be able to 'find herself' properly within them. But even here her very capacity to reject the values that surround her depends on her having access to other grounds of worth which themselves must to some extent be given. An individual who was incapable of identifying with anything, who had no sense of the distinction between the worthwhile and the worthless, would, we have seen, be in a pathological state, akin to the syndrome Erikson diagnosed as an identity crisis. Individuals who do not experience such misfortune owe their sense of self, however indirectly, to the activities of others. For it is only through the activities of others that languages live and cultures flourish. Furthermore, at least in many cases, individuals are dependent on a broader community of others not just for the conditions of their identity but for its content. That is to say, their sense of the dignity or worth of their lives is bound up with their membership of some group. In traditional societies – where the category of an 'individual' admittedly has less of a hold – the sense of sharing an ancestral lineage with others, for example, plays a crucial self-defining role. Even the highly individuated agents of modern societies typically define themselves at least in part through some identification with non-personal others. An individual's allegiance, say, to the city of his birth, or his local football team, or the school he attended may be crucial to his identity. Or it may be the sense of belonging to a community of believers, or sharing an ethnic background, or participating in the class of the struggling oppressed that contributes to the self-definition. In such cases, individuals acquire a sense of the weight or importance of their lives through identifying with something like a larger project, a project with its own history and distinctive purpose, which essentially includes non-familiar others.

Taylor suspects that the need to participate in a life larger than the individual's own is an anthropological constant. It manifests itself in one form or another, Taylor thinks, in all human societies. But in *modern* societies it acquires particular importance. Taylor is convinced that unless we take it into account, the characteristic social and political predicaments of modernity will be unintelligible. The first philosopher to see this clearly, according to Taylor, was Hegel. Equipped with an expressivist theory of subjectivity, one that took seriously the expressive or constitutive relation between particular individuals and the social whole, Hegel was able to spell out a fundamental dilemma facing modern societies. The dilemma arises from the need to reconcile participation in a larger collective life with the modern ideal of freedom.

A free people, according to the modern understanding, is a people of equals. It is made up of individual citizens who enjoy the same moral standing irrespective of creed, occupation, ethnicity or whatever local allegiances they have. No matter what your religion, job, ethnic or cultural background, in a free society you enjoy the same basic rights as your fellow citizens. But Hegel observed that if, in the eyes of the citizens, the *sole* purpose of political society were to protect those individual rights, if it were *just* an instrument enabling individuals and commonly interested groups of individuals to realize their own partial ends, it would not be an expression of their freedom. For the individual citizens would be *externally* related to such a society. They would follow the laws only when it suited them (or when they could not get away with doing otherwise) and they would be ill-prepared to defend it when necessary. Individuals and groups who, despite their formal equality before the law, were disadvantaged in other ways – the poor, for example – would feel even more alienated. Freedom, Hegel concluded, cannot simply be a matter of enjoying individual rights, rights inscribed in an essentially alien law and protected by a neutral instrument of arbitration (the state). On the one hand, such freedom would be unstable: the citizens would be divided amongst themselves and alienated from their collective life. On the other hand, it would be contradictory: a people that did not give the law to themselves would not really be free at all.

The ideal of freedom, then, seems to require more than the enjoyment of individual rights. It requires self-determination or autonomy in the stronger sense of participating in political society. But this seems to imply that *everyone* must participate: if some did not, they would be unfree, and if some citizens are unfree then all are, for the laws would not be an authentic expression of the will of *the people*. Second, it seems to imply that everyone must participate *fully*: if some participate more than others, it leaves the others less free, which again compromises the state's claim to give proper expression to a free citizenry. Furthermore, the fully participating citizens must reach *agreement* over the laws: without total consent, the laws would not express the will of everyone. But as Hegel saw, freedom through full participation and the creation of a unanimous general will has its own self-destructive costs. By eliminating local allegiances – based on work, religion or cultural background, for instance – it homogenizes the citizenry. It makes all citizens fundamentally the same. But a homogeneous, undifferentiated citizenry is not itself a viable object of identification. Something else would have to provide the motivation to participate in political society, something that was also capable of securing a unanimous will and suppressing social differentiation. However this is achieved – militant nationalism and totalitarian ideologies are two such means – it is bound, as Taylor puts it, to 'depreciate or even crush diversity and individuality', and so to undermine freedom and democracy itself (*HMS* 116).

So the dilemma facing modern societies is that the freedom of individuals is essential to their self-definition and self-legitimation – they define themselves as free societies, as democracies, and their political regimes could not hope to justify themselves otherwise – yet the two models of freedom just sketched are ultimately self-negating. Taylor agrees with Hegel that neither the liberal democratic state whose exclusive purpose and legitimacy resides in protecting the rights of individuals, nor the 'Jacobin' state whose purpose is to generate a unanimous will through the full participation of a homogeneous citizenry, are capable of delivering freedom to the individual. Much of Taylor's political and social thought is devoted to unravelling at once the appeal and the folly of these options. The former model finds its way into certain forms of liberalism, including libertarianism and what is now known as 'procedural liberalism'. It is characterized by its 'negative' conception of liberty, the primacy it gives to individual rights, and a certain conception of the neutrality of the state. Taylor's critique of this model, in essays such as 'Atomism' (1979) and 'What's Wrong with Negative Liberty' (1979), provides the basis for his reputation as a communitarian critic of liberalism.[1] The problems with this approach to the individual's freedom, according to Taylor, stem from the inadequacy of its ontological categories. Its defenders, he argues, more or less explicitly subscribe to a conception of agency that blots out the politically significant ways in which an individual's identity is dependent on others. Their concept of freedom is thus ontologically flawed and the measures they invoke for securing freedom politically are self-undermining. Their atomist ontology, Taylor argues, must be replaced by a holist one. But holism itself is just the ontology favoured by the second self-negating concept of freedom – the 'Jacobin' model. In Taylor's view, Jacobinism finds its way into certain versions of modern republicanism, nationalism and Marxism. It is inadequate, according to him, because it lacks the resources for dealing with the multiplicity of identities that characterize a free society. It replaces the notion of 'negative' freedom with a concept of 'absolute' freedom which is hostile to difference.

As a solution to the dilemma, Taylor proposes a concept of 'situated' freedom (*HMS* 160). Only situated freedom, Taylor argues, is capable of reconciling holism and pluralism. It is thus the only model of freedom appropriate to the increasingly differentiated, multicultural condition of modern societies. We shall examine Taylor's case for situated freedom, for a 'liberal holism' as opposed to liberal atomism, in the following section of the chapter. We shall then see that within the liberal holist outlook various options open up. This becomes clear when we turn to the issue of 'recognition' and contemporary calls for a politics of 'difference'. In the second section of the chapter we shall consider Taylor's influential reflections on this topic and the related issue of multiculturalism. This brings us to the problem of exclusion, of how possession of common identities functions to exclude people from the democratic process. In the final section of the chapter we examine Taylor's diagnosis of the patterns of democratic exclusion in the modern world and his suggestions for remedying them.

Liberal Holism

According to an influential strand of liberal thought, a society is morally well-ordered to the extent that it protects the rights of individuals. In John Locke's classical formulation of liberalism, the individual by nature enjoys an absolute and unconditional right to life, happiness and the possession of property.[2] A morally well-ordered society, according to Locke's theory, is one in which individuals are able to exercise this right without interference from others. The role of the state is to provide sanctions against individuals who encroach upon the rights of others. Given the chance, right-minded individuals would consent to such sanctions as it is in their long-term self-interest. In a morally well-ordered society, then, individuals go about their business as they choose with minimal interference from outside powers. Robert Nozick propounds a similar version of liberalism.[3] Like Locke, he asserts the unconditional and absolute right to freedom of the individual, though he is less persuaded than Locke of the long-term interest individuals have in maintaining even a minimal state. Now in Taylor's view, an important consideration for assessing the merits of this kind of liberalism is the way it construes the relationship between individual rights – rights that enshrine the freedom of the individual – and the collective good of sustaining a well-functioning community. As Taylor puts it in 'Atomism', Locke and Nozick affirm 'the primacy of rights' when they ascribe certain rights to individuals unconditionally but 'deny the same status to a principle of belonging or obligation' (*PHS* 188). They regard the latter, the obligation to belong to or to sustain a well-functioning society, as 'derivative'. The individual has only a conditional obligation to belong and to conform to the laws. So, for instance, we might be held to have an obligation to sustain a society *if* it is to our long-term advantage, or *if* we undertake some kind of contract with the state. But the rights of the.individual are not derivative or conditional in this way. The rights of the individual are primary.

There are all sorts of objections one could make to the 'primacy of rights' thesis as defended by Locke and Nozick. For instance, one could point to the arbitrary way in which these theorists posit the absolute right to freedom in the first place. Where does the right come from? Or one could question the primacy of rights on normative grounds. For example, one could present a picture of a well-ordered society that was less individualistic in its focus; or one could point to injustices that are likely to arise when individuals and groups are left to themselves to acquire property without substantive interventions by the state or some other regulatory body. Taylor would by no means find such objections unpalatable. But the argumentative strategy he actually adopts is different, and slightly less direct. In order to see the basic flaw in the primacy of rights thesis, Taylor argues, we have to turn our attention to the ontology it presupposes. That is to say, we need to reflect on the kind of being that is capable of exercising rights. If we do that, and we also consider the conditions that need to be in place for such a being to benefit from the rights ascribed to him, then we see, so Taylor argues, the basic incoherence of the idea that rights are primary.

The key to Taylor's argument is his claim that it only makes sense to ascribe the right to freedom within a 'context of affirming the worth of certain capacities' (*PHS* 196). He first notes that the exercise of the right to freedom does indeed involve a capacity: the capacity to make free choices. Like other capacities human beings have, this one is not given to individuals fully formed at birth. It needs to develop and mature. Furthermore, it only makes sense to ascribe the unconditional right to agents who possess or who have a chance of possessing such a developed and mature capacity. For otherwise, how would they benefit from the right? The whole point of the right is to protect freedom. But the worth of freedom is bound up with its exercise in mature forms. Taylor's next move is to point out that the agent's mature capacity for free choice requires certain background conditions to be in place. Above all, the agent has to belong to a society. Taylor calls this 'the social thesis'. Without society, there would be no maturation of the capacity for freedom. From this, Taylor concludes that the right to freedom of the individual cannot be divorced from the 'obligation to belong'. For if the capacity to make free choices can only develop and mature in society, then we cannot commit ourselves to the sustenance and protection of individual freedoms without at the same time committing ourselves to the sustenance and protection of the society that makes them possible. It is incoherent, then, to affirm individual rights unconditionally on the one hand, and on the other, to affirm the 'obligation to belong' to a wider community conditionally, as if the latter were an 'optional extra'.

Taylor acknowledges that not all the individual rights championed by classical liberalism refer to socially conditioned capacities. Clearly the right to life, for instance, is worth having whatever the degree of maturation of one's capacities. One does not need to have cultivated capacities to enjoy the benefits this right brings. As far as mere life is concerned, the social thesis as Taylor has defined it is therefore irrelevant. It only comes into play once we turn to capacities that require specific social and cultural conditions to develop. But the central goods prized by the liberal theory – autonomy and freedom – are precisely such capacities. They can only flourish given a background socialization process and a certain stock of cultural resources. And it is this dependence, rather than an individual's dependence on family or friends, for example, that in Taylor's view generates a specific obligation to political society. The various social and cultural forces which shape the modern individual – and it is important to stress that the modern individual is a historically specific phenomenon – create 'a significant obligation to belong for whoever would affirm the value of this freedom; and this includes all those who want to assert rights either to this freedom or for its own sake' (*PHS* 206).

Taylor's critique of the primacy of rights doctrine has prompted a number of critical responses, mainly from liberal theorists worried by what they see as the illegitimate threat to individual freedom posed by Taylor's communitarian line of reasoning. Will Kymlicka, for instance, attacks Taylor for surreptitiously subsuming the individual under the community.[4] According to Kymlicka, Taylor's anti-individualistic bias comes out in his construction of the way individuals both acquire and judge their self-defining projects. Whereas for Taylor life projects are acquired 'only by treating communal values as "authoritative horizons" which "set goals for us"', liberals rightly insist 'that we have an ability to detach ourselves from any particular communal practice'.[5] No individual is (or ought to be) compelled to align herself with any particular goal or purpose, however 'authoritative' it may be within the community. There is no such thing as a particular social practice that commands authority 'beyond individual judgement and possible rejection'. Taylor underestimates the capacity of individuals to stand back from their surrounding culture and decide for themselves their own allegiances. In a free, liberal society, individuals are able to determine for themselves the kind of life that is right for them. They are certainly under no natural obligation to conform to cultural horizons that are 'given'. Kymlicka is here giving voice to a widespread suspicion that Taylor's portrayal of the relation between the individual and the community is at once arbitrarily weighted in favour of actually existing communities and unduly conservative in its moral and political orientation. It seems to lock the individual in to a particular social practice. And the liberal not unreasonably finds this thought counter-intuitive both at the descriptive level (it is not how individuals in fact relate to their surrounding culture) and at the normative level (it is not how they would relate to it in a free society).

Is the suspicion well-grounded? It is certainly a mistake to interpret Taylor as advocating some kind of *a priori restriction* on the individual's capacity to make his own judgements of worth. Taylor is not proposing that in any particular case the individual must 'side' with the community. It is up to the individual to endorse this or that practice as he sees fit. The target of Taylor's argument is not the capacity for individual self-determination as such, but rather a failure to appreciate the *ontology* required to make sense of this capacity. When Taylor says that horizons are 'given' and purposes are 'set for us' he is not, as Kymlicka interprets it, addressing the issue of how projects are acquired and judged. He is making a claim about the *intelligibility* of the projects we do acquire and the judgements we do make about them, whatever the content of those projects and judgements. Taylor is far from denying that any particular interpretation of the good is immune from revision. His point is that for critique and affirmation of conceptions of the good to make sense at all, some background must be given to the individual. And if this is true, individuals are dependent on something 'social' *in* their capacity for self-determination. At the same time, the background does not come from heaven. It does not live off its own means, as if it could flourish and reproduce itself without the input of individuals. On the contrary, it can only function properly as background in so far as individuals contribute to it and express themselves through it. There must be some intertwining of the self-defining purposes of the individual and the community. This is why the right to freedom cannot be unconditional in the manner Lockean liberalism proposes.

But Kymlicka's mistake is an instructive one. For it shows the need to distinguish between two levels of enquiry that are easily conflated.[6] On the one hand, there is the transcendental problem, 'what are the conditions of possibility of a particular practice?'. In Taylor's view, transcendental reflection, or enquiry into the conditions of possibility of a practice, yield conclusions with ontological significance – at least they aim to yield such conclusions. And if one can then show that a certain interpretation of a practice is inconsistent with the conditions spelled out in the transcendental argument, we are forced to amend the interpretation. This is what Taylor claims to have shown in his argument against the primacy of rights. On the other hand, there is the empirical problem of how agents go about judging practices and deciding for themselves the worth of the options before them. At this level of enquiry, it also makes sense to advocate certain ways of relating to the practices judged. Now if we fail to distinguish between these two levels of argumentation, we are liable to misconstrue Taylor's transcendental or ontological case against liberalism as an advocacy of a particular empirical stance – and an extremely conservative one at that – towards existing social practices. And this is precisely what Kymlicka does when he chastises Taylor's 'communitarian tendency to endorse existing social practices uncritically as the basis for political deliberations about the good'.[7] If we keep the two levels of enquiry distinct, we see that Taylor's transcendental argument of itself tells us nothing about the stance an individual should take towards any particular conception of the good. However, the argument does reveal an inconsistency in the stance the Lockean liberal advocates towards rights. For it shows that the primacy of rights fails to meet its transcendental conditions.

It is important then that we do not allow our procedure for justifying ontology to pass unnoticed into our procedure for justifying a particular moral standpoint. To do so is to risk reifying or hypostatizing the options that face us. But the slippage can also take the other direction. That is to say, the procedure we adopt for justifying the worth of practices can illicitly determine the shape of our ontology, with equally distorting consequences. Taylor is convinced that this frequently happens in classical liberal and libertarian theory. In Taylor's view, it helps explain this version of liberalism's reliance on a rather implausible atomist ontology. According to atomism, society is comprised of an aggregate of self-sufficient individuals. There is nothing more to a society than the individuals who make it up, and the individuals could be who they are without belonging to a particular society. An ontology like this would justify the primacy of rights if it were true, but it compares very badly with the social thesis. Atomism would have no credibility at all, Taylor thinks, if it were not for the tendency among Lockean liberal theorists to ontologize the procedure by which they imagine autonomous individuals evaluate their options. The procedure involves taking up a distanced, reflexive stance to the surrounding culture and then choosing prudently from the goods on show. And it has to be said that one can find evidence of such ontologization of procedure in Kymlicka's own defence of liberalism. When he writes, for instance, that 'what is central to the liberal view is not that we can perceive a self prior to its ends, but that we understand ourselves to be prior to our ends in the sense that no end or goal is exempt from possible re-examination',[8] it is hard to resist the thought that a reflexive justifying procedure is illicitly finding its way into the very constitution of the self.

Once we take into account the different levels of Taylor's argumentation certain problems with his social thesis disappear. Others, however, remain. The remaining problems hinge on Taylor's rather awkward expression 'an obligation to belong'. In the first place, it is not clear how any kind of belonging can be an object of obligation. Belonging, after all, involves a certain kind of sentiment, a sentiment of attachment, of feeling 'at home' in whatever it is one belongs to. But what sense does it make to say that I have an *obligation* to feel a certain way? Belonging is a matter of affect, and affects cannot be summoned by obligations. The obligation, so to speak, arrives on the scene too late: if my sense of belonging has deserted me no amount of obligation talk is going to bring it back. Second, why should any acknowledgement of the *conditions* of my self-formation entail my allegiance to them? Taylor's response to this question, it seems to me, is weak. He simply asserts that 'since the free individual can only maintain his identity within a culture/society of a certain kind, he has to be concerned about the shape of this society/culture as a whole' (*PHS* 207). While that is surely true, it is not clear why the concern should generate an obligation as such. It is one thing to acknowledge the social and cultural conditions of my developed capacities but it is another to specify the obligations incurred by such conditioning. And even if we assume that an obligation can be derived, to what or to whom exactly is the obligation owed? What is the communal entity to which I am obligated? It is certainly not clear that I have any special obligation to the state on account of the social and cultural conditions of my identity. All the more so if I do not feel that I belong to it, if I feel excluded or marginalized. Taylor is well aware that modern societies generate significant alienation amongst their members. In fact, in Taylor's view there is nothing more important for social and political theory to do than to explain the origins of modern alienation and to assess the resources for overcoming it. It is questionable, however, whether he needs the notion of an 'obligation to belong' to prosecute this theoretical task.

To be fair, Taylor soon drops all talk of an obligation to belong. It has no place in later works, such as 'Cross-Purposes: The Liberal–Communitarian Debate' (1989),[9] where Taylor brings into sharper focus the challenges facing liberalism and the democracies liberalism strives to defend. The question Taylor now poses is this: what categories must liberalism have available if it is to make sense of a viable modern democracy? The question needs to be asked, Taylor thinks, in view of the currency of what he calls 'procedural liberalism'. Procedural liberalism envisages a free and just society as one that facilitates the individual life plans of its members on a fair basis. It recognizes the diverse conceptions of the good held by individuals and does what it can within the bounds of fairness to assist them. It does so – and this is the key point – without appealing to or espousing any particular conception of the good. A democratic society, according to this version of liberalism, is defined by the fairness of its procedures for arbitrating between the competing claims of individuals and groups. At least some of these claims will be informed by the conceptions of the good with which the individuals and groups identify. It is important, then, that the procedures themselves do not reflect or express a particular conception of the good. For otherwise they would discriminate against those who had a different conception. There can therefore be no 'socially endorsed conception of the good' in a democratic society, and this view gives procedural liberalism its distinctive character (*PA* 187). The issue Taylor raises, then, is whether a theory that excludes a socially endorsed conception of the good has the categories available for making sense of a viable modern democracy.

Taylor argues that if it does, it must be able to articulate in its own terms what Taylor takes to be the chief insight of the 'republican' or 'civic-humanist' tradition of political thought. Taylor calls it the 'republican thesis'. The republican thesis is that free, non-despotic regimes require a strong sense of patriotic identification from their citizens. The argument supporting the thesis is that unless the citizens of a community have a strong sense of patriotism for it they lack the necessary motivation to carry the inevitable burdens of life in a political society. They must pay taxes, observe inconvenient laws, fight wars if necessary, and so forth. In non-free or despotic regimes, such sacrifices are forced out of people directly by means of physical coercion or indirectly by the fear of punishment. But in a functioning free republic, the citizens must make the sacrifices willingly. They must carry the burdens themselves. And this can only happen, the argument runs, if the citizens identify themselves strongly enough with the political community, if they regard the community as a genuine expression of themselves. Furthermore, the life of a *free* people has burdens of its own. It requires some active participation in the political culture, something an unfree people leaves to someone else. Self-government is onerous, it needs a strong source of motivation, and the only thing that can provide such a source is patriotic allegiance. For these reasons, the republican thesis proposes an inseparable link between freedom and patriotism. It claims that a free society is viable only if the citizens have the energy and commitment to maintain it. And it locates the source of this energy and commitment in the patriotic bond.

Having outlined the republican thesis, Taylor's next move is to reflect on the categories that are required to express it. The first feature he notes is that patriotic solidarity is a good, or in the terms introduced earlier, a strong value. On the one hand, it is of intrinsic and not merely instrumental significance to the people who possess it or aspire to it. It may be a useful means of acquiring or preserving other goods – public services, for instance, or defence. But it is also valued for its own sake, and so can be called a non-instrumental good. On the other hand, it informs the people's sense of identity. One's patriotic allegiance expresses something important about who one is; it is a self-defining characteristic. But as well as being a good, it is also essentially a *common* good, or as Taylor also puts it, an 'irreducibly social good'.[10] A common or irreducibly social good is both non-instrumental and 'non-decomposable'. It is non-decomposable in the sense that its worth is essentially bound up with its common possession. As such, Taylor distinguishes irreducibly social goods from contingently common goods (or interests) that individuals can enjoy only if they are provided on a collective basis. My personal security, for instance, is a good for me; it is in my interest, as my neighbours' is for them. And the only practical means of obtaining it is for a police force, or perhaps a neighbourhood watch, to protect it for everybody. It just so happens that my security cannot be served without others' being served by the same means. The *worth* of the value in question here, my personal security, would be the same if I were able to ensure it myself. The 'public good' of an effective police force or neighbourhood watch serves individual interests that happen to converge. But the common good of patriotism does not arise from the convergent but decomposable interests of individuals. It is both non-instrumental (good in its own right, not just a means to an external good) and essentially possessed together: its common possession is essential to the worth it has as a good. Put otherwise, the identity patriotic solidarity defines belongs to an 'us' and not merely an aggregate of commonly or convergently interested 'I's. The republican thesis thus requires us to think in terms of 'we-identities as against merely convergent I-identities' (*PA* 192). It requires us to deploy a category of the common good. Without such a category, a free society bound together by patriotic solidarity is unintelligible.

If the procedural liberal accepts the truth of the republican thesis, Taylor continues, she is thereby committed to the existence of a common, irreducibly social good. She therefore has to abandon atomism (if indeed she began with it) in favour of liberal holism. Furthermore, if she is to remain a procedural liberal, she has to find a way of articulating the idea of the common good without committing herself to the notion of a socially endorsed conception of the good. And she can do this, Taylor acknowledges, by construing the principles of *right* as the common object of allegiance. That is to say, the procedural liberal can affirm the indispensable role of the patriotic bond in a democratic society, she can concede the essential 'we-identity' of a free people, while constructing the object of identification as something that is neutral with respect to the various conceptions of the good life pursued in the society. The solidaristic bond then expresses a commitment to the principles of equality, impartiality, equal freedom, the rule of law and the like; that is, it expresses a commitment to the procedures for justly arbitrating between the competing claims of individuals and groups. Moreover, the principles around which the citizens bond need not be abstractly universal: they can be 'ethically patterned' around the customs and traditions of a particular historical community, as in Habermas's model of 'constitutional patriotism'.[11]

Taylor does not seriously engage with Habermas's sophisticated version of procedural liberalism, but he doubts it is the right direction for liberal holism to take. While admitting it is an open question, Taylor suspects that this kind of approach is unable to capture the particularity of the object of the patriot's allegiance. Patriotism essentially sustains a 'specific historical set of institutions and forms' and this, Taylor thinks, 'is and must be a socially endorsed common end' (*PA* 198). The liberal democratic state cannot be neutral between patriots and non-patriots; patriotism is a good it cannot but endorse. But patriotism is always a 'love of the particular', and in this sense the common good it endorses is not neutral or procedural. It should be said that Taylor does not explore the possibilities open to procedural liberalism here, though elsewhere he acknowledges both the possibility and desirability of forms of patriotic allegiance that are not primarily directed at something historically pre-defined.[12] Future-oriented allegiance, allegiance to a project that has not yet been realized, can motivate common action as well as if not better than patriotism to a historically given form of life in modern, increasingly globalized free societies. Taylor's second source of doubt concerns the procedural model's marginalization of active participation as a good in itself. In Taylor's view, participation in a democratic culture is essential for sustaining the solidaristic bonds of a free society, both because it channels patriotic energies in productive ways, and because the practice of self-rule feeds back into and further strengthens the patriotic sentiment. But again, it is not clear why a sophisticated proceduralism cannot embrace this feature too.

The position we have reached is that if procedural liberalism accepts the republican thesis, it is bound to accept at least one socially endorsed common good: the good of patriotic allegiance. It is important to see that Taylor is not positing this good simply as a norm. The point of the argument is not that societies *ought* to have such built-in allegiances, as if societies or individuals were in some sense morally reprehensible for lacking patriotism (though Taylor's earlier talk of an 'obligation to belong' invited a reading along these lines). Rather, Taylor claims to be identifying a *functional* requirement of viable democracies. The claim of the republican thesis is that patriotism is a necessary condition of a viable democracy, irrespective of the judgement one makes on the value of democracy or its supporting conditions. But even if the republican thesis is true as an ontological claim (a claim about the nature of the viable or self-sufficient entity 'a free people'), Taylor has not shown what the object of this allegiance must be. Constitutional patriotism is one option, and Taylor himself suggests that a future-oriented patriotism may be more suited to contemporary conditions than the classical republican model. But we are now entering into a debate *between* liberal holisms. And to be fair to Taylor, the main purpose of his one explicit intervention in the liberal–communitarian debate is to show that this is where the real argument begins.[13]

Particularity and Recognition

Taylor owes his understanding of the republican thesis to the civic humanist tradition exemplified in the writings of Macchiavelli and Montesquieu. But the republican thesis also resurfaces later in the history of thought, in the Romantic/expressivist tradition pioneered by Rousseau and Herder. Moreover, thinkers like Herder formulated the republican thesis in a way that lends it even greater contemporary relevance. Like civic humanism, expressivism conceives democracy as the form of life of a free people. Both traditions emphasize the importance of citizen participation in public life and citizen identification with the political community. Only if a free people is bound by patriotic solidarity can they act effectively together, and they must be capable of effective common action if they are to realize common purposes, most notably self-preservation in times of crisis. Expressivism then gives this idea a distinctively modern complexion by connecting it to the notion of expressive freedom or authenticity. Expressive freedom or authenticity is, on the one hand, a capacity that all human beings have irrespective of their social or cultural location. A society can only be called free if it recognizes and respects this capacity in everyone, and in this sense expressivism is more radically egalitarian than its predecessor. On the other hand, the standards of authentic self-expression vary enormously, both at the individual and at the collective level; or in the terms introduced earlier, at the level of 'we-identity' as well as 'I-identity'. An expressively free people, accordingly, is one that is able to pursue its own common purposes as expressed in its own distinctive language and culture. It cannot be authentic, or enjoy expressive freedom, if it has an alien language, culture or set of strong values imposed on it. For this reason, expressivism is more radically particularized than traditional humanism. There is no single, universalizable formula of authentic self-definition. There are as many formulations as there are viable 'we-identities'. Furthermore, there can be no final, settled formulation of any one 'we-identity', for according to the expressivist theory, self-definition is a constantly changing and unending process. Authenticity is an always incomplete project.

In Taylor's view, the contemporary relevance of the expressivist model of freedom is evident in the numerous ways in which identity provides the focal point of political contestation. Taylor begins his highly influential essay, 'The Politics of Recognition' (1992), by drawing attention to the real sense of injury and oppression experienced by people whose identity is demeaned or marginalized in the public culture, if not excluded from it altogether.[14] The aboriginal peoples of post-colonial societies have suffered acutely from misrecognition of this sort, and they are increasingly vocal in their demands for proper respect of their distinctive traditions and ways of life. To take another example (discussed by Taylor elsewhere),[15] migrant groups generally expect to retain at least some aspects of their original cultural heritage; they do not expect to relinquish their language and customs when they emigrate, and they feel unjustly treated if they are forced to do so (especially where other migrant groups are not forced to conform to the dominant culture). More established national minorities may strive to liberate themselves from the shackles of the majority culture if they feel sufficiently alienated from it and if they are adequately mobilized around their own national identity. Political mobilization around an identity happens in other ways too, of course, for instance amongst blacks, women and gays. The goal for at least many engaged in the black liberation, women's and gay liberation movements is the acceptance and affirmation of their difference. These examples illustrate how political conflicts arise from the failure of some dominant culture to give full and proper recognition to a minority one.

Taylor then considers the scope available to liberal societies for meeting such demands. He notes that a liberal society is defined, in the first instance, by the equal status enjoyed by its citizens under the law. This equality is based on the 'equal dignity' of its members, their capacity to choose their own way of life. A liberal society recognizes the equal dignity of its citizens by granting them the same basic rights: the right to life, free association, freedom of speech, religious freedom, and so forth. Everyone is entitled to these rights simply in virtue of their common dignity as human beings. With regard to their fundamental liberties, the citizens of a liberal society are entitled to equal treatment, and if they are discriminated against on account of their particularity, they in turn suffer a damaging form of misrecognition. The misrecognition results not from 'difference-blindness' but from 'sameness-blindness'. In Taylor's view, difference-blindness with regard to fundamental liberties is an essential feature of a liberal society and it circumscribes the scope available for the recognition of particularity. A society in which demands for recognition are satisfied at the expense of basic freedoms is not liberal. No version of liberalism can countenance it.

But Taylor observes that liberalism often goes much further in its insistence on difference-blindness. For it can construe the difference-blind procedures for interpreting and redeeming basic individual rights (by judicial review) as definitive of the liberal polity as such. It can define the end or purpose served by the liberal democratic state exclusively in terms of impartial or difference-blind procedures for protecting the equal dignity of individuals. That is to say, liberalism can present liberal democracy as neutral with respect to the issue of identity, or as it is also put, neutral with respect to the good. This procedural model of liberalism, Taylor notes, is the dominant form of liberalism in the United States. Now we have already seen that there is something disingenuous about the proceduralist's construction of the neutrality of 'the right' in regard to 'the good': the viability of a liberal democracy depends on citizen allegiance to it, where the allegiance expresses an essentially shared identity, a shared commitment to a common good. So there must be a sense in which the citizens' common good is expressed (rather than side-stepped or neutralized) in the procedural republic's set of difference-blind principles. And in this sense it is not really neutral with respect to the good. But worse, the people may not conceive of the common good served by liberal democracy in these terms at all. To the extent that they are forced into conceiving it or relating to it in that way, they are subject to just the kind of misrecognition of particularity we considered above. The charge Taylor puts to procedural liberalism, then, is that while it is justly difference-blind at the level of basic liberties, it is unduly restrictive in its construction of the expressive possibilities consistent with the protection of those liberties, and this makes it difference-blind in an oppressive way. That is to say, it can contribute to the exclusion, marginalization and alienation of groups whose self-definition as a free people departs from and in crucial ways comes into conflict with the norms of the procedural liberal republic.

Taylor backs up the charge by considering the predicament of liberalism in Canada. The matter is extremely complex, but we can see its relevance for the question at hand without going into details (I shall further discuss Taylor's contribution to the Canadian constitutional debate in the next chapter). Taylor records some of the difficulties that have arisen from Canada's adoption of the proceduralist model. In particular, the model has alienated Quebeckers who regard themselves as belonging to a 'distinct society' within Canada with their own particular 'we-identity'. 'It is axiomatic for Quebec governments', Taylor writes, 'that the survival and flourishing of French culture in Quebec is a good' (*MPR* 58). And in the circumstances Quebec finds itself in, this good – the good of *survivance* – can only be secured by actively promoting it in public policy. The provincial government of Quebec has introduced a series of measures aimed at securing *survivance*, laws that can hardly be considered 'neutral' with respect to the good. Most notably, it has implemented a number of language laws which, amongst other things, enforce French-language education on the children of immigrants and prohibit commercial signs in languages other than French. Taylor is by no means uncritical of the measures Quebec has taken to ensure *survivance*. But he does accept that *survivance* is a legitimate goal for the Quebec government to pursue. There are inevitable costs: certain individual 'immunities and privileges', like the freedom to display commercial signs in English, have to be sacrificed for the common good. Moreover, in Taylor's view *survivance* requires more than policies that make the French language 'available for those who might choose it'; it cannot merely be left to individual choice. If the policies are to work, they must '*create* members of the community' by 'assuring that future generations continue to identify as French speakers' (*MPR* 58–9). In

both these respects, the promotion of *survivance* seems incompatible with procedural liberalism. For from the perspective of procedural liberalism, such policies violate individual rights and are
inherently discriminatory. They give precedence to a collective goal
over individual freedoms and they unfairly favour the group whose
conception of the good they serve.

Yet if the Quebeckers were to follow the procedural path, they
would be putting at risk the basis of their own distinctive identity,
if not guaranteeing its demise. To the extent that the rest of Canada
has sought to impose procedural liberalism upon them, they have
been subject to an oppressive form of difference-blindness. A liberal
society can avoid this kind of outcome, Taylor suggests, if it allows
for the pursuit of collective goals, while 'respecting diversity, especially when dealing with those who do not share its common goals',
and by providing safeguards for the *fundamental* liberties. Taylor
concedes that 'there will undoubtedly be tensions and difficulties
in pursuing these objectives together' (*MPR* 59). But he seems con-
fident it can be achieved. In any case, Taylor suspects that the recent
growth of societies that contain 'distinct' societies or cultures within
them will soon make procedural liberalism obsolete. For such societies are bound to include 'more than one cultural community that
wants to survive' (*MPR* 61), and such communities will demand a
politics of difference that recognizes the importance of socially
endorsed collective goals.

For Taylor, then, a liberal multicultural society at once protects
basic freedoms and has mechanisms in place for ensuring the survival of minority cultures. But it does not base the good of cultural
survival on the notion that different cultures are of equal worth. The
idea that different cultures deserve equal recognition on account of
possessing equal value, Taylor observes, underlies a popular stance
in debates over multiculturalism in education. Advocates of multicultural curricula in the humanities, for instance, sometimes argue
that the traditional western 'canon' has been arbitrarily enforced. It
owes its privileged place in the curriculum not to its superior worth,
but to the parochialism and ethnocentrism of traditional educa-
tionalists. The challenge now is to discard this parochialism, the
multiculturalists argue, and to give due recognition in the curriculum to other cultures which presumably have the same worth. Now
Taylor has sympathy for the 'presumption of equal worth' as a point
of departure or 'starting hypothesis' for the study of another
culture. The chances are 'that all human cultures that have ani-
mated whole societies over some considerable stretch of time have

something important to say to all human beings' (*MPR* 66). It would be arrogant not to approach the study of a culture with this presumption. But the worth of a culture cannot be determined without actually engaging with it. To assert the equal worth of cultures independently of such engagement, to lay it down as a general principle of curriculum design, defeats the purpose of the reform. On the one hand, to collapse the distinction between cultures that deserve the recognition of serious study and those that do not homogenizes them as effectively as the traditional canon did. And on the other hand, if one reasons that all cultures have the same right to inclusion because there is really no such thing as a difference in worth, it makes comparative judgements a simple matter of taking sides. This in turn betrays a certain arrogance, as it implies we have nothing to learn from comparative study. In the previous chapter we saw that relativism (or an extreme formulation of it) backfires in its well-meant endeavour to overcome ethnocentrism. Taylor discerns the same self-undermining logic at work in this approach to multiculturalism.

While there may well be something 'half-baked' about the relativism Taylor attacks, it is not clear that he gets the motivation of his opponents in the multicultural debate quite right. In Taylor's view, the presumption of equal worth is legitimate because it is likely that enduring cultures have something to teach everyone. But when the revisionists call for the inclusion of a culture in the curriculum they need not and typically do not have this goal in mind. Their concerns may be more local, their ambitions less universal. They might then see Taylor's anti-subjectivist argument (the hermeneutic argument against the levelling of the superior/inferior worth distinction) as beside the point. Taylor himself notes that 'the demand for inclusion is *logically* separable from a claim of equal worth. The demand could be: Include these because they're ours, even though they may well be inferior' (*MPR* 68). Taylor does not take this to be the demand multicultural revisionists do in fact make, but surely it would not be unreasonable if they were to make it. A culture may be a worthy – in the sense of a 'fit' – object of study simply because it is 'ours', that is, without it having the kind of worth picked out by cross-cultural comparisons. It deserves a place in the curriculum simply because it reminds us of who 'we' are, and it does not need to contribute to a general understanding of the human condition to serve this function. All the more so if the 'we' in question is a minority whose culture and history has been neglected or suppressed in the traditional canon. And of course it is just such cultures and histories that drive the multiculturalist agenda. As Susan Wolf observes in her 'Comment' on Taylor's text, the main reason for including African, Asian and Native American cultures in the American curriculum is that they are 'the cultures of some of the groups that together constitute our [American] community'.[16] It has little to do with the worth or merit they possess in comparison with other cultures.

Clearly, a dominant culture that denies the existence or importance of constituent minority cultures is oppressively 'difference-blind' in Taylor's sense. His remarks about the equal worth of cultures thus need to be taken in context. According to Taylor's view, the collective good of cultural survival is something that liberal societies can and sometimes should socially endorse – that is, integrate into public policy – depending on its compatibility with the preservation of basic liberties. The argument is *not* that only those cultures which prove themselves to be superior to others through cross-cultural comparison are *entitled to survive*. Taylor's 'presumption' that relatively enduring cultures have something to teach everyone is a relevant consideration for determining the content of a curriculum (though as we have just seen, not the only one). But it should not be taken further than that. When Habermas, for instance, writes that 'Taylor's politics of recognition would be on shaky ground if it had to depend on the "presumption of equal value" of cultures and their contribution to world civilization',[17] he is of course right. But this is not the way Taylor does in fact argue when he is dealing with the issue of survival and its place in public policy. Taylor's discussion of the presumption of equal value reflects his impatience with the US humanities wars. His main interest, however, is the challenge cultural diversity presents for liberal politics. At the heart of this challenge, in Taylor's view, is the demand made by minority cultures for recognition of their common goal of survival. This is a demand which, according to Taylor, procedural liberalism cannot meet. In its place, Taylor proposes a model of liberal politics that is difference-blind at the level of fundamental liberties (it is *liberal* politics), while difference-sensitive at the level of public policy (it is a politics of *recognition*). Does he pull off the trick?

First of all, we must bear in mind that Taylor's model is premised on the thesis that procedural liberalism lacks the resources for dealing with the politics of recognition. But the premise might seem unwarranted. Habermas argues this way in the article just cited above. Habermas's argument is complex but we can grasp its basic point without getting caught up in the details. His case rests on the idea that far from opposing individual rights and sensitivity to cultural differences, procedural liberalism properly conceived binds them together inseparably. It does this by asserting what Habermas calls 'the equiprimordiality of private and civic autonomy'.[18] In modern liberal societies, Habermas observes, private autonomy is enshrined and protected through individual rights. And these are ingrained in the law. But the law itself, according to Habermas's theory, is itself only legitimate if those subject to it can regard themselves as its co-authors. The morally binding force of the law is grounded in its claim to express a common will formed through a procedure of uncoerced dialogue. As co-authors of the law, the citizens exercise their civic autonomy. The two kinds of autonomy, private and civic, are thus internally related. The civic autonomy of citizens is just what enables them to secure for themselves the social and cultural conditions of their non-civic identity. So the opposition Taylor sets up between individual and collective rights is artificial: 'the democratic process of implementing equal individual rights', Habermas writes, extends naturally 'to guaranteeing the equal protection in co-existence of various ethnic groups and their cultural lifeforms'.[19] According to Habermas's theory, then, the responsibility to recognize and respect cultural difference in law has the same basis as the responsibility to recognize and respect individual rights. Both are grounded in the procedure of uncoerced, intersubjective will-formation. The recognition of cultural difference needs no special justification within a properly conceived procedural liberalism. In other words, a procedurally based principle of equal dignity can do the job without introducing a separate principle of equal recognition.

Habermas thus proposes an alternative framework for understanding the predicament of culturally diverse liberal societies. And up to a point, I do not see why Taylor should object to it. If the theory allows for the provision of different collective goals, and if it makes room for context-sensitive applications of general principles for securing individual rights, so much the better: it can be marshalled alongside Taylor's theory against the problematically rigid difference-blind version of liberalism. All Taylor needs to ask for is first, some acknowledgement at the meta-ethical level that the theory is based on a conception of the good society; and second, a convincing account of how the good served by liberal democratic institutions manages to constitute the identity of citizens, that is to say, provide them with a rich enough locus of patriotic allegiance.

Once the liberal acknowledges that the autonomy that grounds the theory is indeed a good (that it is informed by a vision of the good society based on the ideal of autonomy), and once he shows that autonomy is sufficiently potent as an expressive aspiration to unite a people in effective common action, he has moved beyond the orbit of proceduralism as Taylor understands it. Whether a liberal theory can concede these points and remain proceduralist is merely a verbal matter. The point is that once it does concede them, the politics of equal dignity espoused by liberalism need not *compete* with the politics of equal recognition. Autonomy and authenticity are not *necessarily* rival ideals, they need not be set up from the outset as incommensurable goods, and there is little evidence to suggest that Taylor does set them up that way.[20]

A more serious objection, however, is that Taylor's version of liberalism is inconsistent with the principle of equal dignity that defines liberal societies. The charge now is that Taylor's model is *incoherent* as a version of liberalism (or if you like, simply incoherent). A number of critics have made this criticism, but none has expressed it more vigorously and provocatively than Andy Lamey, an academic reporter based in Toronto.[21]

Lamey claims to identify a number of serious contradictions in the model Taylor proposes for liberal politics in Quebec. In the first place, Taylor at once advances and resists the case for cultural assimilation within Quebec. Speaking on behalf of the Quebeckers, Taylor writes that Quebec 'political society is not neutral between those who value remaining true to the culture of our ancestors and those who might want to cut loose in the name of some individual goal of development' (*MPR* 58). Those who opt for the latter goal have to adapt to the legitimate pursuit of *survivance*; they must be prepared to be assimilated within the culture of the Quebeckers' ancestors. By supporting the language laws aimed at preserving and passing on the French culture, Taylor effectively endorses 'cultural homogeneity across generations'. But this position, Lamey objects, hardly squares with Taylor's liberal commitment to pluralism, with his ideal of a liberal culture that is open to others, and with his conception of cultural interaction as a 'fusion of horizons'. On the contrary, the whole point of inscribing the goal of *survivance* into Quebec political society, Lamey argues, is to cocoon the ancestral culture, to immunize it from invasive outside influences. Lamey points out that not so long ago, prior to its 'Quiet Revolution' of the 1960s, Quebec was still a deeply Catholic and not especially liberal society. If the old Catholic establishment had implemented Taylor's model of 'liberalism', it could have secured a permanent position of power for itself by forcing future generations to assimilate to its culture. The kind of policies Taylor supports effectively imprison future generations in whatever is the contemporary self-understanding. They also leave future generations hostage to the prejudices – perhaps quite illiberal – of the past and present. Taylor's commitment to cultural openness seems to fall short when it comes to the Quebec French culture. If he were to advocate cultural transformation through the fusion of horizons consistently, he would surely allow French-speaking Quebeckers to send their children to schools whose language of instruction was something other than French. Yet the language laws Taylor supports prevent it. Taylor seems to be recommending cultural openness and horizon-fusing for all except the French-speakers. He effectively advocates 'a silent privileging of the majority culture' in Quebec.[22]

Taylor thus seems to have double standards when it comes to the issue of cultural assimilation. On the one hand, he is opposed to the assimilation of Quebec's francophones within English-speaking Canada. On the other, he favours the assimilation of non-French-speakers within francophone Quebec. This is particularly problematic, Lamey points out, when one considers the situation of immigrants. Minority immigrant groups have their own cultures and languages, and as we have seen, one of the main issues a politics of recognition must address is the justified need of minority groups in multicultural societies to retain their distinctive cultural identities. However, it is hard to see how such demands for recognition can be facilitated by laws explicitly aimed at *creating* members of the francophone community, still less a community whose members identify with the culture of the Quebeckers' ancestors. Lamey accepts that it may be useful, in a place like Quebec, to urge minority groups to assimilate into the dominant culture. Conversely, it might be appropriate to accept and to affirm the minority cultures without qualification or interference. The problem with Taylor's position, though, is that he seems to want both at the same time. He at once advocates assimilation of immigrants for the sake of *survivance* and due recognition of the immigrants' background cultures and traditions. And in a parting shot, Lamey claims to expose one more contradiction in Taylor's politics of recognition that arises from the migrant's predicament. To suppose, as Taylor does, that immigrants 'live the life of diaspora, whose centre is elsewhere' (*MPR* 63) is to allow that cultural identity at least for them is not constituted dialogically or by structures of recognition at all. It presents the identity of the immigrant as 'monological', as already fully formed, apparently in flagrant contradiction of Taylor's thesis that identity involves a life-long process of dialogue with others.

In assessing these objections, it is important that we distinguish between Taylor's use of the Quebec case to illustrate the limitations of procedural liberalism and his advocacy of a particular stance within the Quebec debate. Taylor is certainly sympathetic to the grievance expressed by Quebeckers that procedural liberalism threatens their cultural identity by excluding the pursuit of collective goals. Given the particular circumstances of Quebec – a French-speaking culture bordering with an anglophone cultural superpower – some collective action needs to be taken to ensure the continuity of its distinct identity. But proceduralism seems to prevent such measures and this generates the grievance. Taylor is sympathetic to it as a nationalist because he acknowledges the legitimacy of the aspiration to pursue common goals around a national identity. He is sympathetic to it as a liberal to the extent that the common goal pursued is consistent with the protection of basic freedoms. Whether the form of nationalism that prevails in Quebec is as liberal as it should be, however, is another matter. When Taylor identifies the culture of the Quebeckers' ancestors as the object of their allegiance, he is describing a matter of fact. This is how Quebec nationalists see themselves, at least many of them. But Taylor is not advocating that they *should* see themselves that way, still less that migrants should be forced to adopt the same form of patriotism. At times, Taylor even suggests that the backward-looking, ethnic orientation of traditional Quebec nationalism is as much a danger to the continuation of a distinct Quebec as procedural liberalism is. By locking itself into the past, such a national identity is incapable of dealing with the challenges of the present, and in particular the challenge (and opportunity) posed by multiculturalism. To be sure, it is sometimes hard to tell when Taylor is simply describing the grievance the Quebec nationalists have with proceduralism and when he is advocating a certain response to the grievance. But to present Taylor as a spokesperson for the more reactionary wing of Quebec nationalism is certainly misleading. In Taylor's view, contemporary Quebec provides a circumstance in which core liberal values are reconciled with the social endorsement of a particular conception of the good. It shows that a regime can pursue the collective goal of cultural survival while respecting basic liberties. To this extent it illustrates a general model that can serve as an alternative to procedural liberalism. Within the model, however, there is much room for manoeuvre.

A couple of other points should be made in Taylor's defence. First, Lamey exaggerates the extent to which Taylor's proposals endorse francophone cultural homogeneity and non-francophone assimilation. On the one hand, the policies justified by the goal of *survivance* are quite limited in scope. They are designed to promote the use of the French language in the public culture both in the present and in future generations. But it is not clear why this goal must homogenize the culture. After all, the dominance of one particular language in other societies does not inhibit cultural diversity. On the other hand, it could be argued that the promotion of the French language is likely to bring about a less homogeneous outcome than no intervention at all. For without some kind of intervention along the lines of the language laws the English language would become dominant by default. While it is true that Taylor effectively advocates a 'privileging' of the majority francophone culture in Quebec, he does not privilege it arbitrarily. Given the historical and geopolitical circumstances, it needs a certain amount of protection. It may not be the only culture that needs protection, and indeed as the dominant cultural group within Quebec, the francophone nationalists will generate other minorities who will in turn have their own special claim to recognition. But this does not invalidate the Quebeckers' original demands, nor does it undermine the basic principle of Taylor's politics of recognition. It just means that the principle of recognizing collective goals consistent with a commitment to basic liberties needs to be applied in ways sensitive to the particular context.

The second point to make on Taylor's behalf is that the features Lamey describes as contradictions in Taylor's theory reflect real conflicts on the ground. In the case of immigrants, for instance, Taylor does want to say that if they are to live in a thriving democracy, they must be assimilated to the extent of having a strong patriotic allegiance to the new home country, while at the same time unassimilated to the extent of retaining much of their original cultural identity and having that identity recognized. There is clearly a tension in these two requirements. Taylor acknowledges as much, though he is convinced (perhaps too readily) that the conflict can be resolved. If ultimately it cannot be, if the two conditions are really incompatible, we could call this a contradiction in Taylor's theory. Alternatively, however, we could call it a contradiction in modern democratic societies themselves. That is to say, if it ends up being the case that modern immigrant societies are unable to achieve unity in diversity, it will be the forms of life, and not Taylor's theory, that go under.

Democratic Exclusion

In Taylor's view, the Quebec case illustrates a 'standing dilemma' facing modern democracies.[23] On the one hand, the basic principle of democracy, self-rule or rule of the people by the people for the people, is a principle of inclusion. *All* the people, not just the members of a particular caste, class or gender, are due a say in the democratic process. The inclusion of everyone is (at least partly) what makes politics democratic. In belonging to a self-governing 'people', the members of democratic societies share a common identity. They are all party to the people's will and doings. It is important that this is true even in cases where individuals or groups do not find their particular will expressed in specific laws. An individual or group may be outvoted, they may disagree with the majority decision, but they still consider themselves free to the extent that they belong to and identify with the larger sovereign entity, the 'people'. So long as they feel part of the sovereign – as they are clearly more likely to do if they have been included in the process through which the people expresses its will – they recognize the legitimacy of the law and consent to it. The law expresses the will of the collective agent, the free people, with which the individual agents identify. At least that is how it must seem to them in a well-functioning democracy. The legitimacy of the modern democratic state depends on the people imagining themselves as 'one', as a 'deliberative unit' with a common identity.[24] Besides being required for the legitimacy of the state, a strong sense of collective identity is also important for providing citizens with the motivation to participate in the burdensome activity of self-rule. As we have already seen, Taylor is convinced by the republican thesis that democracies need patriots of some description, and that patriotism necessarily involves collective identification. In modern democracies, where the distribution of the burdens of citizenship is liable to be uneven (for instance, in the payment of taxes), a high degree of trust between citizens is also important. Again, a sense of shared identity helps to create and maintain the trust. For these reasons, Taylor thinks it indispensable that democracies engender strong common identities. Democracy requires people who *imagine* themselves to constitute 'a free people'.

Democratic inclusion, then, is essentially inclusion in a form of life bonded by a sense of common identity. But this very sense of a common political identity is also responsible for generating exclusion. Taylor distinguishes three circumstances in which exclusion can happen. First, there are cases where an outside group may be excluded because they threaten the dominant political identity. So-called 'ethnic cleansing' is the most brutal form of such exclusion, but Taylor also sees its logic at work in the old apartheid system in South Africa (where blacks were deemed citizens of the 'homelands' external to the state), as well as in regimes which try to assimilate or enforce the inclusion of a minority group by denying its separate existence, as the Kurds find in Turkey. A second pattern of exclusion occurs in immigrant democratic societies whose political identity is bound to a sense of ethnic unity. A political identity based on the common possession of a language, culture and ancestry can be reluctant to include immigrants in its citizenry. The obvious example of a society like this is Germany, which refuses to grant its population of *Gastarbeiter* citizen status. But Taylor also includes his native Quebec in this category. The exclusion of immigrants is reflected in talk of 'us' and 'them', where 'they' are talked about either as a problem or as a possible resource, rather than as equal partners in political or public debate. Even ethnically heterogeneous societies, like the United States, have perceived waves of immigration as a threat to their democracy. The third kind of exclusion Taylor mentions is motivated not so much by the perceived threat to a dominant ethnolinguistic culture as by the need to impose a single rigid formula of citizen identity. Taylor has the French Jacobin tradition in mind here. Immigrants and others are not excluded from the outset on account of their ethnic or cultural origins but for failing to conform to the uncompromising standards the republic demands of its citizens. Finally, all modern liberal democracies emerged historically in political societies dominated by men, and women continue to feel excluded from the dominant public cultures.

In these ways the exigencies of collective agency run athwart legitimate demands for inclusion. The dilemma arises because the people of a democratic society need to imagine themselves as belonging to a particular community – this is an essential condition of both legitimacy and survival – yet in doing this they are drawn into an exclusionary orientation, one which conflicts with the basic legitimating principle of democracies, namely popular sovereignty or the inclusion of all in the process of self-rule. One way of responding to the dilemma is to try to dissolve it by denying the necessity of one of its elements. So, for instance, one could argue that if exclusion arises from people imagining themselves to share a common identity, the way around it is to restrict the role of such imagination in the self-understanding of the democracy. Liberal critics of nationalism sometimes argue this way. If imagining oneself to belong to a nation leads one to support the exclusion of non-nationals from political society, so much the worse for the national political identity, or whatever the identity is that generates the exclusion. Clearly, though, Taylor must reject this option. For without some form of common identification the democracy ceases to function. The only way forward, Taylor thinks, is to acknowledge the dilemma, to accept that some degree of exclusion is inevitable, and to try to minimize or 'compensate' for democracy's intrinsically exclusionary dynamic. The correct way of addressing the problem of exclusion, in Taylor's view, is to examine the modes of social imaginary that prevail in modern liberal democracies, to make explicit the kinds of political society to which democratic peoples imagine themselves to belong, and in doing so to open up the possibility of more inclusive models of common identification. The challenge is to articulate the social imaginaries that at once under-pin inclusion and exclusion and where possible to bring out an unfulfilled potential for further inclusion.

As Taylor has remarked, the task of articulating modern social imaginaries for the sake of exposing the sources of democratic exclusion is taken up, albeit as yet in a rudimentary fashion, in much of his more recent work in political theory.[25] One of the most potent sources of exclusion, as Taylor notes, is the nationalist imagi-nary. Nationalists imagine themselves to belong to a pre-politically defined entity – the nation – and their demands that it be made congruent with the political entity (the state) cannot but cause exclusionary havoc in modern culturally diverse societies. If the community with which the co-nationals identify is understood as possessing a monopoly of power over some territory of origin, it must either remove the non-nationals from the land claimed on behalf of the nation (ethnic cleansing) or accept them as disen-franchised minorities. Both options are at once morally objection-able and counter-productive for democracy. At the same time, however, Taylor is adamant that such radically exclusive politics follows only from a certain mode of nationalism; it is not a necessary consequence of nationalism as such. He argues that in its original (Herderian) formulation, nationalism was a pluralist doctrine: it was powered by a sense that all nations deserve equal respect. And it is hard to imagine how, at least in certain parts of the contemporary world, struggles for self-rule could take any other form than struggles for national self-determination. The aspiration to self-rule on the part of an imagined community of nationals can serve as well as hinder democracy. It can lead to more or less exclusionary forms of democracy. And this is just as true, Taylor suggests, of the 'republican' imaginary. The idea of belonging to a 'free people' committed once and for all to a founding constitution is just as incapable of adapting to historical change, and so just as liable to cause unnecessary and illegitimate exclusion, as the idea of a nation frozen in time by its original occupation of a territory.

In Taylor's view then, there is no way around the dilemma of exclusion. The people of a democracy have to imagine themselves as belonging to a shared community. But the traditional ways of imagining this community – as the 'nation' or as the 'republic' – run aground in the contemporary world of culturally diverse societies. How else, then, might they be imagined? Where are the social imaginaries that at once secure social cohesion and include cultural diversity? 'These', Taylor admits, 'are a lot harder to find.'[26] But Taylor does make one general proposal. It is simply the idea that the imagined location of identity has to be something negotiated in the present by the citizens themselves, rather than something merely received or inherited from the past. Citizens who resist taking their political identity as pre-given – as established once and for all by a constitutional settlement (founding a republic) or by some original occupation of a land (founding a nation) – can adapt creatively to new demands for inclusion. The challenge is to create new loci of identity through interaction with others. Taylor calls this the idea of 'sharing identity space'.[27] Taylor concedes that he is unable to spell out what sharing identity space would mean in practice, but he adds that the details are a matter for citizens themselves to work out in their own particular and changing contexts. Taylor has some thoughts on what it would mean in the Canadian context and I shall consider these in the next chapter. As a general principle, though, it is hard to avoid the impression that rather than solving the problem of exclusion, the idea of sharing identity space merely restates it. It simply seems to enjoin citizens with traditional sources of political identity to change themselves given the modern reality of cultural diversity. But the very problem with these traditional sources is that they are *not* open to change and negotiation. If they were, they would not be in the predicament of identity-threatening exclusion. At the general level, then, it is not clear that the notion of sharing identity space tells us anything we did not already know from our understanding of the dynamics of democratic exclusion. But we must reserve judgement about its practical utility until later.

Rigidly exclusive political identities represent a serious danger to contemporary democracies. But they are by no means the only one. Besides requiring strong solidaristic bonds between their citizens, democracies must meet other conditions. In 'Liberal Politics and the Public Sphere', Taylor lists three.[28] First, the mass of the people must be able to participate in the political culture; they must be given a meaningful say in the decisions that determine their collective identity. Second, in having their say they should not be subject to coercion or manipulation, for instance by more or less subtle forms of propaganda. And third, their say should to some extent be informed and well-considered. Each of these conditions must be met if the democracy is to function effectively. Democracies need publicly visible fora of opinion-formation, discussion and debate, places envisaged within the democratic imaginary as independent of the state: namely, the dimension of civil society called 'the public sphere'. Taylor agrees with deliberative theorists of democracy that an inclusive and 'flourishing public sphere is essential to democracy' (*PA* 279). But he refuses to accept the traditional way of imagining the public sphere as singular and external to the political system. The old model needs to be rejected, Taylor argues, because it fails to address the major ways in which the public sphere is imperilled in contemporary mass societies. The centralization and bureaucratization of government inevitably makes it seem remote from ordinary citizens, and this 'hypercentralization' also impinges on the public sphere. Public debates are conducted through centrally controlled media corporations that have their own exclusive agendas, and this must be bad for democracy. However, as a counter-tendency to hypercentralization Taylor cites the emergence of 'nested public spheres' (*PA* 280). Nested public spheres have a local base and input, they publicly discuss on-the-ground concerns, but they also manage to feed into and shape national (and international) debates. Taylor credits the 'new social movements', such as the feminist movement and the environmental movement, with having created public spheres of this type. In modern societies, Taylor thinks, democracy is better served by decentralized, more inclusive, multiple public spheres in dynamic interaction with the political system, rather than, as traditionally imagined, a single sphere external to the state and watching over it.

A well-functioning democracy, then, has public deliberative processes in place (a public sphere) that allow everyone a free and informed say. The more exclusive the processes, the less conducive they are to democracy. A centralized and bureaucratized public sphere excludes (it prevents many people from having a say, and an informed say), and this breeds alienation. Another mechanism of exclusion, which we have already considered, is lack of recognition. The voices of groups with legitimate contributions to make to public debates may go unheard, or they may be heard in demeaning ways, distorted by prejudice. Of course, cultural or ethnic difference is not the only basis of exclusion: the voices of workers and women, for instance, may also be suppressed. Such exclusions exacerbate the divisions that already exist within the society and can lead to a further undermining of the liberal democracy. Taylor then identifies a third self-destructive mode of exclusion which he calls 'political fragmentation'. The danger of political fragmentation is that of 'a people less and less capable of forming a common purpose and carrying it out' (*PA* 282). Political fragmentation may be driven by an atomistic outlook, that is, by a conception of society as an aggregate of individuals with no common purposes and only their own particular interests and life plans. This denies the very existence of a shared political community. Or it might be driven by a vision of society as so deeply divided by class conflict or patriarchy that invocations of political community appear 'a sham and a delusion' (*PA* 281). But however society is conceived, the effect of fragmentation is to weaken the solidaristic bonds between citizens *as* citizens, and so to disempower the political community as a collective agent. And this sense of the powerlessness of citizens as participants in projects serving the collective good in turn intensifies fragmentation and atomization. With fragmentation, liberal politics becomes more and more a matter of special interest lobbies, of campaigns with narrowly defined, partial objectives, of activities promoting the goals of a minority or a local community. But when political energies are channelled this way it becomes increasingly difficult for citizens to mobilize themselves around common projects. As Taylor puts it, 'a sense grows that the electorate as a whole is defenceless against the leviathan state' and 'the idea that a majority of the people might frame and carry through a common project comes to seem utopian and naïve' (*PA* 282–3). Individuals feel left to their own devices, and as they acquire less experience of effective common action, they become more atomistic in their self-understanding. This makes it even more difficult for them to identify with the political community, and so their sense of exclusion and alienation from the democratic process hardens.

Taylor's reflections on the dangers facing modern democracy exemplify a distinctive understanding of the tasks of political theory. Many political theorists see the aim of their discipline as the clarification of key political concepts such as justice, freedom, rights, democracy and so forth. By way of logical analysis, they seek to clarify the conceptual structure of such notions. According to another commonly held view, the central task of political philosophy is to examine the justification of basic political norms. The main concern of political theory on this view is to assess the legitimacy of state power, to clarify the rational basis of an individual's obligations towards the state and of the responsibilities states have to their citizens, to other individuals, to other states and so on. Clearly, there is considerable overlap between Taylor's conception of political theory and these mainstream approaches: Taylor's concern with the conditions of 'true' democracy is shared by many political theorists. But the primary purpose of Taylor's theoretical reflections is neither the clarification of a concept nor the rational justification of a norm. It is rather the diagnosis of a malady. The focal point of Taylor's investigations is the self-negating features of modern democracy, that is to say, its immanent tendency towards crisis and self-destruction. According to Taylor's analysis, democratic exclusion, political fragmentation and alienation from the political process are the *pathologies* of the modern democratic life form. Unless a remedy is found for them, unless liberal democracies are capable of recovering from their 'critical' state, another form of life will take their place. Generally, Taylor's political theory has the character of a 'clinical' discourse: its aim is to diagnose a social ill and to suggest paths for recovery. In this respect Taylor stands outside the mainstream of contemporary analytic political philosophy, but within the critical tradition of social and political theory that stretches back to Rousseau.[29]

7

Politics and Social Criticism

Taylor's reflections on atomism, proceduralism and 'difference-blind' liberalism can fruitfully be read as contributions to self-contained debates in contemporary political philosophy. Indeed, this is how they are usually presented.[1] Consequently, the dominant image of Taylor, at least amongst political theorists and students of political theory, is that of a communitarian critic of liberalism, or better a liberal holist, who defends a model of participatory democracy. There is nothing wrong with this image as far as it goes. However, if we are to form a fuller, more balanced picture of Taylor's political thought, we need to appreciate that it is set against a background of political commitment and activism. An extensive body of journalism, political commentary and social criticism provides a testament to Taylor's life in politics. In these writings, Taylor addresses an audience engaged in processes of social and political transformation. Early on, in the 1950s and 1960s, Taylor's addressees are mainly radicals, reformists and revolutionaries on the left. Other pieces are written for an audience of citizens – especially in Canada – of no particular political persuasion, as well as policy-makers there. Throughout these writings, Taylor articulates a distinctive conception of the tasks and priorities of social criticism. Though often ignored, they are an important part of his output. For in Taylor's view, the worth of political theory is inseparable from the quality of social criticism it informs, and beyond that, its capacity to transform social life for the better.

In this chapter I shall trace the main developments in Taylor's understanding of the tasks, priorities and responsibilities of social criticism. I distinguish three stages of this development. The first corresponds to his involvement with the British New Left in the 1950s; the second to his activism within the Canadian New Democratic Party in the 1960s; and the third to his contribution to the debates surrounding Canada's constitutional crisis throughout the 1980s and 1990s. The chief task of Taylor's earliest political works is to elucidate the meaning of socialism, the nature of a socialist society, and the role of the intellectual in achieving it. Taylor was an eloquent and influential advocate of 'socialist humanism', an interpretation of socialism that became central to the self-understanding of the New Left as it emerged in Britain in the late 1950s. As we shall see, it is not insignificant that Taylor published most of these writings in an independent, non-hierarchically organized, pluralist, left-wing journal which he himself helped to set up and run. Here, as elsewhere, Taylor's practice of social criticism is informed by and exemplifies a key element of his social theory: the idea that a truly democratic socialist society arises not by way of a self-determining, unified and homogeneous 'will of the people', but from the self-management of spontaneously associated, heterogeneous groups. The second concern, which occupies Taylor throughout the 1960s, is the prospect for democracy, again understood along socialist lines, specifically in Canada. Taylor's writings on this subject dovetail with a decade of involvement with the main socialist opposition party in Canada, the New Democratic Party, and they culminate in a book-length account of the need for a socialist transformation of Canadian politics. We have already touched upon the third area of concern: the Canadian constitutional crisis and, more generally, the question of minority cultural rights. Taylor has discussed this issue in various capacities, as a member of the Royal Commission on Canadian Constitutional Reform and the Future of Quebec and as a newspaper columnist and media commentator during the Quebec referenda campaigns of 1992 and 1995.

Socialist Humanism and the British New Left

Between 1957 and 1960 Taylor wrote a number of articles for the three journals of the British New Left: *New Reasoner*, *Universities and Left Review* and *New Left Review*.[2] The aim of these writings was to contribute towards a retrieval and renewal of socialist politics. To understand what retrieval and renewal mean here, and to grasp why Taylor thought them necessary, we need to attend briefly to the historical context and the versions of socialism that prevailed at the time.

On the one hand, there was the version of socialism variously called 'social welfarism', 'welfarism', 'labourism' and sometimes 'social democracy'. This was the view associated with the main socialist party in Britain, the Labour Party. According to welfarism, the struggle for socialism had essentially been won with the establishment of the welfare state and the rise of consumer capitalism. Post-war consumer capitalism, the welfarists argued, was unlike previous capitalism in two decisive respects. First, it had a less exploitative, more humane distribution of power than its predecessor. Whereas power in previous capitalist societies lay in the hands of a remote, concentrated class of capital owners who exercised their power without consideration for the interests of workers, power in the consumer society was much more diffusely and equitably distributed. This was in large part due to the emergence of a new 'managerial class' who were more responsive to the needs of the workforce and who were able to improve their working conditions. Second, consumer capitalism had brought 'affluence' to a wide range of the population, workers as well as capitalists. All sorts of commodities – washing machines, televisions, motor cars, package holidays and so forth – were suddenly within the purchasing power of most individuals, irrespective of class. It seemed to the welfarists that with this development a key demand of socialism had been met, or was about to be met, within capitalism itself, namely a reasonable degree of material well-being for the vast majority. There was also a safety net for those not able to take advantage of the benignly changing conditions of capitalism: the welfare state. In addition to providing benefits for the poor and disadvantaged, the welfare state would ensure that essential services like medical care, access to education, and decent housing were available to everyone. Again, it thus seemed to the welfarists that a key demand of socialism had been satisfied. The welfarists concluded that the main challenge facing socialism was to consolidate the position of the welfare state and to extend the benefits of consumer capitalism.

The main rival contemporary interpretation of socialism saw things quite differently. On this view, socialism was only possible by means of a revolutionary overhaul of the capitalist system. The main challenge facing socialists was to bring about this revolution, and the best way of achieving that was by supporting Communist regimes throughout the world, in particular the Soviet Union. The Soviet Union represented the most potent threat to capitalism and therefore the most likely agent of its destruction. Moreover, it provided a model for how a socialist society – a society characterized by the collective ownership of the means of production, centralized economic planning and administration, full employment, radical egalitarianism and the overcoming of 'false consciousness' – might actually work. The socialists of this persuasion, commonly referred to as 'Stalinists', organized themselves within the Communist Party. Rigid adherence to the official party line, itself formulated at the top of the party hierarchy, was a distinctive characteristic of this brand of socialism. It was also characterized by a somewhat uncritical attitude towards the actions of the Soviet Union and its Communist satellites.

Like other activists of the New Left, Taylor is opposed to both these models of socialism. He objects to welfarism on three main counts. First, while Taylor concedes to welfarism that capitalism had undergone profound changes since socialist alternatives to it were first conceived in the nineteenth century, he thinks that welfarism mistakenly identifies the changes that have taken place. For the most significant economic development within contemporary capitalism is the rise of the large corporation, or 'multinational'. Rather than diffusing power, the rise of large corporations, and the concentration of capital in their hands, makes the system even 'more homogeneously capitalist' than before.[3] The changing role of managers, in this context, is of little consequence. Even if contemporary managers are more responsive than their nineteenth-century counterparts to the needs of a workforce, the conditions of survival compel the firm to profit or perish, and these conditions are determined objectively by variations in the pattern of capital accumulation, irrespective of any changes in attitude at the workplace. So Taylor's first objection to welfarism is that while substantive economic changes have taken place within capitalism, they have not been conducive to the more equitable distribution of power demanded by socialism.

Taylor's second objection refers to the kind of purposes that in principle can be satisfied by consumer capitalism and the welfare state. He concedes that in advanced industrial societies, where consumer capitalism buffeted by the welfare state prevails, individuals on the whole enjoy a greater degree of affluence and material

well-being than in previous societies. But he denies that this outcome conforms to – never mind exhausts – the legitimate demands
of socialism. This is because the production for profit that drives the
capitalist system is suited only to the satisfaction of 'private' interests, that is, the self-interest of individuals acting independently of
each other in the market place. For the socialist, however, there are
communal needs over and above private interests, shared needs
that are satisfiable collectively if at all. And for common social needs
production for profit is fundamentally inappropriate. Nor can the
welfare state compensate for this deficiency. On the contrary,
since welfare as conceived by welfarism functions as a means for
enabling disadvantaged individuals to compete more effectively, it
actually reinforces the system's tendency to override communal
purposes. By treating state welfare merely as a mechanism for
assisting the underdogs of society, the labour reformists renounced
the best part of their socialist tradition: the 'struggle to establish a
responsibility by the whole community for *all* its members for the
provision of vital human needs'.[4] In other words, the concept
of welfare only takes on a socialist character when backed by a
principle of 'community responsibility'. And this, Taylor thinks, can
only be achieved by a system 'primarily based on common ownership'.[5] Taylor does not have much to say regarding the institutional
structure of common ownership. It suffices for him to reject in the
strongest terms the traditional, highly centralized and rigidly hier-
archical models of state monopoly and paternal bureaucracy, and
to call for more experimentation in the area.

The third objection Taylor puts against welfarism is that it has an
emasculated conception of the good. Taylor chastises welfarism for
lacking moral imagination and for having an ideologically fore-
shortened conception of human potentialities. In the first place, the
welfarists wrongly take people's existing or '*de facto*' preferences –
especially preferences for a life-style geared to commodity consumption – as a given. In doing so, they 'naturalize' this conception
of the good: they make it seem as if it were 'natural' for people to
pursue the good by way of acquiring and consuming commodities.
But far from being given by nature, the predominant images of the
good life in the consumer society are the result of powerful but historically contingent social forces. If welfarism were to think more
historically, if it were to have a greater sense of the historical contingency of predominant conceptions of the good, it would be more
open to alternative, more fulfilling modes of existence. One of the
main tasks of the socialist critic, Taylor suggests, is to point out the

social and historical variability of what appears, through familiarity, natural and given. But the problem with welfarism is not just that it naturalizes a contingent form of life. And the task of socialist criticism is not limited to awakening us to contingency. For the social critic must also rectify welfarism's failure to question the coherence and worth of the conception of the good that does happen to prevail in contemporary capitalist societies. The coherence of a life oriented around commodity consumption is questionable, Taylor thinks, because it cannot sustain the whole course of a life. In addition to its intimate connection to deep-rooted causes of alienation in capitalist society – themselves left unexplored by welfarism – consumption for pleasure is not a 'viable purpose for living' because it is not amenable to growth or development.[6] And even if it were viable, it is not obviously of great worth. One reason for this, according to Taylor, is the hegemony exercised by this conception of the good. Taylor rebukes the welfarists for taking the diversity of life practices in capitalist society at face value. For diversity exists only at a superficial level, that is, within the paradigm of consumption. Contrary to appearances, the overwhelming tendency of capitalism is to homogenize human identities. And a key task of social criticism is to counter this drift towards an underlying uniformity in conceptions of the good.

Taylor therefore flatly rejects the welfarist model of socialism. But like other representatives of the New Left, he was even more hostile to Stalinism. Here too we can identify three main objections. First and foremost, Taylor takes issue with the Stalinist conception of history together with its construal of the historical responsibility of the socialist intellectual. On the Stalinist model, all significant historical change is economically determined and the only significant agents of historical change are economic classes. But the class whose responsibility it is to effect the transition from capitalism to Communism, the proletariat, is for various reasons either unaware of its historical role, or incapable of acting as a class on that awareness. If the critic is to further the goal of freedom, she must realize her place in history, and that means being of service to the agent of world-historical change, the proletariat. The highest responsibility of socialist critics and intellectuals, accordingly, is to function effectively within the 'conscious wing' of the proletariat class – namely, the Communist Party. Hence, on the Stalinist model, the socialist intellectual's primary responsibility is neither to herself nor to any concrete human being, but to history as judged by the party. Once seen in this light, Taylor takes the folly of Stalinism, and its unsuitability as an interpretation of socialism and the demands of social criticism, to be self-evident.

Taylor draws out a further consequence of the view of history on which the Stalinist model of socialism is based: the transition to socialism is supposed to come about as a quantum leap from one kind of society to another. This model of transformation encourages the Stalinist to neglect vital questions concerning the practical instantiation of the socialist ideal of communal responsibility. With its commitment to economic determinism, the Stalinist model looks exclusively to the collectivization of the means of production as the harbinger of a new, socialist society. It just assumes that other social changes will follow automatically from the overhaul of the economic relations. Unsurprisingly, Taylor utterly rejects this approach to historical change on account of its reductionism. But he makes a further objection. For the Stalinist also commends a certain practice of revolutionary social transformation, and this, if it is misguided, has to be challenged on different grounds. Taylor does this by pointing to the way in which the socialist project must look as much to continuity as discontinuity if it is to realize its purpose. He warns that 'the attempt to build new primary societies cannot be based on the existing ones alone. *But it cannot start without them.*'[7] This insight has a crucial implication for the priorities of socialist social criticism. For it follows, on Taylor's view, that socialists should orient themselves 'to rescue the old communities', for instance by promoting economic revitalization, planned urban development, and the regeneration of centres of local creative activity.

A third feature of Taylor's polemic against Stalinism is the latter's *a priori* presumption of harmony between socialist goals. It is characteristic of the Stalinist outlook, Taylor states, to assume 'a harmonious set of values already there waiting to be conceived'.[8] In particular, Stalinism dogmatically assumes a harmony between the goods of creative self-expression and communal solidarity. That is to say, it takes it for granted that the socialist transformation of society will simultaneously unfetter human creative powers and strengthen the bonds of human solidarity. Again, Taylor doubts that this belief is warranted theoretically. But he is more concerned here with the implications of shaping political practice around such a dogma. For it offers no guidance in circumstances where, as a matter of historical fact, the goods are in tension. It leaves the socialist critic hopelessly under-resourced in such circumstances, even though it is precisely conflict rather than harmony between the demands of creative self-realization and communal solidarity that characterizes our age.

According to Taylor, this defect in the Stalinist version of socialism can be traced back to Marx. The alleged affinity between Marxism and Stalinism was a moot point for the New Left, but while Taylor was more inclined to point to the similarities rather than the differences between these two versions of socialism, his relation to Marx was ambiguous. In later pieces, however, Taylor reiterates and accentuates his disagreements with Marxism. Before moving on to these later reflections, a few more points need to be made about what Taylor took the retrieval and renewal of socialism to mean in the context I have been describing.

For the reasons I have just adumbrated, Taylor and others on the New Left sought to retrieve socialism from welfarism and Stalinism – the degenerate models then holding sway. But the fundamental problem facing the socialist project was that people would not identify themselves with it unless socialists found new modes of articulation. It was precisely to explore the possibilities for such a renewed articulation of socialist politics that Taylor and the other co-founding editors of the *Universities and Left Review* launched the journal. The aim of the journal was to make socialist ideas alive again, to show why they really matter, and to enable some kind of identification with socialist purposes. Neither welfarism, with its narrow focus on piecemeal economic and administrative reforms, nor Stalinism, with its reliance on alien dogmas, had the power to express people's fundamental concerns.[9] The new journal would not therefore be limited to narrowly defined economic and political issues, issues that have only an external impact on people's lives. Rather, it would be concerned with how all aspects of life appear from a socialist point of view. Only in this way would socialism affect people internally, so to speak, in their very identity: 'Our concern is with man', Taylor and his co-editors announced, 'in the concrete richness and fullness of his life – all of it'.[10]

As Taylor saw it, the contemporary situation called for an expansive view of the tasks of criticism. In the first place, the left critic had to take on board the problem of motivating people to adopt a critical, socialist politics. Taylor and the New Left saw apathy as one of the main obstacles to the realization of socialist purposes – indeed the movement became closely associated with the slogan 'out of apathy'. The way to combat indifference was to clarify the relevance of socialist values to each individual's life. To do this, the socialist critic must be able to indicate how the quality of life would be superior in a socialist society, and this meant having an account of the qualitative transformations of life experience socialism would bring: 'If life appears to be fragmented and meaningless to more and more people today, the socialists must know what they mean when they speak of a "meaningful life".'[11] The socialist critic will only be able to address such issues if she adopts a holistic approach to criticism. That is to say, the New Left critic must seek 'some vantage point from which to make a deep criticism, not merely of some institutions, but of a whole culture – a way of life, under capitalism'.[12] But *Universities and Left Review* was not just to be a forum for holistic criticism, that is, for exploring an alternative comprehensive conception of the good. It was also to be pluralistic. The editors emphasize that the journal is designed as an 'open forum for debate' amongst left critics rather than as a platform for propagating a particular version of the 'One True Socialism'. Taylor's preference for a holist, pluralist practice of social criticism – evident in recent debates with liberals such as Rawls, Dworkin and Habermas – thus dates back to his youthful engagement in the British New Left and his confrontation with welfarism and Stalinism.

But Taylor's socialist humanism was not without its own tensions and difficulties. These come out in the way Taylor situates himself in relation to Marx. In his earliest writings Taylor has an ambivalent relation to Marx and Marxism. On the one hand, he follows Marx in identifying the capitalist order as the underlying source of contemporary dehumanization: 'before us', he writes, 'stand the inhuman priorities of capitalism: the *only* political question is how we can understand and change them in order to achieve an enlargement of freedom and responsibility'.[13] The whole problem with welfarism, according to Taylor, is its failure to grasp the interconnectedness of the economic, political and cultural spheres. The basis of his critique of social welfarism is that we need to undertake a systematic, holist critique of a way of life, to point out the necessary interconnections between the economic system, alienation and cultural impoverishment. In these ways Taylor seems close to Marx. On the other hand, he distances himself from Marxism on account of the proximity he sees between it and Stalinism. According to Taylor, while Marx is not guilty of all the errors of Stalinism, his position not only lends itself to such distortion, it also shares some of Stalinism's fundamental errors. Taylor's growing hostility towards Marxism is evident in works dating from the 1960s, but it is most clearly expressed in his retrospective essay on the New Left, 'Marxism and Socialist Humanism'.[14]

In this work Taylor attacks Marxism on four counts. First, in a criticism that echoes one made against Stalinism in 'Socialism and the Intellectuals', he objects that Marxism is incapable of dealing with democratic conflict. By taking over the Jacobin ideal of a unified community, Marx allegedly transposes atomist self-determination to a social subject. As we have already seen, for Taylor the Jacobin model of self-determination, in which disagreement is seen as an imperfection of the system, gives the wrong 'unanimist' picture of democracy and self-rule. Its conception of democracy is misguidedly 'substitutionist' and centralized. Second, Taylor now explicitly rejects the Marxist idea that the values of freedom and solidarity must be co-instantiated. Markets, Taylor concedes, are an important feature of a free society, even though they are inevitably divisive and exploitative. And even if the goods of autonomy and solidarity could be reconciled, a socialist society could be disastrous in other ways, for instance as an agent of environmental destruction. Finally, Taylor suspects that orthodox Marxism's insensitivity to ecological issues reflects its impoverishment as a spiritual stance. Its 'militant atheist materialism' defines too narrowly the range of human expressive needs. While Taylor acknowledges that the Marxist conception of freedom has an appealing expressive dimension, even here – with the exception of thinkers like Ernst Bloch and Walter Benjamin – it tends towards a superficially subjectivist interpretation of human expressive powers. It contrasts unflatteringly with post-Romantic outlooks that see the aim of expression as reaching to 'something beyond ourselves'. Taylor chastises Marxism for its barrenness on the existential issues of finitude and the human relation to nature. In sum, Taylor rejects Marxism for the flaws in its conception of democratic freedom, for its reductive model of oppression, for its lack of appreciation of the conflict between goods, and for its overly subjectivist interpretation of the good. And the folly at the root of Marxist practice, in Taylor's view, is to suppose that the deepest human aspirations can be realized together in the single systematic change from capitalism to socialism.

Taylor's criticisms of Marxism thus target a theory of democracy, on the one hand, and a comprehensive theory of human nature, on the other. No doubt Marxism is wanting in both respects. But it should also be said that Marx himself did not say very much on these issues, and most of what he did say is not touched by Taylor's

critique. Marx was much more interested in identifying the contradictions at work in societies organized by the accumulation of
capital than in spelling out the details of a form of life free of those
contradictions. To be sure, in his early work Marx did sketch a
philosophical anthropology: he outlined the ways in which life
under capitalism alienates human beings.[15] Even Marx's more
mature writings, in which he undertook a detailed critique of classical political economy, could be classified as philosophical anthropology to the extent that they expose the contradictions of the
atomist categories deployed by the classical political economists.[16]
Unfortunately, however, Taylor never addresses himself to this, by
far the most significant dimension of Marx's work. It is unfortunate
not just because Marx's analyses are rich in arguments against
atomist ontology and so supportive of Taylor's general philosophical project. More important, even if Marx's theory is *only* insightful
at this level – that is, at the level of exposing the roots of 'economic'
exploitation – that is all the more reason to take it seriously.
One can learn from it without taking on board the whole Marxist
Weltanschauung, whatever that might be. There is no reason why the
social critic must be exclusively oriented by the 'world view'. The
social critic can follow Marx's account of the interconnectedness of
the sources of human misery in a world dominated by capital,
without claiming that *all* forms of oppression have this source.
Furthermore, Marx's critical social theory has the distinct virtue
of being anchored in something unavoidable for the vast majority
of people in the modern world: the sale of labour to meet basic
material needs. By working out the complex ramifications of this
inescapable but contradiction-ridden reality, Marx provides an
important corrective to approaches to social criticism that focus on
the self-negating character of *ideals* or self-interpretations. This is
not to say that Marx's 'materialism' can substitute for interpretative
social criticism – that would indeed be reductive. But a conception
of social criticism that rejected Marx on that account would be
guilty of its own, idealist reductionism. In courting idealism, exclusively interpretative social criticism lends itself to a 'top-down' bias
not dissimilar from the one we noted earlier in regard to Taylor's
conception of the self.

　While much of Taylor's social criticism is guided by the interpretation of ideals, it would be unfair to call him an exclusively
interpretative social critic. As we shall see in a moment, the politics
he espoused in the sixties had a robustly materialist orientation. It
is a pity, then, that his impatience with the 'spiritual' shortcomings

of Marxism should have desensitized him to the power of Marx's material critique.

Democracy in Canada

In 1961 Taylor resigned as an editor of *New Left Review* and returned to Canada. But his engagement in the politics of the New Left was far from over. Indeed it was to intensify considerably over the subsequent decade, mainly due to his activities within Canada's New Democratic Party. Speaking retrospectively of this period, Taylor says that in the NDP of the 1960s he saw a means of making democracy, 'the form of life by which great masses of people are able to rule themselves, . . . more real and more concrete in our world'.[17] The idea that a socialist transformation of politics was required to bring about a more democratic form of life in Canada is the central hypothesis of Taylor's *The Pattern of Politics*. Published in 1970, in response to the landslide victory of Trudeau's Liberal Party in the 1968 federal elections, the book collates many of the views developed by Taylor as policy consultant for the NDP over the preceding decade. The Liberal victory, Taylor notes, had been gained on a platform of modernization and national renewal. With heavy media backing, the Liberal campaign had heralded Trudeau – the so-called New Young Leader – as the mould-breaker of Canadian politics, as the figure who would terminate outdated practices of political antagonism by representing the interests of all Canadians. Taylor then sets out to show why the Liberal 'politics of consensus' cannot deliver the goods it promises. It can deliver only superficial kinds of reform and renewal, Taylor argues, because the Liberal model fails to address structural imbalances in the distribution of power in Canadian society.

What is the source of power that must be challenged if meaningful reform and renewal is even to be on the agenda? It is the autonomy of the large corporation. The first, and the most intransigent, impediment to democracy in Canada is corporate autonomy. Corporate autonomy refers to the ability of large corporations to function without political interference, be it from the state or other forms of citizen representation. This immediately puts Taylor at odds with the liberal model of democracy, as understood at that time. For a central pillar of liberal democracy is commitment to the 'free enterprise' economy, that is, a politically unregulated system of economic production, one shaped exclusively or predominantly

by market forces. On the classical liberal model, the freedom enjoyed by the entrepreneur is essential to a healthily functioning
democracy. The competitiveness of entrepreneurial activity is supposed to ensure economic efficiency; this generates growth and
wealth, which in turn benefits everybody. But entrepreneurial activity is also risky. In making an investment the entrepreneur takes a
gamble: new commodities are produced for which there is an uncer-
tain market; a good price and profit are by no means guaranteed.
On the liberal model it is thus important that risk-taking entrepreneurs are protected from interference from the state. Not only is a
democratic state morally obliged not to interfere too much with the
entrepreneurs' profits – for they are morally entitled to them in
virtue of the risks taken – but it is economically expedient for a
democratic state not to meddle in their activity.

Now Taylor is ready to acknowledge that risk and competition
provide some kind of justification for non-interference in the market
economy. However, he denies that these are the conditions under
which contemporary large corporations actually operate. The riski-
ness of large corporation investment is mitigated by a number of
factors: extensive research prior to the launch of a new product
enables a corporation to predict quite accurately the likely success
of the enterprise, and large amounts of dissipated capital insure the
corporation against possible losses. More important, large corporations are to a significant extent able to determine prices. This gives
the corporation considerably more power than the entrepreneur as
conceived by classical liberalism. Whereas the latter suffers market
conditions, and is rewarded accordingly, the former controls them.
This takes away much of the risk that justified non-interference
in entrepreneurial activity on the classical liberal model. But the
process of establishing prices also strengthens the positive case for
intervention. For in establishing the price of a commodity, the corporation takes into account the costs of production, shareholder
payment, and research for future product development. Taylor suggests that this third segment of the price – the cost of research –
amounts to a development tax: just as citizens pay taxes to the state
for development of public services, so the consumer pays a tax
to the corporation for development of commodities. Unlike other
forms of taxation, however, this one is prosecuted without any
meaningful form of representation. Whereas citizens of a democratic state rightly demand to be represented on tax-raising bodies, the
corporation has no such accountability to consumers. Once we
see large corporations as possessing the equivalent of tax-raising

powers, Taylor thinks, we will be more ready to see them as properly subject to democratic control.[18]

Taylor argues that the expanded power of the large corporation makes the case against corporate autonomy compelling in another, still more important way. The concentration of capital in ever smaller numbers of ever larger corporations, investment in research, and the management of prices diminish competition and risk. But they are not for that reason to be lamented. On the contrary, just these changes enable better-planned, more stable and more efficient production. However, only certain kinds of goods can efficiently be produced and marketed in this way: those that can be sold to individual consumers. It is in the interest of corporations to channel their resources into both the development of commodities designed for a market of individual consumers and the creation of a demand for such commodities. It is also in their interest to discourage the generation of a collective demand for goods and services, partly because it creates alternative markets, partly because it generates a higher tax burden. Either way collective or communal demand challenges their autonomy. Large corporations naturally use their autonomy to invest in the development of goods marketed to individual consumers and to resist government spending on goods and services provided for the community as a whole, such as education, health care, pollution control, transport, urban regeneration and a host of others.

Hence, while expanding corporate power may bring market growth for individually consumable commodities, it squeezes the provision of public services. Nor, Taylor maintains, can private corporations be expected to contribute to the development of the economically deprived regions of Canada. But given the choice, Taylor asks, is this the way that contemporary Canadians would set the priorities of their economy? For Taylor, the answer is obvious: the interest of the vast majority of Canadians lies in reorienting production towards the satisfaction of collective needs. As the most pressing needs are for goods and services such as pollution control, education, health and urban regeneration, as well as aid to the under-developed regions, that is where resources should be directed. But such a change in priorities is only possible if corporate autonomy is challenged, and government, or other forms of citizen representation, take some democratic control over the organization of the economy.

So corporate autonomy is inconsistent with the demands of democracy, first, because corporations now enjoy analogous powers to governments, and second, because they skew the economy in a way contrary to the public interest. Really, these are reasons for questioning the propriety of unlimited corporate power anywhere. But Taylor adduces a third reason for thinking that corporate autonomy undermines the prospects for democracy specifically in Canada. This is the fact that ownership of the large corporations is almost exclusively based in Canada's neighbouring superpower – the United States.

Taylor points to two respects in which US ownership of autonomous corporations poses a special danger to democracy in Canada. First, he argues that the domination of the Canadian economy by large American corporations and their subsidiaries – making it a so-called 'branch-plant' economy – gravely weakens and destabilizes it. At the level of Canada's primary industries, those concerned with natural resource extraction like oil and minerals, American control imposes unnecessary constraints both on marketing outlets and on the future development of resource exploitation. Moreover, the profits realized on resource investments remain in foreign hands. As such, these earnings can be repatriated to the US or used to expand American-owned operations in Canada. Either way Canadian control over the direction of the economy is further inhibited. At the level of the secondary sector, Taylor points to evidence suggesting that the main function of the manufacturing subsidiary or 'branch-plant' is not so much to create profits directly from its own production, but indirectly, by increasing the market for goods and services produced by the parent international corporation. In setting up the subsidiary, the large corporation aims to penetrate the host market and strengthen demand for its own products. As tastes are increasingly shaped for American products, so Canadian purchasing power is channelled to American producers. At the same time, Canadian production, inadequately specialized and consequently uncompetitive, lags behind. The outcome is not only a worsened balance of payments for Canada, but further loss of control over the direction of the economy.

The second way in which corporate autonomy in a Canadian context undermines democracy is that reliance on US-owned investment increases Canada's political dependence on Washington. Weakened by their lack of control over the amount and placement of investment, and by fear of the withdrawal of American capital, Canadian governments have felt obliged to be deferential to the United States on matters jointly affecting them. Taylor lists several instances in which US economic interests prevailed over Canadian ones, for instance in the formation of trade agreements. Taylor observes that such pusillanimity on Canada's behalf seriously weakens the hand of its foreign policy-makers, again undermining democracy in that country. He concludes that any short-term economic advantages accruing from unconstrained American investment are easily outweighed by the adverse effects of economic inflexibility and the inability to plan for development. It is necessary, therefore, to dismantle the system of corporate autonomy and to replace it with a system of economic planning.

In *The Pattern of Politics*, the main obstacle to democracy in Canada resides in the lack of control Canadians have over the economic decisions that affect them: 'The issue of economic dependence', Taylor writes, is in an important sense 'decisive for the whole cast of our political life in Canada' (*PP* 96). For the issue of economic independence puts into focus the contrast between two competing models of political practice: the 'politics of consensus' of the ruling Liberal Party, and a socialist 'politics of antagonism'. The point of departure for the consensus model is the idea that the extant political and economic system basically works well; indeed, in its essentials is the best that can reasonably be hoped for. While the model can accommodate reforms within the system, it precludes any radical challenge to the status quo. Taylor sees the model well-illustrated in the liberal (as opposed to socialist) view that high-quality public services like health, education and pollution control are the luxuries of a profitable market economy. For the liberal, the provision of public services is conditional on the profitability of the economy, and the less interference there is with the market conditions prevailing in the economy, the more profitable it will become. On this view, it is in everyone's interest to have the economic system working as smoothly and efficiently as possible. The liberal thus calls for a politics of consensus that minimizes disruption to the system. As, according to this model, efficiency and profitability are the main conditions of common well-being, everyone should work towards them, irrespective of where control over the economy resides. The fact that power lies outside their hands – namely, with the American owners of the large corporations – should be considered a secondary matter, and certainly not one that legitimates disturbance of the system.

By contrast, the socialist calls for a 'politics of polarization'. This view emphasizes the conflicting interests at stake in the way the economy is organized and the way power is distributed. On this model, the economic system is not 'neutral' in the sense that everybody benefits from increases in its efficiency. The idea that there is a neutral way of defining efficiency is in any case an illusion. If efficiency were to be measured by the standard of collectively satisfiable needs, by the condition of under-developed regions, by the plight of the poor or by the degree of autonomy of ordinary citizens, it would not be so clear that the system was working smoothly and efficiently at all. Moreover, it is no accident, on the socialist view, that a corporate economy does actually have these effects. In order to reverse the priorities of the system, in order to make production efficient in terms of the overall quality of life of the majority of the community, it is necessary to challenge the status quo and bring about a fundamental redistribution of power. The socialist realizes, of course, that her proposals will not please everybody: there is a conflict of interests between the wielders of power in a corporate economy and the potential power-holders of a socialist society. The 'politics of polarization' – or as Taylor also puts it, the 'politics of antagonism' – thus seeks to unveil the fraud played out in the politics of consensus and aims to mobilize deep-seated conflicts for the purpose of bringing about radical social reform.

It is in terms of the contrast between the politics of consensus and a politics of polarization that Taylor frames the difference between the Liberal Party and the NDP. Taylor presents the NDP as offering a real alternative to the consensus politics of the Liberals by aiming to replace corporate autonomy by economic planning. But this is not the only way in which the NDP's 'politics of polarization' seeks to further the ends of democracy. Democracy in Canada is possible only if the economy is managed according to the collectively negotiated needs of Canadians themselves. But democracy is not *just* a matter of collective self-management of the economy: 'The introduction of planning is only a necessary, not a sufficient, condition of real democratization.'[19] Real democratization involves self-rule in all areas of politics. A democracy is a society of self-governing citizens, and that means citizens actually participating in political power.

Taylor then distinguishes between two senses of participation. The first sense refers to citizens 'having a say' in the decisions that commonly affect them. It is important, if this condition of democratization is to be satisfied, that considerable amounts of power are decentralized. In this respect, Taylor observes, the NDP needs to improve upon the models of central planning traditionally deployed by socialist parties, including the NDP's precursor, the Cooperative Commonwealth Federation. In a democratic Canada, the priorities of people expressed at the regional and neighbour-hood levels, rather than at the level of the federal state government, should be decisive. And Taylor proposes a number of mechanisms for making this possible. On the other hand, in a large, modern democracy like Canada, some centralization of power is unavoid-able. The key problem to be addressed is therefore that of attaining the right balance between the 'centrifugal' forces of democratiza-tion – directing power to the regions and neighbourhoods – and the 'centripetal' forces required for efficient state government. Again, Taylor makes a number of concrete policy suggestions, including faster, more efficient dissemination of information, public invest-ment in communication technologies to enable more informed debate, and training of potential local leaders for dealing effectively on behalf of the local community against government. These and other measures are designed both to improve the level of under-standing of the system within which local issues emerge and to promote action at the governmental level that is genuinely in the local interest.

Giving ordinary citizens more of a say in decisions that affect them clearly contributes to the democratization of society. But the other sense of 'participation' to which Taylor draws attention has a more ambiguous relationship to democracy. This is 'the aspiration to participate as recipient and donor in some larger life' (*PP* 110). As we have seen, a central element of Taylor's philosophical anthro-pology is the idea that human beings have a deep-seated need for contact with some significant surrounding reality. The larger life may be, for instance, that of a family, a tradition, a nation, human-ity or a divine kingdom. One receives from this larger reality – it gives one a sense of purpose, fulfilment and power – but one also gives to it, for example by worship or sacrifice. The sense of contact with a larger life is thus bound up with a sense of participation in it and in turn with a feeling of empowerment.

But what does this sense of participation have to do with demo-cracy? On the one hand, it can be harnessed to generate the *illusion* that democratic procedures are in place. If the citizens of a society can be drawn to identify themselves with certain images of a larger life, then by dint of the association between feelings of belonging and empowerment, they can imagine themselves to be participat-ing in the first of the two senses – namely, as having a say in decision-making processes. In such cases, identification with a larger life *substitutes* for real political participation. The main vehicle for this kind of illusion in modern societies, Taylor observes, is

nationalism. In modern societies, or societies that legitimate themselves in terms of the will of the people rather than, say, the word
of God, strong nationalist sentiments can function to mask and compensate for real democratic deficits. Taylor stresses, however, that
nationalism is by no means the only vehicle of such illusion. The
campaign that led to the sweeping victory of the Liberal Party in
the 1968 federal election, according to Taylor, used essentially the
same tactics: an image was presented with which most Canadians
could identify, and without any substantive democratization to
Canada's decision-making institutions, a hunger for participation
was satisfied. Taylor also applies the same argument to the student
rebels of 1968.

The second way in which the satisfaction of the need to participate in a larger life can run counter to democracy is by encourag-
ing the creation of communities bonded by rigid and exclusionary
values. Again, nationalism seems to exemplify this tendency. A
notorious feature of nationalism is the irrational contempt it can
breed for those lying outside the national group, however that is
defined by the nationalist ideology. This feature is particularly
evident in war-time provocations of nationalist sentiment. But more
generally, to think of one's own life as invested with significance in
virtue of participating in the life of a particular nation not only puts
those who have a different national identity – or none – in a less
valuable moral space. It also often makes an enemy of them. There
seems then to be something deeply anti-egalitarian, and so also anti-
democratic, about nationalism.

In these ways participation by way of identification with a larger
reality, especially as exemplified in nationalist sentiment, can
undermine democracy. It can therefore seem preferable to separate
political life and institutions from people's aspirations to participate
in a larger reality like that of a nation. This is the move made by the
modern liberal. Suspicious of the irrational, exclusionary and anti-
egalitarian aspects of nationalism, as well as its tendency to subordinate the individual to collective purposes, the liberal thinks it
better to keep the aspiration to participate in a more significant
reality out of politics altogether. According to the liberal, democratization involves making the aspiration to participate in a more significant reality a 'private' matter, if indeed the aspiration is to have
any role in the lives of democratic citizens at all.

As we know from the previous chapter, Taylor disagrees strongly
with this position. After noting the ways in which this sense of participating in a larger life endangers democracy, he maintains that

some sense of identification with a wider community is none the less essential for a robust, vibrant democracy. Taylor supports this view with two separate arguments. The first, which is stressed in *The Pattern of Politics*, is that most people are unable to participate in some larger reality, and hence find meaning in their lives, outside a community. As an expression of the more or less universal aspiration to participate in a larger reality, nationalism meets a need that must be satisfied somehow. But the 'private' resources of at least most individuals are insufficient for meeting this demand. At the same time, modern technological and atomized societies are not abundantly resourced with alternative sources of solidarity. The resulting frustration breeds alienation, which in turn destabilizes the society.

The second argument – not conspicuous in *The Pattern of Politics* but repeatedly pressed, as we have seen, in subsequent works – is that participation in the decision-making processes of a democracy itself requires strong bonds of communal affiliation. In other words, participation in the first of the two senses distinguished by Taylor is not in the long run separable from participation in the second sense. Unless the citizens of a democracy have a sense of belonging to and participating in a wider community, they will feel alienated from it, and this alienation undermines the viability of the political institutions themselves. Collective self-management – which, as we have already seen, is the defining characteristic of democracy – requires a sense of collective identification.

So the health of Canadian democracy depends not only on economic planning but on the majority of citizens identifying themselves with a wider community and actively participating in the political process. But what conception of a wider community can fulfil this vital role? It is clear to Taylor that in modern democratic societies by far the most significant object of citizen identification and allegiance is the nation. Since the emergence of the nation-state in the eighteenth century, the sense of participating in and belonging to a particular nation has had a decisive role in bringing citizens together in practices of collective self-rule. Yet it is equally clear, for the reasons just considered, that nationalist sentiment has been and continues to be destructive of democracy. The issue therefore arises about what role, if any, nationalism has to play in the future of Canadian democracy.

Rather than dismiss nationalist sentiment as irrational and regressive, it is more appropriate, Taylor suggests, to distinguish between those forms of nationalism that are conducive to democracy and those that frustrate it. We have just considered two main ways in which nationalism can frustrate democracy: it can give the illusion of meaningful participation without altering the underlying process of decision-making; or it can encourage the creation of closed, exclusionary communities. The liberal response is to separate the political process from questions of identity. Taylor's view in *The Pattern of Politics* is that this undermines democracy as much as the separation of the political process from questions of economics. The liberal preference for keeping questions of identity 'private' fails to take seriously enough the solidaristic requirements of a properly functioning democratic polity. But this leaves an apparent dilemma. For on the one hand, Taylor shares the liberal's anxiety about the exclusionary character of nationalism, of how modes of political participation grounded in strong solidaristic national bonds exclude and oppress. On the other, the absence of such bonds, or their migration and domestication into the private sphere, threatens to undermine active political participation as such, or rather, participation in activities aimed at the realization of the common good. We saw in the last chapter that, in Taylor's view, a dilemma like this faces all modern, culturally diverse liberal democracies. But it is particularly evident in the constitutional issues facing Canada. Let us look now at Taylor's analysis of these issues and his proposals for resolving the underlying dilemma.

The Dialogue Society and Deep Diversity

While the standing of the Canadian constitution has always been precarious, since 1990 Canada has been in the grip of a constitutional crisis. The chronology of events surrounding the crisis can be summed up as follows. The 'Dominion of Canada' came into being in 1867 with an act passed by the British Parliament, the British North America Act, at the request of the 'Fathers' of the Canadian Federation. It was not until 1931, however, that Canada's sovereignty and independence were formally recognized, again by way of a Westminster statute. Even then, another fifty years were to pass before a written constitution was handed over to Canada or 'patriated'. In order to be patriated, the constitution, as stipulated by the British North America Act, required amendment. But the federal and provincial representatives in Canada repeatedly failed to reach agreement on the necessary amending formula. It was not until 1982, with Trudeau's Constitution Act, that Canada finally took possession of its own constitution.

In addition to bringing the constitution home, Trudeau reformed it by introducing a Charter of Rights and Freedoms. The Charter enshrined a series of individual rights with provision for judicial review not unlike the US model. It also constitutionally established bilingualism and regional (provincial) equality. However, patriation came at a price: it was prosecuted without consultation with the representatives of Quebec, and without their assent. Furthermore, aspects of the new constitution were contrary to the aspirations of the Quebec nationalists. In particular, it failed to recognize their claim to distinctness (as opposed to their sameness or equality *vis-à-vis* the regions). And it bypassed their commitment to the collective goal of cultural survival (which had the potential of coming into conflict with the individual rights protected by the constitution). In order to make good the claim to legitimacy of the constitution, Quebec now had to be accommodated within the constitutional agreement. To this end, a round of constitutional talks was arranged, this time by the new conservative premier Brian Mulroney, that resulted in the Meech Lake Accord of 1987. The main feature of the agreement, signed by all the provincial leaders, was the recognition of Quebec as a 'distinct society' within the Canadian Federation. However, the agreement provoked widespread criticism in English Canada, and it failed to obtain unanimous ratification from the provincial legislatures. By 1990, with the sense of division between Quebec and the rest of Canada radicalized rather than diminished, the Meech Lake process was defunct. Another round of constitutional talks, following a more open and inclusive procedure, was then initiated that culminated with the Charlottetown Accord in 1992. The accord, which had the signatures of the leaders of the federal and provincial governments, as well as delegates of the indigenous peoples, was put to a nation-wide referendum in October of that year. It was rejected by a significant majority both within Quebec and in the rest of Canada. In 1995 the Quebec provincial government summoned a further referendum on sovereignty association with the rest of Canada. The sovereignty option was defeated by a margin of just 50.6 to 49.4 per cent. The Quebec provincial government has still not given its support to the amended federal constitution.

In the light of these events, Taylor sees the central task of the constitution to be that of recognizing the different principles of unity and identity, principles that have to be met if Canada is to function as a democratic society, in Quebec and in Canada outside Quebec. In Taylor's view, the crucial issue at stake in the constitutional debate is the question of Canadian identity or self-definition. It is a matter of providing an answer to the question 'what is Canada for?' that will express the national aspirations of all Canadians, including the Quebeckers and indigenous peoples (*RS* 157).[20] It thus calls for 'practical reason' in the sense we discussed in chapter 4: the clarification of self-defining purposes, in this case the common purposes of all those who identify themselves as Canadians. If the Canadian Federation is to survive, these purposes must summon stronger allegiance than those that divide the country. That is to say, the local allegiances Canadians have must either find expression in the purposes that answer the question 'what is Canada for?' or be overridden by those purposes. While the local allegiances are manifold, the one that most resists expression at the federal level and that is least likely to be overridden by the self-defining purposes of the Canadian Federation is Quebec nationalism. Of the many centrifugal forces tending towards disintegration, so to speak, Quebec nationalism is the most potent. Unless it is more than matched by the centripetal force of Canadian national allegiance, Canada will split into pieces. The constitutional problem is thus an existential question concerning the very survival of the Canadian identity. Taylor believes that if the Canadian identity is to survive, it must prove itself capable of self-transformation through a reflective or deliberative process of practical reason.

Taylor first notes that all the parties to the constitutional debate subscribe to the basic liberal values of equality, non-discrimination, the rule of law, representative democracy and social welfare provision. This had not always been the case – Quebec had only recently turned its back on the traditional values of ultramontane Catholicism – and Taylor notes the irony that Canada should come so close to breaking up at the very time its basic values have become so uniform (*RS* 156). But precisely this background agreement on basic rights testifies to the importance of two other considerations. First, in addition to the basic individual rights, there is the question of the common purposes the constitution is to serve or facilitate. The Quebeckers, Taylor points out, have a distinct object of strong shared allegiance – *la nation canadienne-française* – and they demand a political regime commensurate with that collective identification. Even before the introduction of the Charter of Rights and Freedoms, this created tension in Canadian society. Nationalists in Canada outside Quebec naturally regarded Quebec nationalism as a threat to their own identity. Not only did it threaten to undermine the object of their allegiance – a unified Canada – but it was also perceived as a kind of rejection, as if this identity was not good enough for the

Quebeckers. On the other hand, the Quebeckers for their part reacted with suspicion to calls for unity, as if they were being asked to sacrifice themselves for the sake of the federation. It is important, Taylor thinks, to recall the climate of mutual mistrust that preceded the introduction of the Charter, a climate that was exacerbated by the somewhat autocratic manner in which the Charter was actually introduced. It is important because the episode raises the second consideration to be taken into account in addition to the schedule of individual rights: namely, that the *process* by which constitutional change is brought about is decisive for the legitimacy of the principles instantiated in the change. If the change is to be the outcome of a genuinely democratic process, it must be the product of open, informed and most of all inclusive common deliberations. This is in fact intimately related to the first consideration. For as we have seen, Taylor considers open, informed, inclusive public deliberation in the public sphere as indispensable for *shaping* the identity of citizens in a healthy democracy. And it is important to distinguish between one's right to participate in such deliberative processes (about which there is no disagreement) and the schedule of individual rights that can issue from it (the proper scope of which is the subject of conflicting opinions).[21]

Assuming that the conditions of proper constitutional debate are in place, what principle of unity should the constitution inscribe? It has to be one that recognizes the legitimacy not only of plural Canadian identities, but plural *ways of having* a collective Canadian identity. In *The Pattern of Politics*, twenty years before the constitutional problem came to a head, Taylor proposed that Canada would only survive if it became what he called a 'dialogue society'. Taylor's dialogue society is characterized by pluralism of religious faiths, beliefs and moralities, and by a non-dogmatic attitude to the possession of truths. The 'fact of pluralism' enters into the very 'content' of the varied beliefs of the citizens of the dialogue society (*PP* 124–5). Such a society would put 'dialogue itself in the central position occupied in earlier societies by an established religion, and in totalitarian societies by an official ideology'. Canada provides a 'natural focus for the experiment in the dialogue society' because of its entrenched cultural and linguistic pluralism, its different senses of itself as a nation, and its distinct democratic traditions. However, it can only succeed if it gives Quebeckers a 'more meaningful content to the positive sense of being part of a bigger country' (*PP* 140, *RS* 35), a sense that has to be there if a unified democratic Canada is to survive. But Taylor also proposed that the 'meaningful content' in question had to draw on the common purposes embodied in economic self-determination to avoid being merely utopian. Only in this way could the various 'constituents of reform' – 'farmer and worker; rural and urban area; outlying region and metropolitan area; and above all French and English' (*PP* 159) – be brought together in solidarity as participants in common action. On this model, the prospects for democracy turn on the joint resolution of the questions of economic independence and national identity: democracy depends on nationalist sentiment being channelled in the way envisaged in the dialogue society.

By the time of Taylor's 1991 essay 'Shared and Divergent Values', the problem of finding a more meaningful content to the Quebeckers' sense of belonging to a country bigger than Quebec had not disappeared, but the viability of Taylor's earlier solution had. Taylor had long since conceded defeat as a socialist protagonist of the politics of antagonism.[22] Economic planning was now off the agenda, his 'constituency of reform' had fragmented, and the idea of building solidarity around the issue of economic independence was left to wither. The ideal of the dialogue society remained, but it was in danger of being hijacked by procedural liberalism. Procedural liberalism, after all, very much endorses the 'fact of pluralism'. The fact of pluralism even enters into the content of citizens' identity in so far as it is shaped by allegiance to the Charter of Rights and Freedoms. The Charter protects individual rights while promoting cultural diversity. Commitment to it is at once commitment to the Canadian 'multicultural mosaic'. Taylor calls the pluralism secured in this manner 'first-level diversity' (*RS* 182). First-level diversity, of course, is no solution to the constitutional problem. For while it affirms pluralism at the level of cultural identity, it also involves a single conception of what makes for a specifically Canadian identity – namely, commitment to the Charter. As Taylor puts it, the 'patriotism or manner of belonging is uniform' (*RS* 182). As the Quebeckers and the aboriginal communities have different modes of belonging, or different objects of patriotic identification, they find themselves excluded at this level. There is a need, then, for 'second-level or "deep" diversity, in which a plurality of ways of belonging would also be acknowledged and accepted' (*RS* 183). In a society built on deep diversity there would not just be plural conceptions of the good, but plural conceptions of citizenship. Furthermore, the plurality of citizenship or the fact of 'deep pluralism' must itself be the object of allegiance. That is to say, the fact that the Canadians belong to a society that allows for deep diversity must itself be a powerful source of their patriotic sentiment – a more powerful one than the national sentiments that divide them. The Canadians are invited to unite around this idea, to bond around the common purpose of deep diversity.

The problem now, however, is that deep diversity looks like an even more utopian solution to the problem of unity than the dialogue society. While Taylor acknowledges this problem, he remains optimistic about its viability. First, a united federal Canada serves purposes that all Canadians recognize: Taylor mentions 'law and order, collective provision, regional equality, and mutual self-help' (*RS* 183). John Horton makes the objection here that these are *instrumental* reasons for keeping the federation together, and on Taylor's own account unity must be based on something more substantial than an 'alliance of convenience'.[23] This is not quite right, as the particular form of law and order to which Taylor refers, the preference for collective rather than private provision, as well as the promotion of regional equalities as a matter of principle, are in Taylor's view distinctively Canadian values. They are expressions of the Canadian identity, and they play an important role in distinguishing the Canadian way of life from the American. However, even if they are not for this reason instrumental goods, it is another thing to say that they are sufficient for sustaining a common allegiance to the Canadian federation, especially amongst the Quebeckers. The second point Taylor makes in defence of the viability of deep diversity is that societies around the world are having to move towards it. Canadians are not alone in 'exploring the space of deep diversity'. Taylor points to the development of the European Union and the 'breathing space' it has given to regional societies like the Bretons, Basques and Catalans (*RS* 184). But as Horton rightly observes, this is a rather rose-tinted view of the European Union's democratic pedigree.[24] The European Union is hardly a paragon of democratic virtue and it is a long way from eliciting the kind of patriotic allegiance required for the Canadian federation. The third reason Taylor adduces is that the problem is here to stay: even if Canada were to split, the two successor states would have to tackle the demands for recognition of their aboriginal populations. Again, however, it is not clear why the persistence of the challenge means that the challenge will eventually be met.

Towards the end of the previous chapter, we noted that Taylor's idea of 'shared identity space' restates rather than solves the general problem of democratic exclusion. Shared identity space is in fact the same thing as the 'space of deep diversity', and it is not clear that the idea fares any better as a solution to the particular problem of the Canadian constitution. Taylor writes that the citizens of Quebec and Canada, like those of others in contemporary liberal democracies, must recognize that their 'identity space is not static', and that they 'cannot all share the same historical identity'.[25] They must do this if their democracies are to survive. Survival thus requires a fundamental reorientation of their patriotic allegiances. These allegiances must now be *constituted* through dialogue with others, they must be constitutively open to change, and they must have a future orientation that is alien to the traditional nationalist and Jacobin models. Taylor is optimistic that such rechannelling of solidaristic energies can be achieved. But those who share his optimism might wonder why constitutional patriotism is any less viable an option. That is, they might ask why it is any less realistic to suppose that democratic citizens can mobilize themselves around procedural principles of right. And those who do not share the optimism will no doubt want to see the new patriotic identity in action before agreeing to Taylor's claims about it.

8

Modernity, Art and Religion

Taylor has no doubt that liberal democracy is one of the great achievements of the modern world. Freedom is an unquestionable good and modern liberal democracies realize freedom on an unprecedented scale. On the whole, the members of modern liberal societies imagine themselves as free and they value this freedom strongly. Many are proud of the fact they belong to a free society – to a 'land of the free' – and they find it hard to imagine a 'good life' otherwise. But Taylor is just as sure that modern societies are in important ways at odds with themselves. They breed alienation, unease and discontent. In part, this is due to their not really being as democratic as they are imagined to be. They legitimate themselves by a standard – the ideal of freedom – they do not properly meet. Much of Taylor's political philosophy is concerned with locating the mechanisms by which modern democracies fall short of their measure as democracies. As we have seen, Taylor regards their propensity to exclusion, the difficulty they have in recognizing and affirming cultural particularity, and political fragmentation as the chief culprits. Each is a potent source of political discontent in the modern world. But the unease with modernity is by no means solely due to the quality of its democracy. There are other features of modern culture and society that generate discontent, conflict and unease. Taylor has put a lot of effort into understanding their origins: he has tried to formulate a 'diagnosis of the times', an account of the *Zeitgeist* or 'the spiritual situation of the age', which explains the pervasive sense of malaise within modern civilization.

A diagnosis of the times requires a theory of modernity, and theories of modernity, Taylor suggests, fall into two broad classes. On the one hand, there are 'acultural' theories. Acultural theories explain the transition to modernity in terms of some 'culture-neutral' operation, where a culture 'defines specific understandings of personhood, social relations, states of mind/soul, goods and bads, virtues and vices, and the like'.[1] A paradigm case of a culture-neutral operation is rationalization. Modernity, according to many acultural theories, is the form of life that arises from the rationalization of structures of thought and action. Weber and Habermas propose theories of this type. Durkheim's theory of modernity as the passage from 'mechanical' to 'organic' forms of social integration also invokes a culture-neutral operation. For Taylor's purposes, the central point about acultural theories is that they explain the transition to modernity in terms of a general function that need not refer to the *content* of the particular cultures involved. The function is defined independently of the cultural 'input': rationalization, for example, is something that any mode of thought, or any social practice, could in principle undergo. In acultural theories, then, 'modernity is conceived as a set of transformations that any and every culture can go through'.[2] In Taylor's view, most theories of modernity are of this type. But for all their merits, Taylor argues, such theories tend to generate two sorts of misunderstanding: they are prone to misclassify historically contingent cultural changes as ineluctable outcomes of 'development'; and they overlook features that do not fit the culture-neutral explanatory schema. They leave important characteristics of modernity out of focus and they are wont to misrepresent the features they do focus on. According to Taylor, both defects can be avoided by adopting the perspective of a cultural theorist. Cultural theories of modernity, as Taylor conceives them, take a comparative approach to their subject-matter; they attend to the internally generated pressures that forced one particular culture (in the sense defined above) to evolve into another. They attempt to reconstruct the intrinsic appeal of the values and standards that help constitute modern culture, as they arose out of mutation from the values and standards of the predecessor culture. They concentrate on how the content of the culture – its dominant strong values, its conceptions of the good, its self-definitions – came to summon the allegiance of modern subjects. In other words, cultural theories attend to the rise of a certain kind of *identity* in the modern world. In Taylor's view, we need to have a 'portrait of the modern identity' in place before we can diagnose its ills. This is just what Taylor set out to do in *Sources of the Self*, though he does not consider himself to have completed the task in that work.[3]

In this chapter I shall examine Taylor's portrait of the modern identity in so far as it feeds into his diagnosis of the times. My main aim is to bring out the distinctiveness of Taylor's contribution to the contemporary philosophical debate about modernity and to indicate some of its strengths and weaknesses. In this debate, the idea of a 'project of Enlightenment' figures prominently. The expression can mean various things, all hard to pin down precisely. At a very general level, it denominates a commitment to the modern ideals of freedom and reason. It can refer to the project of reforming life in the light of these ideals – something that gets under way in the West well before the historical Enlightenment – or it can refer to the project of justifying the ideals philosophically (as the Enlightenment famously sought to do). Now most of the participants in the modernity debate agree that the Enlightenment project is a major source of unease. But they disagree about the precise source of the trouble and how to respond to it. In the first section of the chapter I look at Taylor's understanding of this problem. As we shall see, Taylor's understanding of what is at stake in the Enlightenment project departs significantly, and not unfavourably, from some widely held approaches – though Taylor's model is not without difficulties of its own. Another point of agreement amongst the many voices in the modernity debate is the idea that unease with the Enlightenment project finds its way into modern conceptions of the tasks of art. There is convergence on the idea that modern art in some way corrects or compensates for the excessive rationalism of the Enlightenment project. Modern art is often invoked as a kind of antidote to the malaise of Enlightened modernity. Again, as we shall see in the second part of the chapter, while Taylor is sympathetic to this view he has a distinctive interpretation of the cultural significance of artistic modernism and its relevance for a diagnosis of the times. Finally we shall look at Taylor's understanding of the 'secularity' of modern culture, and in particular his staging of the confrontation between Enlightened modernity and religious belief.

The Sources of Enlightenment Naturalism

For better or worse, much contemporary philosophical discussion of modernity takes its departure from the idea of a 'project of

Enlightenment'.[4] The idea contains a descriptive, a diagnostic and an epistemic claim. The descriptive claim is that modern culture and society is stamped by a certain kind of freedom and reason. Modern freedom is sometimes called 'subjective' or 'negative' freedom; its reason is known variously as 'subjective', 'formal' and most commonly 'instrumental' reason.[5] The diagnostic thesis is that the predominance of instrumental rationality in the modern world gives rise to social and cultural pathologies. It is responsible for oppression, alienation, discontent, malaise. The damage caused by instrumental reason is interpreted along a number of lines. For Adorno and Horkheimer, and before them Nietzsche, for instance, instrumental reason leads to the destruction of 'life': by reifying experience and human relations it stifles the human potential for genuine well-being and true sociality. It does violence both to subjects and to objects. For Habermas, instrumental reason primarily threatens the communicative bonds between subjects: it brings about injurious intersubjective and intrasubjective division, and it undermines the moral order of agents interacting with each other without coercion. For MacIntyre, instrumental reason also threatens morality, but for the quite different reason that it is destructive of the virtues. Alongside the descriptive and the diagnostic thesis, there is also an epistemic claim at stake in the debate: that the Enlightenment project of justifying morality on the basis of subjective freedom and instrumental reason fails. This too generates a malaise of sorts, for it seems to leave open the possibility that morality cannot be justified at all. It opens up the prospect of moral nihilism, as Nietzsche saw.

There is general agreement, then, that a philosophical diagnosis of the times requires a critique of the Enlightenment project which is at once a critique of instrumental reason. Different interpretations of instrumental reason's essential destructiveness have been offered, and corresponding to this, discrete conceptions of the basis of the critique have been proposed. Habermas, for instance, draws on hidden or unacknowledged norms in the Enlightenment project itself. The modern norms of freedom and reason need to be salvaged from their subject-centred, instrumentalist distortions. For Habermas, the problem with the Enlightenment project is that it is 'incomplete': we require an 'enlightened Enlightenment', as he puts it, one that is properly equipped to justify morality on the basis of (non-instrumental) reason and (non-subjective) freedom alone. Only then are we really able to locate the practices that fall short of the requirements of morality. In Nietzsche's view, by contrast, the

Enlightenment project is beyond redemption; but its failure, and the nihilism that follows in its wake, should be no cause of grief. For it is only by leaving the project of Enlightenment behind that we can move on to an authentic, perhaps postmodern, ethic of life affirmation. MacIntyre has a different take again. He agrees with the Nietzschean view that the Enlightenment project is finished; he also doubts that modernity has the resources to support morality. For MacIntyre, both the orthodox theoretical languages of modernity and the dominant social practices they reflect alienate us from morality. But far from embracing a postmodern ethic MacIntyre turns to traditional models of moral community for redemption. Such models, in MacIntyre's view, do not belong to the culture of modernity but they may be able to transform it.

Let these brief remarks on some of the key positions in the modernity debate suffice as stage-setting for Taylor's intervention. Taylor accepts the basic terms of the controversy. While he rarely refers to the 'Enlightenment project' as such, he does use the expressions 'Enlightenment naturalism' and 'Enlightenment rationalism' to designate 'perhaps the dominant outlook of modern Western technological society' (*SS* 234). This outlook is in large part characterized by a subjective or instrumental conception of freedom and reason. Taylor thinks it true both that instrumental reason is a dominant social and cultural force in modernity and that it generates a widespread sense of moral/spiritual discontent. He also agrees that the project of grounding morality on ideas of subjective freedom and formal or procedural reason is doomed to failure. He thus accepts that something like the Enlightenment project is at least partly responsible for the malaise of modernity. Taylor also has some sympathy for each of the responses to the malaise just mentioned. Like Habermas, for instance, Taylor aims to 'enlighten' the Enlightenment about itself. He agrees that Enlightenment naturalism is inarticulate about its underlying standards; he also agrees that a rearticulation of these standards is crucial for grasping modernity's true normative potential. But Taylor has a very different idea of what it is 'to understand naturalism better than itself' (*HAL* 6, *PHS* 6), one that opens up the normative potential of modernity even more than Habermas's account. Like MacIntyre, Taylor thinks that the way forward in the modernity debate is to reflect on the good and the internal connection between identity and the good. But unlike MacIntyre, Taylor does not doubt that a genuine good is at stake in the Enlightenment project. Taylor also takes on board Nietzsche's call for an ethic of affirmation as an antidote to the modern malaise. But in opposition to the Nietz-schean diagnosis, Taylor does not see this as requiring a departure from the moral horizon of modernity as such.

So while Taylor is to some extent sympathetic with the critical responses to the Enlightenment project proposed by Habermas, MacIntyre and Nietzsche, for example, he also finds them unsatisfactory. Moreover, in Taylor's view their positions – like others in the debate I have not mentioned – are inadequate for the same reason: they have a too narrow definition of the goods that make up the modern identity. One of Taylor's chief tasks as a theorist of modernity is to correct this narrowness. He will try to do it partly by drawing attention to dimensions of the modern identity not contained within the Enlightenment project. But he will also try to show that even the project of Enlightenment – or 'Enlightenment naturalism', to use Taylor's favoured expression – has much richer and more complex moral motivations than theorists of modernity with diagnostic ambitions generally recognize.

We can appreciate this richness and complexity, Taylor argues, only if we place Enlightenment naturalism within a cultural theory of modernity. We need to reconstruct the intrinsic appeal of the values embedded in the Enlightenment outlook as it emerged historically through a contrast with the preceding moral horizon. Taking such an approach, Taylor identifies three key 'transvaluations' in the transition to modernity. First, there is the emergence of a new conception of freedom. This is the freedom of an individual who stands back from his given situation to shape an identity in the light of his own desires and convictions. Freedom defines a new, distinctively modern conception of human dignity: the dignity of the rational, 'disengaged' subject. The disengaged subject assumes, or strives to assume, nothing on authority; traditional beliefs about self and world are submitted to the independent, critical assessment of the individual. The subject transforms what is 'given' to it by tradition or by nature into a rational belief or desire. The emergence of this ideal, Taylor notes, is reflected in the value accorded to reason and individual conscience by the Protestant Reformation in early modern Europe. The Reformation movement contrasted the dignity of self-defining, sober subjectivity with an outlook it took to be enslaved by religious 'enthusiasm', superstitious beliefs in the sacred and unquestioned obedience to the corrupt authority of the church (SS 191). By adopting the disengaged stance, the early modern subject emancipates himself from the 'white magic' of the unreformed church. As Taylor puts it in his Gifford Lectures, the disengaged self is 'buffered' from the enchanted world of spirits and demons. The disengaged subject takes sober, adult control of his environment rather than allowing himself to be bewitched and dominated by it. The thought then emerges that in taking control the subject realizes his true dignity as a human being. Impressed by the dignified quality of the buffered self's existence, the Enlightenment project commits itself to a form of life in which rational, disengaged subjectivity can flourish. It is a form of life that enables individuals equally to shape themselves by reaching their own beliefs, forging their own plans of life, associating freely with others and binding themselves to others through contractual consent – all in the context of a dominant rather than submissive relation to nature.

The second transvaluation concerns the goodness of what Taylor calls 'ordinary life'. Ordinary life designates 'those aspects of life concerned with production and reproduction, that is, labour, the making of things needed for life, and our life as sexual beings, including marriage and the family' (*SS* 211). It is integral to the Enlightenment outlook, Taylor insists, to see the pursuit of happiness through work and family life as a perfectly legitimate human aspiration. This might seem a banal truth, but there are two points that turn it into an extremely significant one. The first is that on Taylor's interpretation ordinary life is not simply a resource of '*de facto*' goods. It is not simply an efficient means for the satisfaction of wants; rather, it has the status of a *strong* value. It designates a form of life that is qualitatively superior to one in which ordinary life is not affirmed. The second, related point is that ordinary life does not enjoy this status in all cultures, and more pertinently, it was not deemed to have a place in the 'higher' life in modernity's predecessor culture. On the contrary, the higher was defined in contrast to the ordinary. For the medieval monastic cultures, one had to transcend the ordinary life of production and the family to attain the highest moral ideal. But with the onset of modernity, ordinary life is no longer scorned or denigrated as a lower form of existence. Economic activity and family life are now regarded as intrinsically worthwhile goals. Again, it is a crucial part of the Enlightenment project to reshape society in a way that affirms the intrinsic dignity of ordinary life.

The third transvaluation Taylor identifies brings the dignity of disengaged rational subjectivity and the affirmation of ordinary life together. It is the idea that the moral life should be directed towards alleviating the suffering of the whole of humankind and implementing a system of universal justice. Drawing on the ethic of ordinary life, it regards the minimization of creaturely pain as the true moral goal. And drawing on the dignity of disengaged self-defining subjectivity, everyone counts equally in the true moral order. The project of Enlightenment is thus committed to a form of life in which the suffering and burdens of everyday life are mini-mized for all individuals. The contrast here is with a conception of the 'higher' as contemplation of the divine on the one hand, and on the other with a conception of the good society as hierarchically structured. In the former case, Enlightenment naturalism chastised the wastefulness of scholastic devotion to matters of little practical utility. Instead it enjoined people to use their abilities to take control of their situation for the purpose of ameliorating the condition of humankind. In the latter case, it attacked the injustice of a social order whose purpose was to protect the inherited privileges of church and state elites. In the light of the new ideal, the laws and public institutions should be reformed for the benefit and welfare of everyone. From the perspective of Enlightenment naturalism, Taylor observes, disengaged freedom, the affirmation of ordinary life and concern for the welfare of humankind amount to real moral progress. They constitute a high, perhaps the highest, degree of moral stature and maturity.

Already we can see Taylor departing from some of the standard ways of thinking about modernity and the Enlightenment project. Modernity is often attacked for its obsession with mastery and control. It is accused of giving unchecked rein to instrumental reason and the will to power. Its critics often oppose the scientific, objectifying outlook to the 'moral' or 'spiritual' stance as such, as if the Enlightenment project were driven purely by the desire for domination. Indeed, some defenders of modernity, those of a tech-nocratic stripe, argue in a similar way: they deny that there is any-thing moral or spiritual about the Enlightenment stance; it merely reveals the way things look once moral and spiritual obstacles are removed. But unlike the critics, they have no bad conscience about the power instrumental reason brings. For Taylor, however, whether the attitude is pro or con, such an interpretation of the Enlighten-ment project must be based on a misunderstanding. In the first place, it neglects the role played by the *strong* evaluation *of* instru-mental reason. According to Taylor, it is a mistake to see instru-mental reason as *just* a neutral means for bringing about some chosen end. Rather, it functions within the Enlightenment stance as the proper expression of the dignity of the disengaged subject. It has the character of a moral achievement. It is valued strongly *vis-à-vis* the non-buffered, porous self, whose subservience and proneness to self-destructive illusion and superstition are demeaning by comparison. In the second place, the value Enlightenment naturalism accords to instrumental reason is bound up with the goods of ordinary life and the alleviation of suffering. Not many critics of the Enlightenment project would want to deny that the affirmation of ordinary life and the universal alleviation of suffering are intrinsically worthwhile goals. Yet they are just as important to the Enlightenment stance as disengaged subjectivity. Furthermore, the critics of the Enlightenment project themselves typically appeal to these values, albeit often implicitly, in the very course of their critique. For instance, they attack the predominance of instrumental reason on the grounds that it leads to unnecessary suffering. Such critics therefore fail to appreciate the diversity of goods contained in the Enlightenment vision. Their conception of it is too narrow. If it were to be broadened, Taylor suggests, they could not but recognize themselves in the culture of modernity they attack.

According to Taylor, then, Enlightenment naturalism is motivated by strong values that often go unacknowledged by both its supporters and its critics. But there is another level of complexity frequently ignored in the debate, one that is still more important, Taylor thinks, for understanding the malaise arising from the Enlightenment project. This is the level of moral sources. A moral source, we may recall, is a constitutive good, contact with which empowers the good. One's identity is shaped by certain strong values, and moral sources empower one to realize the values more fully. In Taylor's view, Enlightenment naturalism could not emerge as the dominant moral outlook of modernity unless its constellation of strong values were backed up by new and potent moral sources. Now if we take a culture-theoretic perspective on modernity, it becomes clear, Taylor argues, that the strong values that drove the Enlightenment project were originally supported by a theistic conception of moral sources. The Enlightenment project got going on theistic moral energy: it was sustained by a conception of the human in relation to God, reflection on which empowered the realization of the life goods it prized. And it turns out that even here, at the level of the Enlightenment project's original moral sources, instrumental reason played a crucial role.

In Taylor's view, the ontological outlook that supports the Enlightenment project has its origins in the 'providential deism' of the eighteenth century. According to Taylor, providential deism

brought about a significant 'anthropological shift' in the understanding of God which paved the way for the thoroughly secular
sources of Enlightenment naturalism. Taylor distinguishes three
'anthropomorphizing' features of deism.[6] The first is the idea that
God not only created the world but designed it in such a way that
human beings would survive and prosper as long as they acted in
accordance with God's plan. Human flourishing is thus central to
God's reasoning in creating the universe. The fulfilment of human
purposes is the means, and the sole means, through which God's
own purposes are fulfilled. The second feature is that human beings
are able to fulfil God's plan and attain happiness through the use
of faculties given to them by God but in no way dependent on God's
grace for their exercise. The crucial capacity given by God for
the realization of the plan, Taylor notes, is instrumental reason.
Through the exercise of their capacity for instrumental reason
human beings are able to discern the providential order, the thread
of God's design, and to shape things to suit the goals of human
self-preservation and flourishing. The design ensures that what is
instrumentally rational for one person harmonizes with the interests and instrumental rationality of others. The prospect of reward
and punishment in the after-life adds extra incentive for us to follow
God's plan, but God also installs a natural propensity in human
beings to follow it. Both measures minimize, indeed negate, the
human dependence on God's grace for the realization of his purposes. Third, the design is such that God's purposes can readily be
discerned by the rational human mind. By subjecting nature to
careful scientific scrutiny, human beings are able to reshape it
according to their purposes. So there is nothing intrinsically mys-
terious about the workings of God. On the contrary, mystery is anti-
thetical to God, as it would amount to a defect in his design, part
of which is the human ability to work out its structure. For providential deism, the world is designed by God in such a way that
human beings can realize their true and highest calling as God's
creatures purely by exercising their natural capacity for instrumental reason.

According to Taylor, then, providential deism construed God as
a moral source in his very capacity as an instrumental reasoner.
Reflection on God as an instrumental reasoner empowered human
beings to carry through God's design. And this, according to Taylor,
provided the underlying motivation for the emerging scientific
stance to nature. Scientific experimentation was part of the human
spiritual vocation in so far as it enabled human beings to reshape

nature in their interest, which in turn preserves God's providential order. In Taylor's words, '*instrumentalizing* things', treating God's creation as the means for self-preservation, 'is the spiritually essential step' (*SS* 232). Seeing nature instrumentally empowers human beings to bring about the goods of ordinary life and the amelioration of the general condition of humankind. While Taylor (along with many others) identifies Bacon as the first major articulator of the new scientific outlook, the key figure in Taylor's account is Locke. For Locke, as Taylor reads him, the moral good is founded on God's command and not on the intrinsic good of things themselves. But God's command is normative for us because it is instrumentally rational to obey it: disobedience carries the terrible punishment of an eternity in hell. This makes God a kind of 'super-player in a game of rational choice', for he 'instrumentalizes our instrumental reason by giving us a law which brings us into line with his purpose of general conservation' (*SS* 242). Instrumental rationality thus becomes 'our avenue of participation in God's will'. By following God's law and acquiring useful scientific knowledge we are able to realize the paramount goods of ordinary life, general happiness and disengaged freedom.

Taylor then retraces the logically short (though historically long) step from providential deism to the secular outlook of Enlightenment naturalism. In the deist outlook, the human power of disengaged reason and nature understood as an interlocking order of purposes are in a sense 'proximate' moral sources (*SS* 315), for they lead us to a further source – God. The transition to Enlightenment naturalism now just required a reinterpretation of these proximate sources as sources in themselves. In Taylor's view, not much is *lost* by way of moral sources in the move from deism to Enlightenment naturalism: the theistic moral source of deism had been anthropomorphized to such an extent that it eventually offered little that could not be provided by reflection on human powers or nature alone. At the same time, however, much stood to be gained: for deism opened the gate for *new* ways of experiencing nature and human capacities as the constitutive good independently of God. With the demise of deism, nature and human capacities would become 'frontiers of moral exploration' (*SS* 314, 408). The early phase of Enlightenment naturalism drew on a morally empowering vision of the intrinsic goodness of human nature. A natural propensity for sympathy with others constituted humans as good and reflection on this could motivate general benevolence. In a later phase, the human power to *cultivate* natural desire through disengaged reason takes over as the key moral source. By disengaging from one's particular drives and passions, by fully realizing one's capacity for self-responsible freedom, we can release a universal love for the whole of humankind. The ability of people to be moved in this way, Taylor thinks, is a unique and unquestionably admirable achievement of modernity (though, as he notes, it has affinities with the ancient stoic tradition).

To recapitulate, Taylor's thesis is that if we are to understand the malaise that surrounds the Enlightenment project we need to examine it at two levels. At one level there is the range of life goods and hypergoods it is committed to. Taylor argues, not unreasonably, that these goods have a validity and a complexity often overlooked by its critics. At the second level there is the ontological vision Enlightenment naturalism propounds; that is to say, the view it has of the constitutive good, the ontological feature that explains *why* the life goods are good. Two features have been explored: nature interpreted as a more or less benign power, and the human capacity for disengaged, self-responsible reason – both, as we have just seen, inherited from deism. In Taylor's view, self-responsible freedom provides the key moral source for most contemporary defenders of the Enlightenment project. It is not only the feature that constitutes the 'moral' goods of benevolence and justice for them, it also *inspires* them to meet their vocation. The question Taylor now poses is: do the two levels, the life goods and moral sources, match up? Is the source of self-responsible freedom up to the task of motivating the Enlightenment project's vocation – its 'moral' hypergood?

Taylor doubts that it is. It is questionable whether self-responsible freedom provides adequate support for the 'far-reaching moral commitments to benevolence and justice' (*SS* 515) that define the Enlightenment project. I will discuss the reasons Taylor gives for this doubt, and the alternative, more 'adequate' source he proposes, a little later. For the moment, it suffices to note that in Taylor's view anxiety about the adequacy of its moral sources contributes to the *malaise* surrounding the Enlightenment project. Modern subjects are committed to the 'moral' life goods of justice, truth, benevolence and the minimization of suffering; but Enlightenment naturalism's ontological vision does not adequately inspire them with confidence or hope that the goods are realizable. To borrow a phrase from Habermas, the Enlightenment project has a 'need for self-reassurance' regarding the adequacy of its sources.[7]

So according to Taylor, a lack of congruence between the 'moral' hypergood and the sources empowering it contributes to the instability of the Enlightenment project. There are other reasons for the instability, but before turning to them it is worth reflecting on Taylor's method and the diagnostic work being done by his notion of moral sources. Taylor's concern is to reconstruct the changes in moral outlook that accompanied the adoption of the modern life goods. This is an important task because moral outlooks refer us to a sense of 'moral reality' – the constitutive good – and this 'sense of reality' informs the quality of will, and the quality of experience, of the people under the outlook. For the most part, the sense of reality is not explicitly formulated; it is 'lived' pre-reflexively by subjects rather than objectively known by them. If this is the case, how are we to tell what our background sense of reality is? It is impossible to say exactly, but the historian can piece together important clues. Taylor's investigations are guided by the thought that the modern moral outlook first emerged in the culture of seventeenth-century Europe. It is therefore appropriate to look back to this time for *explicit* formulations of the outlook. Whereas we find it hard to focus contrastively on our background intuitions, our ancestors *had to* articulate the changes taking place; indeed, the articulations helped bring about the change. Some articulations of the new moral outlook took the form of philosophical theory, but most did not. Certainly, most people were moved by articulations of the constitutive good – they were energized by a moral source – without having been *demonstrated* anything philosophically. From Taylor's perspective, the significance of a moral source lies in its capacity to shape the will, or in its ability to constitute a certain quality of experience, rather than in its validity as the conclusion of a *theory*. The decisive feature about a moral source is its capacity to move people; its 'truth' is inseparable from its force. Moral sources are in this sense '*idées-forces*' (*SS* 203). Taylor's task, then, is a kind of phenomenology of moral experience; his aim is to recover the meaning content of pre-reflective moral life using the method of historical distantiation.

It is the *lived* reality of moral sources that makes them relevant for a diagnosis of the times. It is important, then, that we do not think of sources as theoretical or reflexively generated entities. A comparison can be made here with the distinction between strong value and strong evaluation we discussed in chapter 4. A strong value is something that stands out in a qualitative contrast, but for the most part our understanding of the framework of qualitative contrasts is implicit. Strong evaluation, on the other hand, involves explicit deliberation over some course of action. Unless we appreciate that it is strong value and not strong evaluation that is essential for human agency, Taylor's theory will rightly seem 'intellectualist' and excessively linguistic. Now a similar confusion is liable to arise over moral sources. In order to articulate moral sources, we have to take a reflective stance: we try to make explicit the pre-theoretical understanding of the constitutive good. But while theoretical formulation is an indispensable task for the cultural theorist, it is not necessarily, and indeed is not typically, the way 'agent-understanding' works. To suppose it is would be to reproduce the 'intellectualist' mistake involved in essentializing strong *evaluation*. The denizens of modernity do not need to be reflexively aware of their moral sources in order for moral sources to be a legitimate category for understanding their form of life and the moral conflicts besetting it. Admittedly, Taylor does sometimes refer to moral sources as constitutive goods *reflection* on which empowers the good (*SS* 264). But such talk is misleading.[8] If it were literally true, it is hard to see how moral sources could play such an important role in Taylor's diagnosis of the times, at least without succumbing to an 'intellectualist' distortion.

Just as moral sources are not the inventions of a reflecting or theoretical consciousness, they do not change simply on account of new ideas. It is impossible to understand the evolving moral outlook of modernity without taking into account the accompanying social and political transformations. So, for instance, while providential deism paved the way for the later secular outlook, it could only have done so in conjunction with the 'drive towards reform', or as Taylor also calls it, the 'compulsion to development', that profoundly altered the social and political order of early modern Europe.[9] Reforms such as the poor laws, the dissolution of 'carnival', and the imposition of personal and professional codes of discipline all served to entrench a sense of the new 'moral order'. The strong value accorded by deism to self-reshaping through instrumental reason for the sake of preserving the divine plan was therefore not just an abstract ideal: it was imposed by new regimes of self-discipline and productive work. By pointing to such interconnections between changes in moral outlook and social change, Taylor can fend off the objection that he takes a problematically 'idealist' approach to the formation of the modern identity. In a short 'Digression on Historical Explanation' in *Sources of the Self*, Taylor admits that his theory has an 'unavoidable incompleteness' (*SS* 203). However, his theory is not for that reason 'idealist', he asserts, for he does not propose it as an answer to the causal question: 'what brought the modern identity about?'. His account could legitimately be accused of idealism if it were offered as a historical or diachronic explanation of the modern identity. But as an objection to the interpretative investigations Taylor actually undertakes, the idealist charge is inappropriate. While reductive theories of historical change – 'vulgar Marxism', for instance – focus exclusively on the diachronic-causal question, they are no substitute for a cultural, interpretative approach.

However, one does not need to be a vulgar Marxist to suspect that Taylor's response to the 'idealist' objection is not fully satisfactory. For even if we *remain* at the level of interpretative analysis, it is questionable whether Taylor assigns due significance to the role played by a sense of ultimate moral reality in shaping moral experience and motivating moral action. No doubt a lively sense of the constitutive good can empower moral behaviour. But surely explications of the pre-reflective moral life need not refer us to a sense of the ultimate nature of things. The direct apprehension of the needs of another, or the intuited sense of the requirements of a principle, for instance, may be the relevant motivating feature. Such direct apprehensions and intuitions are of course more the product of a decent upbringing in a loving environment than anticipations of an underlying moral ontology. This is not to deny that contact with moral sources has a motivating role to play as well. It is just to question the weight it should carry relative to other considerations. By way of a reply, Taylor can say that he is not interested in the 'causal' issue of what 'brings about' moral subjectivity. But there would be something disingenuous about such a response, as there is in his denial that he is offering a historical explanation of the rise of the modern identity. For Taylor certainly wants his account to have *diagnostic* validity. He wants to throw light on the malaise troubling the modern identity, with a view to suggesting some remedies. But how can a theory with diagnostic ambition disavow any claim to explanatory truth? The role Taylor accords to moral sources in his diagnosis of the times *tacitly* commits him to a causal story in which moral ontological outlooks play a disproportionately large part. It is therefore not the mere focus on self-interpretations that lends Taylor's theory its 'idealist' character, but the 'top-heavy' content of the interpretations themselves. We could say that the unfortunate 'top-down' character of Taylor's theory of the self is reproduced in his theory of modernity.

Furthermore, while Taylor's concern with moral sources is not as 'intellectualist' as it might seem at first sight, there is something in this charge too. To see what it is, it helps to go back to Taylor's

'Introduction' to the first two volumes of his *Philosophical Papers* (1985). He writes there that his critique of naturalism 'can only be established in an historical account' that would draw out the moral motivations behind the modern 'epistemological' model of the subject (*HAL* 7, *PHS* 7). Such an account would involve 'placing the history of our scientific and philosophical consciousness in relation to the whole development of modern culture, and particularly of the underlying interpretations of agency and the self' (*HAL* 7, *PHS* 7). *Sources of the Self* is 'the larger work which will come to grips with this kind of historical account, and do at least something to meet this demand . . . to explain plausibly the spiritual roots of naturalism' (*HAL* 7, *PHS* 7). It is Taylor's attempt, in hermeneutic social scientific fashion, 'to understand naturalism better than itself'. This sub-plot of hermeneutically refuting naturalism is one of the book's great strengths. By showing how instrumental reason helps constitute the moral stance of Enlightenment naturalism, at the level of both life goods and moral sources, Taylor is able to give a more nuanced critique of the 'Enlightenment project' than the standard accounts. But this success comes at a price. On the one hand, it attaches great importance to strands of modern culture that were influential in shaping naturalist consciousness – deism, for example – though it is far from clear that their impact on contemporary life warrants such attention. On the other hand, it neglects areas of modern culture that can be understood neither as part of naturalism nor as part of the Romantic reaction to it. Taylor wants to diagnose the times and to refute naturalism *at one stroke*. It is not surprising, then, that Taylor's portrait of the modern identity should have an 'intellectualist' hue.[10]

Art and Authenticity

We have just examined how Taylor reconstructs the Enlightenment project as a moral vision. It defines certain life goods and it opens up moral sources for realizing them. The life goods or strong values it affirms are benevolence, respect of individual rights, universal justice, the minimization of suffering, ordinary life, and the dignity of adult rational subjectivity. These goods define what Taylor now calls 'the modern moral order'. It is a vision centred in the first instance on the human power to attain objective knowledge of the order of interlocking purposes, and to control or reshape their inner and outer environment accordingly. The capacity for rational disengagement functions as a moral source, for it is by standing back from one's particular feelings and beliefs, by taking an objective and impartial stance towards the world, that moral energy is released for the realization of the life goods. This idea of the human species realizing itself through the development of its capacity for instrumental reason both lies behind and is entrenched by the drive for reform that characterizes the modern world. However, all the evidence suggests to Taylor that, as a vision of the human good, Enlightenment naturalism is inherently unstable. It is not clear that its moral sources, once articulated, are rich enough to sustain the very goods it affirms. We could say that there is an issue about the *internal* adequacy of its sources, that is to say, about the 'match' between the sources and the life goods. But before we can fully appreciate Taylor's reasons for questioning this match, there is another source of instability we have to consider. For it is questionable whether the package of *life goods* advanced by the Enlightenment project is really desirable. Even if its sources were up to it, is Enlightenment naturalism's conception of human flourishing one we can really endorse?

Taylor answers negatively, and he is convinced that few of his contemporaries would do otherwise. For as well as its commitment to the Enlightenment project, the modern identity has been shaped by the idea, originally formulated by the Romantics, that humans are 'expressive beings'; that is, beings whose flourishing involves a kind of 'expressive self-fulfilment'. Taylor distinguishes two aspects to the goal of expressive self-fulfilment. First, there is the idea of reconciling or integrating elements of human life that are divided in the Enlightenment vision. For example, rationally disengaged subjectivity is attained by standing back from something given pre-reflectively – spontaneous wants and desires, for instance – and then taking control or mastering the object. It thereby creates a division between the intellect and the passions, the cognitive and the affective, nature and spirit. Such division is intolerable from the Romantic/expressive perspective: it alienates the self from nature, from its own 'inner depths', and from other selves. A self divided in this manner cannot attain the 'wholeness' essential for human flourishing. The second aspect of expressive self-fulfilment emphasized by Taylor is the idea that each person has her own standard, a standard each of us must explore and realize for herself. The ideal of being 'true to oneself', of being integrally free or authentic, is also stifled by disengagement and instrumental reason. Authenticity and expressive wholeness call not for distance, impartiality and calculation, but for imaginative self-exploration. It is by exercising one's unique capacities of creative imagination, particularly through works of art, that one is able to bring together the goals of authenticity and expressive wholeness in one's life, and thus flourish as the singular human being one is.

Taylor argues that just as critics of modernity often ignore or oversimplify the moral motivation behind the Enlightenment project, they also fail to appreciate the moral richness and complexity of the Romantic/expressivist ideal of authenticity. The ideal of authenticity, Taylor observes, is routinely attacked for the self-centredness it breeds. It is held responsible for the rise of the so-called 'permissive society', the 'me-generation' and the 'culture of narcissism'. For such critics, there is a 'cult' of authenticity at play in contemporary western societies, an 'abnormal and regrettable self-absorption', as Taylor puts their concern, which 'flattens and narrows our lives' (*MM* 4). Many of those hostile to this culture – Taylor mentions Daniel Bell, Allan Bloom and Christopher Lasch – regard talk of authenticity as something like 'a screen for self-indulgence' (*MM* 16).[11] But in Taylor's view, such diagnoses fail to get to the roots of the malaise. For the ideals of authenticity and expressive fulfilment are as legitimate as those that underlie the Enlightenment project, and just as critics of the Enlightenment project implicitly appeal to Enlightenment ideals themselves, so the critics of authenticity rely on an unacknowledged commitment to the norm of authentic self-expression in making their critique. The diagnosis goes astray by reproducing the pattern we noted earlier: it construes the goods pursued in the culture of modernity too narrowly. We also saw that Taylor attempts to correct the narrow interpretation of the Enlightenment project by examining it from a culture-theoretic perspective, that is, by reconstructing its initial appeal as a moral vision. And he recommends the same approach to the culture of authenticity. Taylor takes us back to the original 'expressivist turn' in modern culture, then he follows it through its subsequent transitions to locate the moral power of the ideal of authenticity. It is only by reconstructing the transitions in the modern understanding of authentic self-expression, Taylor thinks, that we position ourselves correctly for diagnosing the unease that plainly surrounds the contemporary pursuit of authenticity.

The crux of Taylor's argument is that the rise of Enlightenment rationalism and the consolidation of the modern moral order catalysed a counter-current aimed at realizing a 'heightened, more vibrant quality of life' (*SS* 372) through the exercise of the creative imagination. The 'expressivist turn' in modern culture thus affirmed new life goods, goods that contrasted with those of disengaged rational subjectivity and whose appeal arose precisely from that contrast. But if the expressivist turn introduced a new conception of human flourishing, if it sought to realize life goods suppressed by the Enlightenment project, how would it conceive the *constitutive* good in virtue of which the life goods were good? That is to say, how would it articulate the 'sense of reality' of those in possession of the life goods? And how could the articulation be done in a way that brought the constitutive good 'closer', that is, in a way that made contact with the *source* of the life goods, so rendering them more tangible? The problem facing the expressivist turn, as Taylor presents it, is to *bring about* the good of a 'heightened, more vibrant quality of life' by articulating, and so 'making manifest', its constitutive good. With the expressivist turn, the task of formulating the background sense of moral reality, in a manner that makes manifest the constitutive good, falls on the poets (broadly understood). It is a task that calls for the creation of a particular kind of art work: the epiphany.

An art work is epiphanic, Taylor writes, if it is 'the locus of a manifestation which brings us into the presence of something which is otherwise inaccessible' (*SS* 419). The 'something' which the epiphanic art work brings to presence is a source of meaning – it is a constitutive good – and it is brought to presence in a unique, non-reproducible way; namely, in this particular work of art. To realize an epiphany is thus 'a paradigm case' of recovering contact with a moral source: it achieves a 'contact with something, where this contact either fosters and/or itself constitutes a spiritually significant fulfilment or wholeness' (*SS* 425). In the first phase of the expressivist turn – the Romantic movement, including Wordsworth, Shelley, Constable and Friedrich – the creative imagination provides the locus for a renewed contact with nature. The successful work of art gave authentic expression to the subjectivity of the creator, but it did so by activating the 'élan of nature within' (*SS* 370) through previously hidden world-disclosive powers of language. The task of the Romantic poet is 'to make us aware of something through nature for which there are as yet no adequate words' (*SS* 381). The poet has to create a 'subtler' language, to use Shelley's term, to bring his sense of the underlying reality to expression. According to Taylor's interpretation, the thing brought to expression in the Romantic epiphany, nature, was understood as an unambiguous moral source. The Romantic epiphany at once 'celebrated the

218 *Modernity, Art and Religion*

goodness of nature' (*SS* 429) and made the élan of nature more intensely manifest within the subject. The successful Romantic work of art can thus be called an 'epiphany of being', or as Taylor also puts it, an 'epiphany of translucence' (*SS* 431). The Romantic epiphanies of being 'free us from the debased, mechanistic world' by bringing to light 'the spiritual reality behind nature and uncorrupted feeling' (*SS* 457).

Once the expressivist turn was made, however, nature and purely human powers were again opened up as 'frontiers of exploration', only this time for the modern artistic imaginary. That is to say, it became possible to imagine the art work as the locus of a manifestation of something quite different to nature as it was disclosed in the Romantic epiphanies of translucence. Taylor then interprets the main streams of post-Romantic and modernist art as various attempts at articulating in a *more* authentic manner the sense of reality in which the subject is set. The post-Romantic realist art of 'despiritualized nature', for instance, rejects as inauthentic the Romantic ideal of the work of art as a translucent manifestation of an underlying spiritual reality. The 'realist' art of Flaubert, for example, aims not at revealing a hidden meaning in nature but at giving 'meaningless and banal unhappiness the closure and shape of fate' (*SS* 431). Taylor suggests that even here, however, the art work aims at contact with a moral source; for 'the unveiling of things in their meaninglessness involves its own kind of transfiguration' (*SS* 431). The realist movement in any case readily gave way to the affirmation of something – in Courbet's or Manet's case, for instance, 'raw nature' – that shines through the object. Despite the realist aspiration of 'stripping things of meaning' (*SS* 431), it thus still makes sense to talk of a 'naturalist epiphany'. Taylor then considers the rise of a sensibility that finds no positive meaning in nature at all. This movement, exemplified in the work of Baudelaire and taken up by Mallarmé and the Symbolists, involved an even more radical departure from the ideal of translucence. For Baudelaire, nature is too inert and banal to be the source of the worth of art, indeed to be the source of the worth of anything. The task of art is therefore 'to correct nature' (*SS* 438), to redeem life by reconstituting it in accordance with a higher, purely 'spiritual' vision. A third reaction to Romantic expressivism, which also rejects the goodness of nature, is the 'post-Schopenhaurian epiphany' exemplified in the work of Wagner and Lawrence. This strives to articulate and make manifest 'the wild energy of an amoral nature' (*SS* 441). While each of these movements is committed to a fundamentally epiphanic conception of art – that is, to a conception of art as the locus of a manifestation – their epiphanies involve 'a *transmutation* of what is there; despiritualized reality, or fallen nature, or the amoral will; rather than the revelation of a good which is ontically independent of us' (*SS* 446).

Having examined some of the main post-Romantic alternatives to the epiphanies of being, Taylor turns to the exploration of sources in the modernist movement in twentieth-century art. To the modernists, Taylor observes, Romanticism seemed to offer 'trivialized, ersatz, or inauthentic meanings to compensate for a meaningless world' (*SS* 458). In its place, modernism sought a 'retrieval of experience', or as Taylor also puts it, a recovery of 'interiority'. Much modernist art sets itself the task of reawakening the content of primordial lived experience, a content suppressed by the deadening routines, commodified culture and inauthentic modes of reflection characteristic of the modern world. A similar ambition is shared by movements in twentieth-century philosophy, including, as we have seen, the phenomenological movement. The aim is to render experience more vivid or more concrete through a rearticulation. Taylor then distinguishes two general approaches within modernism to the retrieval of lived experience. First, there are movements such as surrealism, futurism and their postmodernist offshoots, which strive for an 'unmediated contact with the fullness of life' (*SS* 469). The futurists did this by affirming the human powers of creation and control; the surrealists sought to break these powers down for the sake of renewing contact with the inner flux of experience and the unconscious flow of primitive desire. But 'whether through a celebration of our own power or through a merging in the depths' (*SS* 472), Taylor argues, this strand of modernism tends towards 'subjectivism' on account of the unmediated quality of the experience recovered in the art. There is no *epiphany* realized in the art: the experience of art replicates experiences accessible through other means (technology, say, or dreams). This strand of modernism has a higher estimation of the powers of the imagination than Romantic expressivism, but the powers are not the locus of a manifestation that is otherwise inaccessible. It tends to celebrate the artist's powers for their own sake, a practice which, in Taylor's view, repeatedly fails in the basic aim of heightening the quality of experience. The second strand of modernism, in his view, is more successful: its access to the sources of fuller experience is indirect, the recovery is mediated through new forms of epiphany. Amongst others, Taylor cites the 'framing' epiphanies of Ezra Pound's poetry, the 'inter-temporal' epiphany of Proust, and the 'constellations' of Adorno and Benjamin as examples of mediated retrievals of experience. The modernist epiphanies recover a sense of inner depth by 'decentring' the subject and by breaking with the 'received sense of identity and time' (*SS* 465). In these ways they manage to disclose experience in a more authentic but less subjectivist manner. Finally, Taylor discusses the 'counter-epiphanic' strand of modernism that practises an 'austere discipline of the imagination' to find a language suited to a time 'devastated' and 'degraded' by totalitarianism and the Holocaust. But even here, Taylor writes, 'the counter-epiphanic can be embraced not in order to deny the epiphanic altogether, not just in order to find a place for the human spirit to stand before the most complete emptiness, but rather to force us to the verge of epiphany' (*SS* 485).

Taylor's argument, then, is that in modernism and post-Romantic art, as well as Romanticism itself, we find the work of art functioning as a locus of moral sources. The epiphany articulates a sense of reality which at once makes that reality more intensely or more concretely manifest. One accesses the reality through the creative imagination – it is only here, in the particular work of art, that we get the disclosure – and in this sense there is something ineradicably 'subjective' about an epiphany. Inwardness or interiority is not an object of scientific discovery: on the contrary, the scientific attitude of disengagement and objectification denatures this realm. It is a *creation* of the imagination, and the reality disclosed is *personally indexed* to the creator. But the 'something' that makes itself manifest in the work of art, the source to which the work owes its power, is not necessarily, and in fact is not typically, a property of the subject. As Taylor puts it, the expressivist turn involves a subjectivation of the 'manner' in which sources are explored, but not necessarily of the 'matter' of the exploration (*MM* 88). It does not follow from the subjective manner in which we articulate our sense of the underlying reality that there is nothing 'beyond the subject' to be articulated and made manifest in the articulation. Taylor has tried to show how modern art has been guided by a search for 'moral sources *outside* the subject through languages which resonate *within* him or her' (*SS* 510). The 'order' which is grasped by the artist is 'inseparably indexed to a personal vision' (*SS* 510). In Taylor's view, the development of human poietic powers in this direction teaches a number of lessons to philosophers concerned with diagnosing the times.

First, while critics of instrumental reason often appeal (rightly) to the liberating power of modern art, they typically have a too narrow understanding of the way art's liberating power works. Regrettably, in Taylor's view, the strand of modernism that unleashes the powers of subjective expression in a direct, non-epiphanic manner – surrealism, for example – often serves as the paradigm. Taylor has Habermas, and before him Marcuse and other members of the Frankfurt School, in mind here. They rightly draw attention to the 'aesthetic' needs that go unfulfilled in a society dominated by instrumental reason. But they fail to appreciate a deeper 'spiritual' dimension of modern art, that is, the role it plays as a locus of moral sources or as a site of the disclosure of a morally significant reality. Critics of the culture of authenticity, in Taylor's view, share this oversight. Like the progressives of the Frankfurt School, conservative critics such as Allan Bloom construe the pursuit of expressive authenticity in subjective terms, only they have a negative evaluation of it. They reject the culture of modernity, as we have seen, for its superficial individualism and narcissistic self-absorption. But this too fails to give credit to the anti-subjectivist thrust of modern art itself; it is blind to the fact that from Romanticism to modernism the pursuit of authenticity turns the artist *away* from merely subjectivist formulations. It is by reaching beyond the subject that art manages to recover a 'heightened, more vibrant quality of life', and so realize its true or authentic vocation. However, the subjective manner of the pursuit of authenticity, and the subsequent proliferation of moral sources, does create a *danger* of subjectivism at the level of content. The personally indexed nature of the vision through which a source is accessed, and its separation from the 'publicly established order of references' (*SS* 491), can mislead us into taking a subjectivist stance in relation to our interiority. The slide to subjectivism is a serious danger – indeed, in Taylor's view it provides the real basis of the malaise over authenticity. It is mistaken, then, to diagnose the 'morally flattened' quality of contemporary experience as the result of the modern pursuit of authenticity as such. For whatever the cause of this malaise in the modern identity, the non-subjective pursuit of authenticity is itself the road to recovery.

So the first main lesson of expressive and post-expressive art is that the retrieval of the fullness of experience, itself an indisputable life good, calls for non-subjectivist articulations of sources. The second lesson relates to the implications this has for other life goods, and in particular the 'moral' good of benevolence. Taylor seems to accept that the initial phase of the expressivist turn, the Romantic epiphany of being, has played itself out. The epiphanies of being showed some 'reality' (nature) to be 'an expression of something', which is 'an unambiguously good moral source' (*SS* 479). Post-Romantic and modernist sensibilities challenge each aspect of this understanding of art, but it is the third aspect that now generates the most worrying doubt. The idea that the non-subjective reality, contact with which retrieves the fullness of experience, is an *unambiguous* source of goodness now fails to carry conviction; and this, Taylor conjects, makes us nervous. For it is possible, and in the minds of many quite likely, that contact with the source of expressive fulfilment *disempowers* us in relation to the 'moral' life goods in a narrow sense, and vice versa. The worry is, in other words, that the pursuit of our expressive fulfilment conflicts with our pursuit of morality. Baudelaire's epiphanies of anti-nature, for instance, and the post-Schopenhauerian epiphanies of nature as a wild amoral force might transform the quality of our experience, but they can hardly be said to elicit a universal love for humankind. On the contrary, the two goods seem to be incommensurable given this outlook. As Taylor notes, Nietzsche took this thought further to challenge the worth of morality itself. If the pursuit of morality inhibited or compromised authentic self-creation and the intensification of experience through art, so much the worse for it: better to drop the moral (Christian) hypergood altogether. Taylor takes seriously Nietzsche's diagnosis of the impoverishment of modern life due to the slavish and ultimately self-destructive obedience to the moral hypergood. To the extent that the reality we contact through the exploration of our interiority is an ambiguous source of goodness, in the sense that it conflicts with our commitment to the life good of benevolence, we face a 'crisis of affirmation' (*SS* 448). How can nature be affirmed if contact with it negates such an important class of goods? At this point Taylor follows Dostoyevsky rather than Nietzsche in suggesting that recovery from the crisis may consist in a grace-given 'trans-figuration' of the world through a transformation in our stance towards it: nature is made good by our seeing that it is so, and we are able to 'see that it is good' by opening ourselves to and participating in *agapē* – the 'divine affirmation of the human' (*SS* 516, 521).

Taylor thus suggests that a theistic perspective is more suited than a non-theistic one for reconciling the modern goods of expressive fulfilment and benevolence. In fact, Taylor seems to think that the hypergoods of expressive fulfilment and morality taken separately are most fully powered by a theist moral source. If Taylor is right, a theist affirmation of the modern identity is the most promising way of sustaining it. But before we move on to consider Taylor's case for theism, a few comments on his account of the expressivist turn and its significance for a diagnosis of the times are in order. The first point that needs to be stressed is that while Taylor's approach conflicts with certain general theories of art, he is not offering a general theory of his own, and he is certainly not proposing a criterion of the 'aesthetic'. In passing, Taylor notes that the kind of investigation he is engaged in would be impossible to formulate within the framework of some of the more popular aesthetic theories (*SS* 487–93). If one is to examine art as the locus of moral sources, one has to do more than analyse the formal properties of different literary genres (as structuralist literary criticism does), and one has to do more than interpret the ways in which the 'inner life' of the poet, her emotions and feelings, are harmoniously rearranged in the work (the line taken by 'New Criticism'). While formalist/structuralist criticism and psychologistic approaches to art and literature are often pitted against each other, from Taylor's perspective they have a common weakness: an inattention to the empowering quality of the art work's world disclosure. Unless we do attend to this feature, we miss out on a claim that at least some modernist work makes on us. At the same time, Taylor is not saying that empowering world disclosure, or the energizing articulation of a sense of reality, *defines* 'the work of art'. He is not interested in 'aesthetics' in the sense of the study of the properties that demarcate art from non-art. Nor is he proposing that the exploration of constitutive goods through the creative imagination is the *only* end, or legitimate end, of modern art or literature, as if there were no other worthwhile purposes directing literary or art practice in the modern world. That would of course be an absurd claim. Taylor's account of modernism must be read for what it is: a chapter in a story about modern moral sources. Its aim is to show how the modern sense of belonging to a meaningful reality, of *having* a meaningful reality, takes unprecedented imaginative forms.

However, it is also true that Taylor seeks a diagnostic purchase from his enquiries. That is to say, he wants to put his story about modern moral sources to work in diagnosing the times. In order to do this, he has to identify the sources of moral energy people actually draw upon in the modern world, and to indicate how they match up with the life goods of authentic, expressive fulfilment we desire. Now in view of this diagnostic task, Taylor's focus on the practices and ambitions of artistic elites seems questionable. Taylor could argue that the retrieval of meaning by way of an articulation of a constitutive good (whether 'moral', 'amoral' or 'immoral') reflects an anxiety over the quality of modern life that stretches well beyond the elites themselves. Or he could maintain that the options opened up by the Romantics, the post-Romantics and high modernists have had a significant if sometimes indirect broader cultural influence. Or again, he could simply hold up his hands and admit that he is only dealing with changes in '*mentalités*', in how the self and its relation to the world have been imagined in modern times, and that he has little to say about the *causes* of such change, or about the mechanisms by which new forms of self-interpretation filter down into the life world at large. But it has to be said that none of these responses is very satisfactory, and for reasons similar to the reservations we expressed earlier about Taylor's historical method. In the first place, it is doubtful that the main obstacle to expressive fulfilment in many people's lives is the potency of their contact with a constitutive good: the boring nature of their daily work, lack of time, family pressures or isolation, for instance, are likely to be more challenging hurdles to overcome. Contact with a constitutive good will certainly be more of an issue for those whose *hypergood* is authentic self-expression, but for many people self-expression has a less demanding status, and can be facilitated by more mundane measures. The point is that if one wants to diagnose the contemporary ill of 'flattened' or meaningless experience, the availability of moral sources is not the most obvious place to look. While Taylor by no means claims that access to rich moral sources *suffices* for the realization of the good – lots of other conditions must be in place – it is *this* condition that takes centre stage in his account of the conflicts of modernity in *Sources of the Self*. Again, one does not have to be a vulgar Marxist to suspect there is something problematically 'idealist' about such an approach to the malaise around fulfilment.

There are other reasons for questioning the appropriateness of Taylor's focus in relation to his diagnostic goal. We have seen that Taylor is reluctant to speculate on the causal agencies of cultural change. Inevitably, however, he has to employ some sort of explanatory model. The view that tends to surface in his work is that cultural transitions, or changes in the dominant modes of self-interpretation, are driven by the activities of elites. The picture is one of conceptual, ideational and broadly speaking 'poetic' innovations

seeping through culture from top to bottom (encouraged or inhibited, of course, by the prevailing social forces, and partly shaping
those forces in turn). Now whatever can be said of this model generally, in the case of modernism it is clearly more plausible for some
strands than others. While surrealism, for instance, has evidently
had a huge impact on many aspects of modern culture, the 'epiphanies' of modernism can hardly be said to have infiltrated very far; at
least not as far as would warrant their central place in Taylor's story.
This is not to deny that the epiphanies of Joyce, Pound, Proust or
Rilke, for instance, transform the experience of those who encounter
them; it is just to make the obvious point that a lot of people do not
encounter them at all. They do not feature in the discontent Taylor is
keen to diagnose, and, alas, it is hard to imagine many people
turning to them for 'recovery'. But the problem is not just that access
to these sources is limited, and likely to remain that way. It is also
that Taylor's focus on high modernism leads him to neglect sources
people do actually draw on for meaning, experiential fulfilment or
exploring their inner depths. A point like this is made by Martha
Nussbaum.[12] Taylor's portrait of the modern identity, Nussbaum
notes, pays little attention to the many art forms of non-western
origin that help shape the sense of self in contemporary western societies. For instance, there is no place in Taylor's account for the contributions made by African culture – via jazz and blues, for example
– to contemporary understandings of expressive fulfilment, despite
their enormous impact and power. Nussbaum is surely right in her
observation that as an account of where people in the modern world
actually turn for spiritual renewal *Sources of the Self* is very one-
sided. This thought might prompt the reflection that *Sources of the
Self* is really a self-clarification of Taylor's *own* sources, that is to say,
a kind of philosophical confession or spiritual autobiography.[13] And
no doubt it is. But it must be read as more than that: Taylor's explicit
aim, after all, is to intervene in the debate about modernity (*SS* ix)
with a view to diagnosing the moral conflicts that 'rage within each
of us' (*SS* 106). The fact that Taylor's portrait of the modern identity
is skewed by a 'monomaniac's' concern with overcoming naturalism
(*HAL* 1, *PHS* 1) might make it partial, but it does not make the project
itself invalid. There is no reason why the project could not be
expanded to include non-western sources, as well as sources more
firmly embedded in popular culture. *Sources of the Self* could even be
read as the prototype for a new paradigm in literary and cultural
studies, one geared towards the description and critical retrieval of
moral sources.

Taylor's account of modern moral sources invites a more formidable objection, however. For one could challenge Taylor's account not so much for lacking comprehensiveness as for lacking coherence, or at least a demonstrated coherence, in its basic interpretative framework. We have seen that Taylor cites the exploration of sources that lie 'outside the subject' but which 'resonate within him or her' as the central aspiration of modernism. The epiphany aims at a fuller, more vibrant quality of experience, something it can achieve only by avoiding subjectivism. In this respect, the epiphanic disclosure of meaning is a key challenge of our time. But are such epiphanies realizable, in fact? Might not the modernist advocates of this conception of human 'poietic powers' be exaggerating them? Could it be that the epiphany really lies *beyond* the productive capacities of language as such, rather than being one possibility of the creative imagination amongst others? To put it another way, one might ask whether there is an unacceptable pre-critical, metaphysically 'realist' assumption built into the very notion of an epiphany. Habermas, for one, takes this line: he questions the very *intelligibility* of the epiphanic work of art.[14] Richard Rorty makes a similar point without going quite so far.[15] Rorty's objection is that Taylor does not demonstrate his claim that the works he interprets as epiphanies must be read as sites of a manifestation of something that lies 'beyond the subject'. The option remains open that they are nothing but a harmonious reordering of human emotions and attitudes – the option initially put forward by I. A. Richards and which Rorty himself recommends.[16] Taylor's reply to these objections, I think, would be that they miss the central point about sources. The sources Taylor describes are not primarily intellectual or theoretical achievements. They are not concepts or propositions; they do not make a claim in the manner of a judgement; and they should not be assessed by the standards of either science or common sense. Rather, contact with moral sources is an achievement of the spirit: the success or 'validity' of the epiphanic art work lies in its bringing about or constituting a certain quality of experience, and beyond that, a way of seeing that orients a form of life. In this sense, their claim to truth is practical rather than theoretical. In Taylor's view, the fact that we recognize the phenomenological inadequacies of subjectivism – that is, its inability to power a deeper, more authentic mode of experience – testifies to the falsity of subjectivism at the ontological level. Of course, the phenomenology can be questioned, and it has to be said that some of Taylor's negative assessments of the quality of experience expressed or constituted by 'subjectivist' strands of modernism – surrealism, for instance – have little backing. But if it is true that an experience can *only* be constituted through the articulation of a non-subjectivist reality, then that reality does have to feature in the 'best account of who we are and what we are living'. And to that extent, there is at least some justification in calling the experience-constituting articulation an 'epiphany'.

Beyond Secularism

Taylor frequently observes that in modern civilization art in some respects replaces religion (*SS* 376, 422). To see Taylor's point, we need to cast our minds back to the particular religion it had to replace: roughly speaking, 'rationalized Christianity'. Rationalized Christianity transformed the moral life by directing it towards the goods of ordinary life, self-responsibility, respect of individual rights, and the amelioration of the condition of humankind through instrumental reason and non-discriminating benevolence. These life goods defined the emerging modern moral order. Alongside this change, rationalized Christianity transformed the underlying sense of the constitutive good. The moral life was experienced as a set of demands on a self 'buffered' from the spirits and demons that inhabited the 'enchanted' world. By standing up to these outside forces – by taking them on, so to speak, and vanquishing them with the God-given weapons of reason and purity of heart – the buffered identity acquired a sense of its own power and invulnerability. This enhanced sense of moral power, Taylor argues, was crucial for building and sustaining the modern moral order. As rationalized Christianity evolved into Enlightenment naturalism, self-responsible reason came to be viewed as a purely human power rather than a divine gift. And while, once the disenchanted cosmic imaginary took firm hold, this power was no longer needed to fend off demons and spirits, it was still required to immure the self from the comforting but regressive illusions of religion and metaphysics, as well as the siren song rising from the subterranean realm of the instincts. The buffered identity thus continued to sustain the modern moral order after the demise of rationalized Christianity, and in fact, in Taylor's view, it is one of the characteristic features of life in a secular age. Modern secular civilization is a form of life that produces and is in turn sustained by buffered identities. But from the beginning, Taylor observes, the buffered identity has been experienced with ambivalence: it is self-enclosed, detached, cut off, and while these qualities enhance its sense of invulnerability, they also breed dissatisfaction. Something had to compensate for the truncated spiritual experience of the modern subject, something that could – in this respect – take the place of religion. Art makes up for the loss by opening the subject to a larger order of meaning through singular acts of creative imagination. The inner 'resonance' achieved through the poetic articulation of an outer reality thus carries echoes of past contacts with the sacred. It is no coincidence that Taylor should choose a term redolent with religious meaning – 'epiphany' – to designate this achievement. The epiphanies of Romantic, post-Romantic and modernist art recreate something of the spiritual intensity that was once the provenance of the sacred. They take us beyond the buffered self and the disenchanted, secularized world it inhabits.

Taylor's argument is thus that one of the central life goods of modern culture – expressive self-realization – needs moral sources that lie outside the subject, that is to say, sources that transcend the horizon of the buffered identity. A modernity that negated or suppressed such sources, that closed itself off to such modes of transcendence, would be incapable of yielding the very life goods that define it. In the value it attaches to art and the life of the artist, the secular modern identity thus shows traces of an enduring religious aspiration. But this aspiration by no means always takes us in the direction of *theism*. It *can* do, and Taylor himself is impressed by the modernisms that take this route. But it can also reawaken a potential for experience that is closer to the pagan mentality, that is to say, a mentality divorced from and at odds with the modern moral order. The 'transcendent' reality made manifest may be not so much the 'order' in which the subject is set as the chaos. As Taylor is aware, a decentring in relation to God is one way of escaping the secular buffered identity, but it is not the only way.

This brings us back to the second class of modern self-defining life goods – the goods of minimized suffering, benevolence and justice. As we have seen, Taylor doubts that the secular sources of Enlightenment naturalism are sufficient for empowering this ideal too. Such uncertainty is widely felt, Taylor conjects, and this also generates a certain anxiety or malaise over the adequacy of the secular sources. Here, Taylor notes an asymmetry with theism. 'Theism', Taylor writes, 'is contested as to its truth . . . But no one doubts that those who embrace it will find a fully adequate moral source in it' (*SS* 317). If theism is true, and God is the constitutive good, it obviously matters a great deal. But human powers and nature are contestable in this respect. For even if one recognizes the dignity of disengaged reason, or the goodness of nature, it remains an issue whether such recognition will empower us to realize the life goods of benevolence and justice. If it is true that human beings possess an intrinsic dignity as rational agents, or that nature constitutes things as good, does that really matter? Or rather, does it matter *enough* for us to lead our lives in a way that meets the standards set by the life goods? The thought that it might not, that reflection on such a constitutive good might fail to energize us into realizing the good, into sustaining the modern moral order, is what makes the question of their 'adequacy' as moral sources so pressing. The threat facing us in the modern secular age is that we might be living 'beyond our moral means' (*SS* 517).

Let us now look at the argument Taylor gives for supposing, first, that the secular humanist outlook overtaxes itself with the high demands of benevolence and justice; and second, that by contrast a theistic outlook does have the moral means for meeting these standards. The argument is sketched in the concluding chapter of *Sources of the Self*, but it is elaborated in a little more detail in *A Catholic Modernity?* (1999). Taylor begins by reiterating the point that 'our age makes higher demands for solidarity and benevolence than ever before' (*CM* 31). It enjoins us to act benevolently towards people throughout the globe, to more and more strangers who can offer nothing in return. Taylor then reflects on how we are able to meet these demands, that is to say, on what motivates us to meet them and the sustainability or stability of the motivations. At one level, we can be motivated into acts of philanthropy on an *ad hoc* basis: we see television images of the suffering caused by a famine in Africa, for instance, and our donation leaves us satisfied that we have done what is expected of a decent, civilized person. Better to give something than suffer the shame of doing nothing. But this is a fragile basis for meeting the demands of benevolence: besides being media-driven, and on that account fickle, it is far 'from the universality and unconditionality which our moral outlook prescribes' (*CM* 31). And as Taylor observes, the thought that such acts of benevolence fall so far short of the proper standard provides a motivation for not acting benevolently at all. A more dedicated commitment to the alleviation of suffering requires a sense of the intrinsic worth of the benevolence. For the non-theistic humanist, the worth derives exclusively from the fact that human beings possess an intrinsic dignity. Their possession of this dignity explains why it is worthwhile pursuing the demanding life of ameliorating the human condition; it motivates the philanthropist to live up to his ideals. The problem with this pattern of motivation, however, is that it is vulnerable to 'the immense disappointments of actual human performance' (*CM* 32). Faced with the many ways in which human beings fall short of their potential, the zealous humanist, who has dedicated himself to the cause of human improvement, easily finds his love of the other human being turning into hatred and contempt. The benevolent impulse degenerates into a source of aggression: the other is forced 'to shape up', as witnessed in despotic socialism at the macro-level, and at the micro-level in coercive 'helping' institutions 'from orphanages to boarding schools for aboriginals' (*CM* 33). The greater the image of the human, 'the more grievously do people fall short and the more severe the turnaround that is inspired by the disappointment' (*CM* 33). Taylor reconstructs a similar pattern in humanistically motivated struggles against injustice. Fierce indignation in the face of sexism and racism, for instance, can turn into hatred of those responsible for it. This can breed a sense of the absolute moral superiority of the strugglers for reform, that is to say, a sense of their immunity from wrong or evil, which in turn ratchets up the hatred and aggression, leading to new and greater modes of injustice.

The argument, then, is that a commitment to benevolence and justice requires a sense of the worth of those commitments. If one has a low opinion of human beings one is not likely to find much worth in a life dedicated to the improvement of their lot either. But the higher one's opinion of them, and the more one invests in ameliorating their condition or bringing about true justice, the more susceptible one is to the danger of destructive reversals in the direction of one's motivation. The more impassioned the initial fervour and respect for the other, the greater the oppression and contempt that results from the reversal. Taylor concludes that 'wherever action for high ideals is not tempered, controlled, and ultimately engulfed in an unconditional love of the beneficiaries, this ugly dialectic risks repetition' (*CM* 33). But then the question arises: are human beings really *capable* of such an unconditional love? If they are not, then it would be wiser, and more honest, Taylor submits, to lower the ideals. As the high standards of universal justice and benevolence are integral to the self-understanding of modernity, this option would inevitably involve some modification to the modern identity. It would, in effect, amount to an admission of defeat. On the other hand, if we think that human beings *are* capable of the unconditional love, what is the basis of this capacity? In Taylor's view, the great advantage of theism, and the reason it represents a kind of 'epistemic gain' over non-theism, is that it provides an answer to this question. It tells us that the unconditional love of one human for another is made possible through a relation to something transcendent, or participation in an infinite, non-human love. Human beings owe their power to realize the highest good to their relation to a transcendent power: the power of affirmation formulated, for instance, in the Christian notion of *agapē*.[17] Openness to the divine source of affirmation empowers the unconditional love that is required for the full realization of the moral standards we recognize. Taylor acknowledges that openness to *agapē* by no means guarantees moral empowerment. It is rather a matter of faith, and just as important, hope: hope that the pursuit of justice and human welfare is not fated to the 'ugly dialectic' that has marred projects of radical reform throughout human history.

It is hard not to sympathize with Taylor's reluctance to forgo a 'radical hope in history' for the sake of a 'stripped-down secular outlook' (*SS* 520). But the argument Taylor gives for theism raises at least as many questions as it answers. Let me make just a couple of points about the first stage of the argument – that is, the exposition of the degenerate reversals of lofty secular humanism. First, it is not clear why, within a secular outlook, dedication to others or a commitment to universal justice has to be based on a high estimation of human powers. It is no doubt true that the higher the expectations we have of our fellows the more disappointed we are in their actual performance, and more to the point, the deeper our hostility. But why should a realistic awareness of the limits of human powers lessen one's motivation to correct injustice or diminish suffering? The epistemic gain at stake here surely concerns a tendency to project, perhaps subconsciously, one's own image of the human onto the other, an image the other may be incapable of living up to, or might reject altogether. Furthermore, it could be argued that theism actually encourages this tendency, or at least is not as well placed as secular humanism for articulating its origins, and so for avoiding it. The second point is that, as a number of commentators have observed (indeed as Taylor observes himself), theism is hardly free of the danger of the 'disconcerting reversals' Taylor finds in secular humanism.[18] The history of Christendom, he recognizes, amply testifies to the ease with which theistically sustained ideals of peace and good will can be transformed into instruments of war, cruelty and hatred. In acknowledging this, Taylor declares that his aim is 'not to score points' but to open up a range of questions about the sources required for sustaining the goods of justice and benevolence (*SS* 518). But scoring points is exactly what Taylor must do if he is to convince us that theism is superior to secular humanism in this respect. After all, the exposition of the ugly dialectic to which secular humanist projects of reform are vulnerable counts for little if theism is just as susceptible to it.

A lot therefore turns on the second stage of Taylor's argument; namely, the claim that human beings are capable of an unconditional love, and that they are capable of it only to the extent that they open themselves to God's grace, *agapē*. The remarkable spiritual careers of Mother Theresa and Jean Vanier, Taylor suggests, testify to the possibility of such unconditional love or compassion. And in Taylor's view, *agapē*, or some equivalent notion in other religions (he mentions Buddhist *karuna*), is the best way of making sense of such lives. It is Taylor's belief that this kind of spiritual life is only possible through some kind of contact with a larger, infinite source of love. He thinks that we can only make sense of at least the Christian and Buddhist faiths 'by supposing that something like what they relate to – God, Nirvana – really exists'.[19] Let me again just raise two brief points. First, Taylor's claim that we can *only* make sense of these spiritualities in terms of what they relate to is itself more an expression of faith (and perhaps more significantly, hope) than argument. It will do little to convince anyone who adopts what Bernard Williams calls 'Feuerbach's axiom'; namely, the principle that if religion is false (and Taylor accepts that there are no guarantees it is true), it ultimately explains nothing and is itself something that needs to be explained.[20] For Taylor's claim really to hold, he would first have to show that all the non-religious ways of explaining religion – ways that do not suppose that something like what the religious faiths relate to actually exists – are themselves false, which is a tall order. But perhaps the more interesting issue, and this is the second point I would like to raise, concerns the reality Taylor thinks we are forced to recognize by his argument. Even if we bracket the Feuerbachian axiom, and we accept that there is some reality the religious experience relates to, what is it? What *kind* of theism does Taylor's argument support? This is a complex question, but as Stephen Mulhall has made clear, the theism that emerges from *Sources of the Self* has two dominant features.[21] First, the constitutive good of theism (God) is nothing if not the source of grace – a view that surfaced, incidentally, in Taylor's critique of Hegel's interpretation of Christianity we discussed briefly in chapter 3. The second, related feature is that as the constitutive good, God cannot be conceived as a human-independent ontic logos. The order in which one is set as the beneficiary of grace is 'personally indexed'; it discloses itself in non-substitutable, subjectively mediated 'epiphanies'. In view of this, it is surprising that in a reply to a similar point made by Michael L. Morgan Taylor should deny that his 'account of religious faith rules out any substantive view, up to the most "transcendent" and non-human-centred'.[22] While Taylor is entitled, on general epistemological grounds, to say that his account does not strictly speaking 'rule out' such traditional, non-human-centred theological views, they are hard to square with his argument, and no less so than the non-theistic view.

If Taylor is right, then the self-defining life goods of the modern identity may require more than secular sources. In his view, secular conceptions of the constitutive good fare badly by comparison with theism as empowering sources both of benevolence and of expressive self-realization. Openness to God's grace and mystery protects us from the dangers of reversal in the pursuit of justice and the 'amelioration of the condition of mankind'; it helps us avoid the slide to subjectivism in the pursuit of authenticity; and it enables, or might enable, a reconciliation of these ideals without too much cost. In other words, theism promises a fuller realization of the modern identity than secularism, and on this account, suggests itself as one route to recovery from the malaise of modernity. But in Taylor's view, theism provides an even more promising orientation than secular humanism for dealing with another contemporary malaise, something which Taylor did not explore in *Sources of the Self* but which he foregrounds in more recent work. For up to this point, we have been considering moral sources in relation to *life* goods and the conflicts that arise from that relation. In addition to life goods, however, there are goods – in the sense of things that matter to us, things that we find or seek meaning in – that go 'beyond life': above all, there is suffering and death.

Taylor calls a moral outlook that takes life goods, or human flourishing, to be the sole location of worth 'exclusive humanism' (*CM* 19). Enlightenment naturalism, the dominant outlook of modernity, is a form of exclusive humanism. Like all forms of humanism, exclusive humanism affirms the good of human flourishing. But whereas non-exclusive humanisms understand human flourishing in relation to something higher, transcendent or 'beyond life', exclusive humanism denies the legitimacy of anything other than the realization of life goods. For non-exclusive humanism, 'the point of things isn't exhausted by life, the fullness of life, even the goodness of life' (*CM* 20). And 'what matters beyond life doesn't matter just because it sustains life; otherwise it wouldn't be "beyond life" in the proper sense' (*CM* 20). To see a good in something beyond life invariably involves a certain renunciation or 'decentring' of the self. And in Taylor's view discomfort, even repulsion, at this provides a powerful motivation for exclusive humanism. Exclusive humanists are sensitive to talk of anything 'beyond life', Taylor maintains, because it threatens to 'reverse the revolution' that introduced the modern moral order of rights, the affirmation of ordinary life, the relief of suffering and so forth. But while, as we have seen, Taylor acknowledges the real gains achieved by the secular revolution (or the Enlightenment project) in this dimension, he does not see them as providing a reason for asserting 'the metaphysical primacy of life' (*CM* 29). For the assertion of the metaphysical primacy of life has led to a 'widespread inability to give human meaning to death and suffering, other than as dangers to be avoided or combated' (*CM* 24). Exclusive humanism, or the idea that there is nothing of intrinsic value beyond human flourishing, is 'dangerously partial and incomplete, particularly because it cannot see that even things that negate this flourishing – solitary death, unremarked suffering, waning powers – can have the deepest human significance, just because they have more than human significance' (*CM* 109). An outlook that opens us to the meaning to be found in suffering and death, without thereby forfeiting the life goods that define human flourishing, is thus much preferable to one based on the metaphysical primacy of life. Again, Christian *agapē* and Buddhist *karuna* are Taylor's exemplars for how this can be achieved. They belong to non-exclusive humanisms in the sense that their affirmation of human flourishing (their commitment to the 'practical primacy of life' that makes them *humanisms*) is powered by a decentred or self-renouncing stance in relation to the transcendent (their commitment to the metaphysical primacy of a constitutive good beyond human life that makes them *non-exclusive* humanisms).

When Taylor announces, on behalf of non-exclusive humanism, that 'the metaphysical primacy of life is wrong and stifling and that its continued dominance puts in danger the practical primacy' (*CM* 29), he could be interpreted as simply expressing his particular religious allegiance, as merely opening up the religious perspective as an option. But there is much more to it than that. For in Taylor's view, there is something about human nature that prevents human beings from resting content with their flourishing. As he puts it, 'human beings have an ineradicable bent to respond to something beyond life' (*CM* 27), and he observes that 'the insufficiency of human flourishing as the unique focus of our lives ... recurs throughout all of human history and cultures, albeit in very different ways' (*CM* 106). This bent towards something beyond life is thus another of Taylor's 'anthropological constants'. One of the central ways in which it manifests itself is in the perennial human fascination with death and violence. Taylor then draws attention to how restlessness with human flourishing as the sole purpose of life finds articulation within a modern, non-theist perspective – namely, in Nietzsche's thought and more generally in 'the immanent counter-Enlightenment'.[23] The Nietzschean immanent counter-Enlightenment 'takes us beyond by incorporating a fascination with the negation of life, with death and suffering', and in this respect it reflects 'our nature as *homo religiosus*' (*CM* 28). But it is an *immanent* counter-Enlightenment because it has no place for a constituting *good* beyond life, that is to say, a good that transcends life. It too puts in jeopardy the practical primacy of life, not as exclusive humanism does, by asserting the metaphysical primacy of life (which it finds 'stifling'), but by having no *further* source beyond life, a source that can reorient us in relation to the destruction of life. Taylor thereby expresses sympathy for René Girard's view that, as Taylor puts it, 'the only way to escape fully the draw towards violence lies somewhere in the turn to transcendence – that is, through the full-hearted love of some good beyond life' (*CM* 28–9).[24]

But as we have seen, there is more at stake in the acknowledgement of a good beyond life than its ability to redirect the human fascination with death and violence back towards life. For there is also the issue of the intrinsic meaning of death and suffering itself. The question of the meaning of death, and the options available to the modern identity for answering it, in a sense departs from the diagnostic agenda set out in *Sources of the Self*. For the central issue of that agenda is the relation between moral sources and the chief life goods of modernity. The malaise Taylor attempts to diagnose relates to an anxiety over the adequacy of secular sources to empower the good, particularly the life goods of benevolence, authentic self-expression and the reconciliation of these ideals. Even the critique of instrumental reason, according to Taylor, should be seen as involving a retrieval of the hidden life goods underlying the Enlightenment project. The work of 'retrieval' undertaken in *Sources of the Self* (*SS* 520) is primarily directed towards uncovering moral sources as empowerers of life goods. But the issue of the meaning of death, and the distinctive forms of anxiety relating to death at large in contemporary secular societies, requires different treatment. It is an issue Taylor takes up in his Gifford Lectures, 'Living in a Secular Age', where he also explores new directions for understanding the discontent arising from the levelling effects of the modern moral order and the secular experience of time.[25]

I began this chapter by remarking on Taylor's celebration of modern liberal democracy, and it is appropriate that we conclude by returning to it. For while in many respects modern secular civilization is dangerously unstable, and while it tends to stifle the needs of the spirit, Taylor has no doubts that in one crucial dimension, secularization represented an unambiguous epistemic gain: it signalled the demise of the 'project of Christendom' (*CM* 17). The secular culture of rights separates itself from any ultimate moral vision, and this has enabled it 'to call political power to book against a yardstick of fundamental human requirements, universally applied' (*CM* 18). In doing so, secular liberal societies have been able to further the goals of freedom and justice that are central to the Christian ethic itself. For this reason alone there can be no question of a return to pre-modern theism. For Taylor, it is the project of modernity, rather than anything like the project of Christendom, that promises a fuller realization of Christianity's basic ideals.

Conclusion

How should we sum up Taylor's achievement? Taylor continues to publish at a prolific rate and for this reason alone it would be rash to answer in a firm voice. The style in which he writes, his preference for clarifying the stakes of an ongoing debate over the construction of systematic theory, also makes it difficult to reach anything like a definitive assessment of his contribution to philosophy and the human sciences. None the less, in the course of this book we have seen that an ambitious philosophical project unifies Taylor's work and that his success in prosecuting his project is uneven. By way of a conclusion, then, let us reflect briefly on some of the main strengths and weaknesses of Taylor's central arguments.

One of Taylor's chief aims is to rehabilitate the idea of an ontology of the human. As Taylor understands it, an ontology of the human – or philosophical anthropology – is an account of the distinctive, essential features of human reality. It is philosophical rather than empirical because it investigates the transcendental conditions of human activity, or in other words, the standards that have to be met if a form of life is to be recognizable *as* human at all. In Taylor's view, a deeply entrenched set of preconceptions about the nature of knowledge impedes this kind of reflection. In the modern world, Taylor contends, there is a widespread *presumption* that genuine knowledge, *whatever its object*, involves the adoption of a disengaged perspective, that is, a neutralization of the meaning or significance things have for us as 'subjects' or 'agents'. If this is a sound presumption, then an ontology of the human is fundamentally misconceived, for the distinctive features of human reality *are* the features that supposedly belong to us as subjects or agents, that is to say, the features excluded from the outset by the modern disengaged or 'naturalist' epistemology. Now Taylor has plenty of arguments to suggest that this presumption is not in fact sound. The idea that human self-understanding must *in principle* conform to a certain object-neutral model of knowledge has been responsible for bad science, and it misleads philosophers into thinking that embodied experience can be captured in a notion of 'sensory data' or 'mental representation'. But more important, Taylor argues convincingly that disengaged knowledge is itself only intelligible on account of the never-fully-articulated 'background' knowledge we have as agents. Admittedly, in developing these arguments Taylor is hardly blazing a trail – there is little he says that cannot be found in the existential phenomenologies of Merleau-Ponty and Heidegger or the philosophical hermeneutics of Gadamer.[1] Taylor's achievement here consists in having clarified and brought out the continuing relevance of their critique of naturalism.

Taylor argues persuasively that if we scratch beneath the surface of the classical debates in modern epistemology and philosophy of mind, we find another agenda, a hidden but deeper set of controversies involving conflicting notions of what it is like to be a human being or a 'subject'. He follows a similar strategy in his thinking about language: by attending to the rival philosophical anthropologies that underlie modern theories of meaning, Taylor forces us to reconsider the basic options facing the philosophy of language. It is evident, Taylor maintains, that language must be understood at once as part of the natural history of the species and as a sphere of autonomous, *sui generis* norms. If we factor in both these requirements, it becomes plausible to suppose that the normativity of language – the fact that in language we are able to 'get things right' – is grounded not, as the standard theories maintain, in the ability of words or sentences to designate objects, but in the primordial human capacity for *expression*. As Taylor makes clear, this is a crucial insight for two main reasons. First, it enables us to think of all kinds of articulated expression, and not just those that correspond to objects in literally true sentences, as bearers of meaning and validity. Poetry as much as prose, stories as much as theories, for instance, are able to 'get it right'. Second, and more provocatively, poetic and narrative articulations are in a sense more fundamental to language, because they draw on powers that must already be in place for us to be able to describe the world in a prosaic or literal way. The *creation* of meaning therefore cannot be treated as a derivative or accidental feature of language, and this is why Taylor calls for a paradigm shift away from the standard designative theories. Of course, Taylor himself is not the originator of the expressivist theory he defends. But he unquestionably breathes new life into the expressivist tradition, he highlights its great significance for contemporary debates, and he provides us with a useful map for finding our way about its complex landscape.

Taylor's expressivism is a pluralist philosophy. It attempts to do justice to human diversity, both the diverse ways of understanding the human (expressed in the arts as well as the sciences) and the diverse ways of being human (expressed across individuals and cultures). But it might seem that Taylor's pluralist aspiration clashes with his desire to rehabilitate ontology. For as we have seen, an ontology of the human concerns itself with putatively *essential* features of human reality. If, as expressivism insists, there are multiple modes of knowing, if there is no single foundation on which human knowledge rests, can the 'essentialist' language of philosophical anthropology really be countenanced? Certainly, many contemporary philosophers are suspicious of such talk. And does not the diversity of human practices, the plural ways of being human, suggest that there is not just something conceptually misplaced about the idea of an ontology of the human, but something practically dangerous too? Again, there are many theorists who regard Taylor's invocation of 'human constants' as a warrant for ethnocentrism. Now one of the great merits of Taylor's expressivism is that it dispels the anxiety motivating these questions. In relation to the first, Taylor offers a model of philosophical argumentation that shows how justified claims about the limits of subjectivity are possible, without supposing them to be incontestable. Such 'transcendental arguments' identify essential features of human reality in a non-essentialist way, although only a thin or formal ontology can be established by this means. In relation to the second question, Taylor manages to show that the human constants identified by an ontology of the human need not place unwarranted or arbitrary limits on our ability to bear witness to diversity. On the contrary, they set the conditions for any appreciation of significant difference at all, that is to say, difference we can either learn from or criticize. Overcoming ethnocentrism, Taylor shows, is a matter of understanding the historical contingency of the limits we do draw rather than abandoning them altogether. While Taylor has been a little short on examples of how his model of the anthropological learning process works in practice, his historical studies of the rise of the modern identity indicate how fruitful an ontologically framed approach to cultural difference can be.

However, it is also true that some of Taylor's ontological claims are insufficiently backed up by his arguments. Most notably, his attempts at fashioning a necessary connection between the self and the good stand in need of further support. So, for instance, Taylor's thesis that the unity of a life must be articulated in a quest-like narrative that situates the self in relation to the good, like his claim that the self must be sustained by moral sources, is not established with the clarity required to earn it a place in an ontology of the human. And while Taylor's conception of the self is not as 'moralist' or 'intellectualist' as some of his critics suppose, Taylor's 'top-down' approach – his focus on ideals and aspirations – does need to be balanced by a consideration of other aspects of identity. But notwithstanding the gaps in Taylor's moral ontology, and the undeniable fact that there is more to the self than the things that matter to it on account of their worthiness, Taylor's challenge to the dominant paradigms in moral philosophy is formidable. The very question of the meaning of a life, and the ability to be moved in qualitatively different ways by contact with constitutive goods, certainly invite more sophisticated treatment than we find in mainstream ethics. Nor, as Taylor shows, is modern moral philosophy's neglect of such issues accidental. For it reflects the predominance of proceduralist theories of practical reason in modern ethics, theories that define 'morality', and the kind of reasoning proper to it, in a narrow, formalist manner. While sketchy in details, Taylor's 'substantive' model of practical reason offers an attractive alternative to proceduralisms, both utilitarian and Kantian. First, it allows the content of a specific moral demand (understood broadly as a strong value), rather than a generalizable testing procedure, to do the work of justification. Second, the work of justification is not abstracted from the motivations a person has to live in accordance with a given demand, since strong values are expressive of a person's identity, not contingent to it. Taylor's substantive model of practical reason can thus rightly treat general moral scepticism as a side-issue that rarely impinges on practice. And third, by redescribing the alleged autonomy of the 'moral', or the priority of 'right', as the expression of a 'hypergood', it shows how the peculiar force that demands for universal justice and benevolence have in the modern world can be preserved internally to an ontologically grounded meta-ethic.

Until recently, the idea that an ontology of the human is required for making sense of contemporary social issues would have seemed quite implausible, at least amongst theorists in the liberal tradition. While many are still sceptical, there can be no doubt that the contemporary scene in political theory is much more hospitable to ontological thinking than it has been, not least due to the impact of Taylor's work.[2] Taylor's exposition of the limits of atomist ontology, the social conditions of self-identity, and the importance of self-identity for politics are now widely appreciated amongst liberals as well as communitarians. Indeed, they are so well appreciated that the debate has moved on, and while it may be a measure of Taylor's success that all liberals are holists now, it does leave some of his earlier work in this field looking a little dated. Taylor's contributions to democratic theory, on the other hand, and in particular his analysis of the dangers besetting modern liberal democracies, testify to the continuing relevance of his ontological framework. The citizens of a viable modern liberal democracy, Taylor shows, need strong sources of common identification; but they must also accommodate – and within limits facilitate – differentiation, especially in view of growing multiculturalism and globalization. Taylor shows great acumen in diagnosing the dilemmas generated by the dynamics of democratic exclusion and inclusion. However, it is fair to say that his analysis of the ills afflicting modern liberal democracies is more convincing than the remedies he proposes for them, as the instabilities in his account of the predicament facing the Canadian federation illustrate. Furthermore, while Taylor's focus on the ontological issue of patriotic self-definition raises a serious challenge to procedural liberalism, it is arguable that he exaggerates the functional importance of common identification in contemporary liberal societies, and that he underestimates the resources available to a procedural but holist theory of democracy for dealing with this problem.

As originally conceived by Marx, the task of a critical theory of society is 'the self-clarification of the struggles and wishes of the age'.[3] By Taylor's own reckoning, the validity of philosophical anthropology turns crucially on its ability to facilitate this task. In his forcefully presented view, the distinctive struggles and wishes of the modern age can only be clarified by considering how modern subjects are situated in relation to the good. Taylor is convinced that in order to understand the struggles for democracy, freedom and justice that characterize the modern world, as well as modern strivings for authenticity, meaningful community and expressive unity with nature, we need to regard them as oriented towards a fuller realization of life goods or strong values. Taylor points out, fairly, that most of the positions in the philosophical debate around modernity fail to accommodate this basic insight. He then argues, in his most distinctive and original contribution to this debate, that the unease surrounding the pursuit of the modern goods (or rather hypergoods) of freedom, universal benevolence and justice, and authenticity has its roots in the questionable adequacy of the sources required for sustaining them. This argumentative strategy works well as an account of the limits of both the 'Enlightenment project' and 'subjectivist' interpretations of art and expressive fulfilment. But as a diagnosis of the times, Taylor's theory is too narrow and it lacks a convincing explanatory framework. Like his approach to the self, his theory of modernity has a regrettable 'top-down' or idealist character.

However, Taylor's reflections on the relative adequacy of secular and non-secular moral sources pose a serious question to those who, again like Marx, are concerned with the preservation of 'radical hope in history' (*SS* 520). In Taylor's view, such hope is groundless unless human beings are capable of radical self-transformation for the good. That human beings do have this capacity, Taylor thinks, is the chief lesson of the Judaeo-Christian experience. By opening themselves to God's unconditional love, by surrendering to his grace, human beings can be energized into realizing the highest moral ideals. Left to their own resources, however, human beings are unable to attain this love; indeed they seem destined to repeat the 'ugly dialectic' that has plagued the radical humanist spirit throughout history. Taylor thus argues that contact with a non-human source of goodness offers the *only* prospect of preserving radical hope in history. Taken by itself, Taylor's argument is not compelling. But for non-theists who are not yet ready to give up their historical hope, it is troubling. For they must ask themselves if they have a better way of sustaining their hope in the human. It is now up to secular humanists to meet Taylor's challenge.

Notes

Introduction

1 Maurice Merleau-Ponty, *Phénoménologie de la Perception* (1945), p. xiv; *Phenomenology of Perception*, tr. Colin Smith (1962), p. xix.

2 Charles Taylor, 'Embodied Agency', in Henry Pietersma ed., *Merleau Ponty: Critical Essays* (1989), p. 2.

3 See Taylor, 'Introduction' to *HAL* and *PHS*, p. 1. Elsewhere, Taylor defines philosophical anthropology as 'the study of the basic categories in which man and his behaviour is to be described and explained' (*EB* 4). The term 'philosophical anthropology' is sometimes used to refer to a particular school of philosophy in Germany, one associated with the work of Max Scheler and Helmut Plessner. Scheler is an important reference point for Merleau-Ponty, but only indirectly, via Merleau-Ponty, for Taylor himself.

4 See Hans-Georg Gadamer, *Truth and Method*, tr. Joel Weinsheimer and Donald G. Marshall (1993).

5 I should also say that Taylor is not an anti-systematic philosopher either. In their very avoidance of systematicity, anti-systematic philosophers – such as Derrida, Levinas and Deleuze – can be as much oriented by system-building as systematic ones, and productive of equally difficult technical vocabularies.

6 Geoffrey Warnock recollects that Taylor was 'commissioned' to instruct the Oxford philosophical elite attending J. L. Austin's 'Saturday Morning' classes of Merleau-Ponty's *Phenomenology of Perception* (see Warnock, 'Saturday Mornings', in Isaiah Berlin et al., *Essays on J. L. Austin* [1973], p. 32). Taylor then participated in A. J. Ayer's Tuesday evening meetings (see A. J. Ayer, *Part of My Life* [1977], p. 183) and Taylor's book on Hegel was initially commissioned by Ayer for

inclusion in a series he was editing for Penguin Press. In 1958 Taylor participated in what Wolfe Mays later referred to as the first public discussion of phenomenology in Britain since Gilbert Ryle's review of Heidegger's *Being and Time* in 1932 (see Wolfe Mays and S. C. Brown eds, *Linguistic Analysis and Phenomenology* [1972], p. 19). The discussion – chaired by Ryle – took place as a symposium of the Joint Session of the Mind Association and the Aristotelian Society. The proceedings of the symposium, including Taylor's paper and Ayer's reply, are reprinted in Harold A. Durfee ed., *Analytic Philosophy and Phenomenology* (1976).

7   Taylor, review of *La Philosophie Analytique. Cahiers de Royaumont*, *Philosophical Review*, 73 (1964), p. 133. The absurdity of the Oxbridge attitude to Continental philosophy is illustrated in the following anecdote from Marjorie Grene, an American phenomenologist: 'Some years ago the then President of the Yale Philosophy Club told me they had two visitors at succeeding meetings. First came Charles Taylor, who publicly avowed his debt to Merleau-Ponty; then came Miss Anscombe, now Professor of Logic and Metaphysics at Cambridge, who remarked, as I'm told she often does, "Of course everybody knows everything written on the continent is just gas," and then asked if there was anything important going on in *British* philosophy, declared, "Yes, there is one young man who is really a philosophical genius, and that's Charles Taylor"' (Marjorie Grene, *Philosophy In and Out of Europe* [1987], p. 37).

When it comes to French post-structuralist thought, Taylor can lapse into the odd contemptuous remark himself. But at least he acknowledges a problem: 'I confess that I have not been entirely cured of the scoffer's disease', he writes (review of Peter Dews's *Logics of Disintegration*, *New Left Review*, 170 [1988], p. 111).

8   'Charles Taylor – un philosophe enraciné dans le monde', an interview with Charles Taylor, *Le Devoir* (14 December 1992).

9   'Charles Taylor en entrevue à La Presse', *La Presse* (16 September 1995).

10   'Charles Taylor – un philosophe enraciné dans le monde'.

11   'Oxford Petition for Disarmament', *The Times* (8 May 1954).

12   Heseltine would later earn a reputation as a bullish critic of the Labour Party's disarmament stance.

13   *The Times* (22 June 1954).

14   See Christopher Driver, *The Disarmers: A Study in Protest* (1964), p. 74.

15   See the Annual Report of the Campaign for Nuclear Disarmament, 1959 (CND archive, Library of the London School of Economics). As reported by Elizabeth Anscombe, Taylor was also 'one of the leaders of the CND revolt against Hugh Gaitskell', the Labour Party leader at that time (G. E. M. Anscombe, 'Mechanism and Ideology', *New Statesman* [5 February 1965], p. 206).

16   The four co-founders were Taylor, Stuart Hall, Gabriel Pearson and

Ralph Samuel. In a reminiscence on the 'exiles and migrants' who made up the founding group, Stuart Hall recalls Taylor as a 'French-Canadian Rhodes scholar (as well as that even more perplexing phenomenon, a sort of Catholic Marxist)'. See Robin Archer and the Oxford University Socialist Discussion Group eds, *Out of Apathy: Voices of the New Left Thirty Years On* (1989), p. 28. Whatever the accuracy of this recollection, it is an intriguing image.

17 As recorded by April Carter in John Minnion and Philip Bolsover eds, *The CND Story: The First 25 Years of CND in the Words of the People Involved* (1983).

18 George Clark, 'Second Wind – The Story of the Campaign and the Committee of 100', Workshop Publications (1963).

19 Peter Sedgwick, 'The Two New Lefts', in D. Widgery ed., *The Left in Britain 1956–1968* (1976), pp. 131–55, p. 132.

20 'Charles Taylor – un philosophe enraciné dans le monde'.

21 Taylor addressed a francophone audience with his contributions to the Montreal journal *Cité Libre*. This was a liberal, reformist, anti-clerical and anti-separatist publication, established in 1950 by a group including Pierre Elliott Trudeau. The journal played its part in Quebec's 'Quiet Revolution': the liberalization of Quebec's rigidly Catholic and conservative political culture in the post-war period. Between 1962 and 1966 Taylor contributed many articles to the magazine, and was an editor from August 1964 to February 1966. The other main forum for Taylor's journalism in the 1960s was the anglophone bimonthly, *Canadian Dimension*. Taylor was a founding associate of the journal, its Quebec correspondent from its formation in 1963 to 1965, a contributing editor the following year, and a regular contributor of articles until 1971. Like the *Universities and Left Review*, *Canadian Dimension* was a journal of the New Left that prided itself on ideological and financial independence. It also showed a commitment to openness and pluralism within a broad left perspective, and was characterized by a similar humanist optimism: 'we have not become so disillusioned, so swamped by commercialism, so paralysed by the bomb', the editor declares in the first issue, 'that we have halted the search for "the good society" and the use of reason as a guide for action' (*Canadian Dimension*, 1 [Summer 1963], p. 1). The journal also invites comparison with *Universities and Left Review* and *New Left Review* on account of its extraordinary initial success, reaching 5,000 sales by the end of its third year, a remarkable number for a journal of its kind in Canada.

22 As Taylor recalls in an interview in 1989, Trudeau spoke for Taylor at platform meetings in the 1963 campaign. Taylor describes a 'great moment of reminiscence' when, waiting to be interviewed by Radio Canada on Trudeau's retirement in 1984, he saw footage of 'a much younger Pierre and behind him, "votez Charles Taylor"' (*Idler*, 26 [November and December 1989], p. 27).

23 See André Lamoureux, *Le NDP et le Quebec 1958–1985* (1985), p. 145.
24 See Desmond Morton, *The New Democrats, 1961–86: The Politics of Change* (1986), p. 64. In his memoirs, Trudeau recollects that Jean Marchend – whom the Liberals were particularly keen to recruit – had negotiated with them 'safe' ridings (seats) for Gerard Pelletier, ex-editor of *La Presse*, and himself, as part of a deal that would see all three of them join the party. See Pierre Elliott Trudeau, *Memoirs* (1993), p. 77.
25 For the record, in 1962 Taylor gained 6,388 votes (12.5 per cent of total cast); in 1963, 8,855 votes (19.3 per cent of total cast); and in 1965, 14, 929 votes (29.1 per cent of total cast). The NDP vote in Quebec over the three elections was 4.4 per cent, 7.1 per cent and 12.0 per cent respectively. Figures drawn from the *Canada Chief Electoral Office Reports*, and Lamoureux, *Le NDP et le Quebec*, p. 205.
26 Morton, *The New Democrats*, p. 86. For reports that Taylor had been earmarked as incumbent national leader, see 'NDP Looking for Youth to Lead Party to Power', *Financial Post* (18 February 1967), p. 13; *MacLean's Magazine*, 82 (October 1969), p. 5; and 'Report from Parliament Hill', *Monetary Times* (February 1969).
27 See, for example, 'Federal-Provincial Planning' (20–2 November 1964), 'Towards a Canadian Nationalism' (August 1966), 'A Budget of Urban Problems', NDP Discussion Papers (11 September 1969), in the National Library of Canada.
28 C. W. Gonick, 'Taylor's Socialism for 1970: A Comment', *Canadian Dimension*, 5, 8 (February 1969), pp. 41–3, p. 41.
29 These were published as 'The Stakes of Constitutional Reform' and 'Shared and Divergent Values', both republished in *RS*. For more on the context of these works, see Guy Laforest, 'Philosophy and Political Judgement in a Multinational Federation', in J. Tully ed., *Philosophy in an Age of Pluralism* (1994). Taylor's contribution to the 1985 commission was 'Alternative Futures: Legitimacy, Identity, and Alienation in Late-Twentieth-Century Canada', also in *RS*.
30 See, for instance, Taylor, 'Où est le danger?', *Liberté*, 83 (June 1989), pp. 13–16.
31 See Charles Taylor, 'Les Ethnies dans une société "normale"' (1) and (2), *La Presse* (21 and 22 November 1995).
32 See 'Group Wants Healthier Post-referendum Climate', *Gazette* (10 April 1996).
33 'Charles Taylor – un philosophe enraciné dans le monde'.

Chapter 1 Linguistic Philosophy and Phenomenology

1 P. F. Strawson, 'The Post-Linguistic Thaw', *Times Literary Supplement* (9 September 1960). The article was published anonymously. Its author is identified by Jonathan Rée, 'English Philosophy in the Fifties', *Radical Philosophy*, 65 (Autumn 1993), pp. 3–21.

2 As Gilbert Ryle put it: 'The distinction between the vehicle and what it conveys is what distinguishes factual enquiries like psychology and philology, from conceptual enquiries, like logic and philosophy', in A. J. Ayer et al., *The Revolution in Philosophy* (1957), p. 8.

3 For accounts of the relation between the linguistic school and earlier analytic philosophy, see the essays by Strawson and Warnock in Ayer et al., *The Revolution in Philosophy*; and James O. Urmson, *Philosophical Analysis* (1956).

4 Taylor, 'Phenomenology and Linguistic Analysis', *Proceedings of the Aristotelian Society*, 33 (supplementary volume, 1959).

5 Ibid., p. 109.

6 Ibid., p. 110.

7 Taylor, 'The Pre-Objective World', co-authored with Michael Kullman, in *Review of Metaphysics*, 12, 1 (September 1958); reprinted in M. Nathanson ed., *Essays in Phenomenology* (1966).

8 Maurice Merleau-Ponty, *Phénoménologie de la Perception* (1945), p. xi; *Phenomenology of Perception*, tr. Colin Smith (1962), p. xvi.

9 Taylor, 'Phenomenology and Linguistic Analysis', p. 93.

10 Taylor and Kullman, 'The Pre-Objective World', p. 123, and 'Phenomenology and Linguistic Analysis', p. 95.

11 Taylor, 'Phenomenology and Linguistic Analysis', p. 95.

12 Cited in Taylor and Kullman, 'The Pre-Objective World', p. 122.

13 Immanuel Kant, *Kritik der reinen Vernunft* (1787), B 75, A 51; *Critique of Pure Reason*, tr. Norman Kemp Smith (1929).

14 Taylor and Kullman, 'The Pre-Objective World', p. 132.

15 Ibid., p. 134.

16 Ibid.

17 Ibid., p. 135.

Chapter 2 Science, Action and the Mind

1 See Thomas Nagel, *The View from Nowhere* (1984).

2 See Bernard Williams, *Descartes: The Project of Pure Enquiry* (1978).

3 Taylor, 'Understanding in Human Science', *Review of Metaphysics*, 34, 1 (September 1980), p. 31.

4 See Clifford Geertz, 'The Strange Estrangement: Taylor and the Natural Sciences', in J. Tully ed., *Philosophy in an Age of Pluralism* (1994), pp. 83–95. Stephen Toulmin makes a similar criticism in Robert Borger and Frank Cioffi eds, *Explanation in the Behavioural Sciences* (1970), p. 22.

5 See, amongst other places, Richard Rorty, 'A Reply to Dreyfus and Taylor', *Review of Metaphysics*, 34, 1 (September 1980). For further criticisms of Taylor on this score, see Joseph Rouse, *Knowledge and Power* (1987).

6 Taylor, 'Understanding in Human Science', p. 28.

7 These questions are addressed most systematically in *EB*. Other works in which Taylor examines the plausibility of behaviourism are 'Psychological Behaviourism', in Paul Edwards ed., *The Encyclopaedia of Philosophy* (1967), pp. 516–20; and 'The Explanation of Purposive Behaviour', in Borger and Cioffi eds, *Explanation in the Behavioural Sciences*. Taylor also summarizes his position on behaviourism in his contribution to Paul Ricoeur, *Main Trends in Philosophy* (1979), pp. 149–54.

8 Taylor, 'The Explanation of Purposive Behaviour,' p. 64.

9 Even before the publication of *The Explanation of Behaviour* behaviourism was a dying force. As Taylor later wrote, 'my first book was a vicious attack on, a stab to the heart of, behaviourist psychology'. But 'the victim was dead before the knife entered its vitals' ('Reply and Re-articulation', in Tully ed., *Philosophy in an Age of Pluralism*, p. 236).

10 Taylor, 'Peaceful Coexistence in Psychology', originally published in *Social Research*, 40, 1 (Spring 1973), pp. 55–82.

11 An almost identical conclusion was reached *vis-à-vis* earlier forms of behaviourism by Merleau-Ponty in *La Structure du Comportement* (1942), a text Taylor refers to in *EB*. For the English translation see *The Structure of Behaviour*, tr. Alden L. Fisher (1963).

12 Stuart Sutherland, in Borger and Cioffi eds, *Explanation in the Behavioural Sciences*, p. 138.

13 See, for example, Norman Malcolm, 'Explaining Behaviour', *Philosophical Review*, 76 (1967), pp. 97–104.

14 Richard J. Bernstein, *Praxis and Action* (1971), p. 298.

15 Thanks to David Macarthur for pointing this out to me.

16 A point raised by Bernstein in *Praxis and Action*.

17 See, among other places, Taylor, 'Philosophy of Mind', contribution to *The Concise Encyclopaedia of Western Philosophy and Philosophers*, new revised edition (1991); 'Overcoming Epistemology', in Kenneth Baynes, James Bohman and Thomas McCarthy eds, *After Philosophy* (1987) (reprinted in *PA*); and 'Foundationalism and the Inner–Outer Distinction', in Nicholas H. Smith ed., *Reading McDowell: On Mind and World* (forthcoming).

18 Taylor, 'Philosophy of Mind', p. 235.

19 As Taylor puts it, starting with the notion of embodied agency 'entails abandoning the inner/outer sorting altogether, and hence the portmanteau categories of "mind" and "mental" '. Taylor recommends an approach to human subjectivity that takes us 'outside the classification in which the "philosophy of mind" figures as a term'. Ibid., p. 237. Taylor, 'Lichtung or Lebensform', originally published in German translation in Brian McGuiness et al. eds, *Der Löwe spricht . . . und wir können ihn nicht verstchen* (1991).

20 See also Taylor, 'Sense Data Revisited', in G. F. Macdonald ed., *Perception and Identity* (1979).

21 In S. Mitchell and M. Rosen eds, *The Need for Interpretation* (1983). Reprinted in *HAL* as 'Cognitive Psychology'.

22 See Taylor, 'Peaceful Coexistence in Psychology'.
23 See Taylor, 'What is Involved in a Genetic Psychology?', in Theodore Mischel ed., *Cognitive Development and Epistemology* (1971). Reprinted in *HAL*.

Chapter 3 The Romantic Legacy

1 I use the term 'Romantic tradition' loosely enough to include Hegel, though Hegel explicitly distanced himself from the Romantic movement in a stricter sense. I also use it to include philosophers not normally identified as Idealists, such as Herder.
2 Taylor, 'Genesis', review of *The Structure of Behaviour* by Merleau-Ponty, *New Statesman*, 70 (3 September 1965), p. 327.
3 Taylor, 'Reply and Re-articulation', in J. Tully ed., *Philosophy in an Age of Pluralism* (1994), p. 234.
4 In a couple of more recent interviews, Taylor indicates that it was indeed Hegel's theory of modernity that aroused his interest, and it is this aspect of Hegel's philosophy that continues to be most important for him. See 'Balancing the Humours' and 'From Philosophical Anthropology to the Politics of Recognition: An Interview with Charles Taylor', *Thesis Eleven*, 52 (February 1998), pp. 103–12. That there may also have been a theological motivation for engaging with Hegel is suggested by Taylor's article 'Clericalism', *Downside Review*, 78 (1960).
5 Taylor, 'The Validity of Transcendental Arguments', originally published in *Proceedings of the Aristotelian Society* (1978–9).
6 Kant, *Kritik der reinen Vernunft* (1787), A 112; *Critique of Pure Reason*, tr. Norman Kemp Smith (1929).
7 Taylor's central interpretative claim about Hegel is that he continued and radicalized the method of transcendental argumentation initiated by Kant. Like Kant before him, Hegel in the *Phenomenology of Spirit* sought to expose the contradictions at play in the empiricist theory of knowledge and to move beyond it in a manner satisfactory to reason. But Hegel departs from Kant in his understanding of where transcendental reason takes us once the old model has been left behind. Taylor's sympathies here are mixed, and at times hard to decipher. While in Taylor's essay 'The Opening Arguments of the *Phenomenology*' (in Alasdair MacIntyre ed., *Hegel: A Collection of Critical Essays* [1972]), and parts of *H*, he clearly sides with Hegel for drawing out the anti-representationalist implications of transcendental reason more thoroughly than Kant, he also repudiates Hegel, as Kant would have done, for carrying the claims of reason too far. As we shall see presently, if Kant understates the power of transcendental argument, in Taylor's view, Hegel overstates it.

8   See G. W. F. Hegel, *Phenomenology of Spirit*, tr. A. V. Miller (1977).
9   Taylor, 'The Opening Arguments of the *Phenomenology*', p. 186.
10 Taylor acknowledges that Kant, Hegel, Merleau-Ponty and indeed the later Wittgenstein are not the only philosophers to attack the mentalist conception of the subject. Nietzsche and neo-Nietzscheans also target it. But the problem with Nietzsche's approach, according to Taylor, is that it does not replace the representationalist conception of knowledge with a better one. While this is right, there is something question-begging about it. For the anti-representationalist stance of the Nietzschean may not be motivated by epistemological considerations at all. I pursue this line further in 'Reason after Meaning', *Philosophy and Social Criticism* 23, 1 (1997), pp. 131–40.
11 For a defence of Hegel from Taylor's charge that Hegel's philosophy is incompatible with Christian faith, see Stephen Houlgate, *Freedom, Truth and History* (1991), pp. 188–97.
12 This makes it arguable that Hegel was not an expressivist at all (Michael Rosen, *Hegel's Dialectic and its Criticism* [1982], p. 124). For the expressivist, according to Taylor, thought is shaped and constituted by its medium. But for Hegel, Rosen remarks, the progress of consciousness is 'the process of emancipation of Thought from such an expressive dependence on its medium'. It is the fact that language is capable of communicating thought without shaping it that makes absolute or philosophical truth possible. In reply, Taylor could concede that in the end reason or philosophy and not art is the most adequate medium of expression for Hegel, and this is where he departs from expressivism. Moreover, Taylor would reject Rosen's overly 'metaphysical' reading of Hegel, which takes Spirit to have its own element, 'Thought', which is 'independent of its embodiment' (Rosen, *Hegel's Dialectic and its Criticism*, p. 132).
13 The non-metaphysical turn in Hegel interpretation is summed up and advanced by Paul Redding, *Hegel's Hermeneutics* (1996). The trend is traced back to a study of Hegel that pre-dates Taylor's: Klaus Hartmann's 'Hegel: A Non-Metaphysical View', in MacIntyre ed., *Hegel*. Later, it is exemplified in studies of Hegel such as Alan White, *Absolute Knowledge* (1983); David Kolb, *The Critique of Pure Modernity* (1986); Terry Pinkard, *Hegel's Dialectic* (1988); and most influentially, Robert Pippin, *Hegel's Idealism* (1989).
14 Pippin, *Hegel's Idealism*, p. 9.
15 Ibid., p. 247.
16 Ibid., p. 206.
17 Ibid., p. 12.
18 Another of the post-metaphysical interpreters of Hegel, Terry Pinkard, follows Taylor in reading Hegel's dialectic as a chain of transcendental arguments, but denies that Hegel tries to squeeze any strong ontological claims out of them. In fact, it is just the ontological weakness of Hegel's dialectics *vis-à-vis* Kant's transcendental arguments that

makes him more anti-metaphysical than Kant. According to Pinkard, 'whereas Kantian transcendental arguments attempt to establish a necessary and unique solution to questions of possibility, Hegelian speculative arguments (as understood here) *cannot* establish uniqueness. They can merely offer up one alternative that is justified, if at all, by its superior explanatory power' (Pinkard, *Hegel's Dialectic*, p. 7). Taylor would have no problems with this as a philosophical position, though he might question whether it is the position Hegel had himself. If all that Hegel meant by 'rational necessity' was demonstrably superior explanatory power relative to some alternative, that would be fine. But Taylor thinks Hegel has a more emphatic conception of necessity in mind, one which confers uniqueness *retrospectively* once the final stage in the dialectic is reached.

19 Though Taylor does insist, as Artno Laitinen pointed out to me, that for Hegel the categorial dialectic traced in the *Logic* corresponds to ontological contradictions or contradictions in reality (for example, *H* 131). I am also grateful to Artno Laitinen for alerting me to two useful discussions of this matter, Ludwig Siep's 'Hegel's Idea of a Conceptual Scheme', *Inquiry*, 34 (1991); and Thomas E. Wartenberg's 'Hegel's Idealism: The Logic of Conceptuality', in Frederick C. Beiser ed., *The Cambridge Companion to Hegel* (1993).

20 Pinkard, *Hegel's Dialectic*, p. 174.

21 Pippin, *Hegel's Idealism*, p. 236.

22 Pippin presents a powerful case for such a quietist position *vis-à-vis* nature in 'Leaving Nature Behind, Or: Two Cheers for Subjectivism', in Nicholas H. Smith ed., *Reading McDowell: On Mind and World* (forthcoming). Elsewhere, Pippin suggests that we should not be concerned by the fact that his approach 'seems to avoid rather than answer the central question, What *kind* of beings are we?': Robert Pippin, *Idealism as Modernism* (1997), p. 12.

23 Generally, while the post-metaphysical Hegelians chastize Taylor for confusing logic with ontology (something he does not do – the fault lies in his hastiness in introducing ontological considerations to explain key transitions between categories), they tend to fudge the issue of what ontology Hegel does have in view. Kolb, for instance, writes that 'Hegel's opinions about what exists and how it exists are expressed through the overarching unity of the system, not through metaphysical claims' (Kolb, *The Critique of Pure Modernity*, p. 44). But then what are we to make of the *necessity* Hegel insists is the mark of the real? Taylor is surely right to say that Hegel does not see himself as merely proposing one interpretation of being amongst others, mere *opinions* about what exists and how it exists. The 'overarching unity of the system' is meant to capture something essential about the unity in diversity of what there really is. So, for instance, Taylor is entitled to attribute to Hegel the view that finite determinate being does not exhaust being, but there exists infinite being as well.

Taylor's objection is that Hegel does not demonstrate this claim, and so show up the necessity of infinite being, its identity with rational necessity.

24 Redding, *Hegel's Hermeneutics*, p. 166.

25 Kolb, *The Critique of Pure Modernity*, p. 40.

26 Taylor, 'The Importance of Herder', originally published in Edna and Avishai Margalit eds, *Isaiah Berlin: A Celebration* (1991).

27 Actually, the examples Taylor draws on at this stage of the argument refer to communication arising between animals and their human trainers, rather than the training that takes place within the species. Taylor does not consider how the bonds between animals and humans draw on a capacity the animals must already have for bonding between themselves.

28 Taylor, 'Heidegger, Language and Ecology', originally published in Hubert Dreyfus and Harrison Hall eds, *Heidegger: A Critical Reader* (1992).

29 Axel Honneth, in his 'Nachwort' to *Negative Freiheit?* (1988) (one of the German translations of Taylor's philosophical papers), notes that the development of the subject's creative capacity lessens her reliance on the formulations of her linguistic community, which both make possible and constrain her expressive potential. The members of a linguistic group can differentiate themselves 'contrastively' from the members of other groups. But as soon as a subject has thoughts or feelings for which the tradition does not have the appropriate means of expression, Honneth observes, she can only make herself intelligible through innovative transgression of the limits of the collective linguistic horizon. As Honneth observes, 'the expressive potential of a communal language is thus extended little by little through the expressive practices of speech of the individual'. This point is not emphasized as much as it could be by Taylor himself, however.

30 See Taylor, 'Theories of Meaning', *Proceedings of the British Academy*, 66 (1980), reprinted in *HAL*; and 'Language and Human Nature', also in *HAL*.

31 See *HAL* 273–92; and Taylor, 'Heidegger and Davidson' (unpublished ms).

32 Just as Merleau-Ponty's phenomenology shows that a perception always 'announces more than it contains', so there is a non-capturable surplus to the meaning of linguistic articulations. The expressivist theory of perception complements the expressive theory of language.

33 See Martin Heidegger, *Being and Time*, tr. John Macquarrie and Edward Robinson (1962).

34 Especially in Heidegger's later works such as *Das Ding* ('The Thing') and *Bauen Wohnen Denken* ('Building, Dwelling, Thinking'). English translations in Martin Heidegger, *Poetry, Language, Thought*, tr. Albert Hofstadter (1971).

Chapter 4   The Self and the Good

1   See Taylor, 'What is Human Agency?', in T. Mischel ed., *The Self* (1977). Reprinted in *HAL*.

2   See Harry Frankfurt, 'Freedom of the Will and the Concept of a Person', *Journal of Philosophy*, 67, 1 (1971), pp. 5–20.

3   See Owen Flanagan, 'Identity and Strong and Weak Evaluation', in Owen Flanagan and A. O. Rorty eds, *Identity, Character, and Morality* (1990).

4   See Amelie O. Rorty and David Wong, 'Aspects of Identity and Agency', in Flanagan and Rorty eds, *Identity, Character, and Morality*, p. 36.

5   Ibid., p. 31.

6   See Martin Heidegger, *Being and Time*, tr. John Macquarrie and Edward Robinson (1962).

7   See Alasdair MacIntyre, *After Virtue* (1984).

8   See Taylor, 'Explanation and Practical Reason', in *Wider Working Papers* (1989). Reprinted in *PA*.

9   See Habermas, *Moral Consciousness and Communicative Action*, tr. Christian Lenhardt and Shierry Weber Nicholson (1990), and *Justification and Application*, tr. Ciaran Cronin (1993).

10   In fact, Habermas had to modify his moral theory, and soften his Kantianism, to accommodate the logic of strong evaluation. For another attempt at incorporating the notion of strong evaluation within a broadly Kantian framework for thinking about justice, see Paul Ricoeur, *The Just*, tr. David Pellauer (2000).

11   For Taylor's specific criticisms of Habermas's proceduralism, see 'Language and Society', in Axel Honneth and Hans Joas eds, *Communicative Action* (1991), and 'The Motivation behind a Procedural Ethics', in Ronald Beiner and William James Booth eds, *Kant and Political Philosophy* (1993). For Habermas's response, see his reply to Taylor in Honneth and Joas eds, *Communicative Action*, and *Justification and Application*. For a more detailed assessment of the debate, see my *Strong Hermeneutics* (1997), ch. 6.

12   For a defence of proceduralism (especially Habermas's) from this point of view, see Shane O'Neill, *Impartiality in Context* (1997).

13   See Emmanuel Levinas, *Otherwise than Being or Beyond Essence*, tr. Alphonso Lingis (1991).

14   For further development of this argument, see my 'Levinas, Subjectivity and the Sacred', *Synthesis Philosophica*, 29–30, 1–2 (2000), pp. 129–43. See also Paul Ricoeur, *Oneself as Another*, tr. Kathleen Blamey (1992).

15   Besides *SS*, see Taylor, 'Iris Murdoch and Moral Philosophy', in Maria Antonaccio and William Schweiker eds, *Iris Murdoch and the Search for Human Goodness* (1996), pp. 12ff; and Taylor, 'Leading a Life', in Ruth

Chang ed., *Incommensurability, Incomparability and Practical Reason* (1997), pp. 173ff. Life goods do not exhaust strong values because there are some goods which are 'beyond life' (*CM* 20). The good which lies beyond life takes us onto the 'transcendent' or religious plane of meaning, which I shall discuss in chapter 8.

16 In another formulation, Taylor describes moral sources as constitutive goods 'insofar as we turn to them in whatever way is appropriate to them – through contemplation, or invocation, or prayer, or whatever – for moral empowerment' (*SS* 310–11). Elsewhere (for example, *SS* 93) he says that love of (not reflection on) moral sources empowers the good.

17 See Ricoeur, 'Le fondamental et l'historique', in Guy Laforest and Phillipe de Lara eds, *Charles Taylor et l'interprétation de l'identité moderne* (1998).

18 Rorty and Wong, 'Aspects of Identity and Agency', p. 33.

Chapter 5   Interpretation and the Social Sciences

1 See Michael Martin, 'Taylor on Interpretation and the Sciences of Man', in Michael Martin and Lee C. McIntyre eds, *Readings in the Philosophy of Science* (1994); and James F. Bohman, David R. Hiley and Richard Shusterman eds, *The Interpretive Turn* (1991).

2 See Taylor, 'Interpretation and the Sciences of Man', *Review of Metaphysics*, 25, 1 (September 1971), pp. 3–51. Reprinted in *PHS*.

3 See Terry Pinkard, 'Interpretation and Verification in the Human Sciences: A Note on Taylor', *Philosophy of the Social Sciences*, 6 (1976), p. 166.

4 Ibid., pp. 167, 169.

5 Ibid., p. 170.

6 Martin, 'Taylor on Interpretation and the Sciences of Man', p. 265.

7 James Bohman, *New Philosophy of Social Science* (1991), p. 113.

8 Ibid., p. 250, n. 27.

9 To be fair, while Taylor's account of validity in interpretation is certainly not 'subjectivist', it is sketchy. For a more detailed treatment of the topic that could be used to firm up Taylor's approach, see Alessandro Ferrara, *Reflective Authenticity* (1998).

10 See Taylor, 'Neutrality in Political Science', in P. Laslett and G. Runciman eds, *Philosophy, Politics and Society* (1967). Reprinted in *PHS*.

11 See Taylor, 'Social Theory as Practice', in Taylor, *Social Theory as Practice* (1983). Reprinted in *PHS*.

12 Taylor, 'Understanding and Ethnocentricity', originally published in Taylor, *Social Theory as Practice*.

13 See Peter Winch, *The Idea of a Social Science and its Relation to Philosophy* (1958); and 'Understanding a Primitive Society', *American Philosophical Quarterly*, 1 (1964), pp. 307–24.

14 Taylor, 'Rationality', originally published in Martin Hollis and Steven Lukes eds, *Rationality and Relativism* (1982).
15 Bohman, *New Philosophy of Social Science*, p. 133.
16 Taylor does reflect on ways of giving meaning to death in the 1999 Gifford Lectures, 'Living in a Secular Age' (forthcoming).
17 See David Couzens Hoy, 'Is Hermeneutics Ethnocentric?', in Bohman et al. eds, *The Interpretive Turn*. Hoy reiterates his case in his contribution to Hoy and Thomas McCarthy, *Critical Theory* (1994), pp. 204ff.
18 See Taylor, 'Comparison, History, Truth', in Frank Reynolds and David Tracey eds, *Myth and Philosophy* (1990). Reprinted in *PA*.

Chapter 6 Individual and Community

1 See Taylor, 'Atomism', in Alkis Kontos ed., *Powers, Possessions and Freedom* (1979); and 'What's Wrong with Negative Liberty', in A. Ryan ed., *The Idea of Freedom* (1979). Both reprinted in *PHS*.
2 See John Locke, *Two Treatises of Government*, Peter Laslett ed. (1960).
3 See Robert Nozick, *Anarchy, State and Utopia* (1975).
4 See Will Kymlicka, *Liberalism, Community and Culture* (1989).
5 Ibid., p. 50. The quotations of Taylor are from *HMS* 157–9.
6 I draw here on a distinction made by Sabina Lovibond in *Realism and Imagination in Ethics* (1983).
7 Will Kymlicka, *Contemporary Political Philosophy* (1990), p. 222.
8 Ibid., p. 212. These goals and ends make up what Kymlicka calls 'the cultural marketplace' (ibid., p. 217).
9 See Taylor, 'Cross-Purposes', in Nancy L. Rosenblum ed., *Liberalism and the Moral Life* (1989). Reprinted in *PA*.
10 See Taylor, 'Irreducibly Social Goods', in Geoffrey Brennan and Cliff Walsh eds, *Rationality, Individualism and Public Policy* (1990). Reprinted in *PA*.
11 See Jürgen Habermas, *Between Facts and Norms*, tr. William Rehg (1996), p. 500.
12 See, for instance, Taylor, 'Globalization and the Future of Canada', *Queen's Quarterly*, 105, 3 (Fall 1998), pp. 331–42.
13 Against those who deny that the republican thesis *is* true as an ontological claim about *contemporary* liberal democracies, Taylor makes two points. First, even in democracies where the norm of participatory self-rule plays a minor role, such as the United States, patriotic identification is rife, particularly at times when the democratic basis of the society is threatened. In Taylor's view, the citizen outrage occasioned by the Watergate scandal testifies to this. Second, it betrays an ethnocentrism to suppose that all democratic aspirations have to follow the procedural liberal model. It ignores the value placed on (and functional necessity of) participatory self-rule in other cultures.

14 See Taylor, 'The Politics of Recognition', in Taylor, *Multiculturalism and 'the Politics of Recognition'* (1992). An expanded, paperback edition of this volume was published with the title *Multiculturalism: Examining the Politics of Recognition* (1994). Taylor's essay is also reprinted in *PA*. My page references are to the original 1992 publication.

15 See, for example, Taylor, 'Democratic Exclusion (and its Remedies?)', in Alan C. Cairns, John C. Courtney, Peter Mackinnon and David E. Smith eds, *Citizenship, Diversity and Pluralism* (1999), pp. 278–9.

16 Susan Wolf, 'Comment', in *MPR* 81.

17 Jürgen Habermas, 'Struggles for Recognition in Constitutional States', *European Journal of Philosophy*, 1, 2 (1993), p. 141. Reprinted in *Multiculturalism* (1994). All page references are to the original publication.

18 Ibid., p. 131.

19 Ibid., p. 141.

20 Maeve Cooke, in 'Authenticity and Autonomy: Taylor, Habermas and the Politics of Recognition', *Political Theory*, 25, 2 (April 1997), defends Habermas's claim that liberalism can go as far as it ought to in recognizing difference simply by drawing on the principle of autonomy. There is no need to bring authenticity into the picture. For Cooke, Taylor offers a useful corrective to Habermas's approach simply by reminding us that liberalism is a 'fighting creed', a substantive ethos or conception of the good that excludes those not committed to the ideal of autonomy. While, if my interpretation is correct, this construction exaggerates the conflict between authenticity and autonomy in Taylor's own account, it confirms the ease with which Taylor's and Habermas's liberalisms merge into each other.

21 See Andy Lamey, 'Francophonia For Ever: The Contradictions in Charles Taylor's "Politics of Recognition"', *Times Literary Supplement* (23 July 1999), pp. 12–15.

22 Ibid., p. 14.

23 Taylor, 'Democratic Exclusion (and its Remedies?)', p. 279.

24 Taylor, 'Democratic Exclusion (and its Remedies?)', p. 271.

25 See Taylor, 'Preface' to *Philosophical Arguments*, pp. x–xi. Works in this category include 'Invoking Civil Society', 'Liberal Politics and the Public Sphere' (both in *PA*), 'Nationalism and Modernity' (in Robert McKim and Jeff McMahan eds, *The Morality of Nationalism* [1997]), 'Modes of Secularism' (in Rajeev Bhargava ed., *Secularism and its Critics* [1998]), as well as 'Democratic Exclusion (and its Remedies?)'.

26 Taylor, 'Democratic Exclusion (and its Remedies?)', p. 280.

27 Ibid., p. 281. See also Taylor, 'Sharing Identity Space', in John E. Trent, Robert Young and Guy Lachapelle eds, *Quebec–Canada: What is the Path Ahead?* (1996).

28 See Taylor, 'Liberal Politics and the Public Sphere', in *PA* 273.

29 On the concept of pathology as it features in the tradition of critical social philosophy, see Axel Honneth, 'Pathologies of the Social: The

Past and Present of Social Philosophy', in David Rasmussen ed., *The Handbook of Critical Theory* (1996).

Chapter 7 Politics and Social Criticism

1 See, for instance, Will Kymlicka, *Contemporary Political Philosophy* (1990); Stephen Mulhall and Adam Swift, *Liberals and Communitarians* (1992); and Ruth Abbey, *Charles Taylor* (2000).
2 See especially 'Socialism and the Intellectuals', *Universities and Left Review* (hereafter *ULR*), 2 (Summer 1957), pp. 18–19; 'The Politics of Emigration', *ULR*, 2 (Summer 1957), pp. 75–6; 'Marxism and Humanism', *New Reasoner*, 2 (Autumn 1957), pp. 92–8; 'Alienation and Community', *ULR*, 5 (Autumn 1958), pp. 11–18; 'What's Wrong with Capitalism?', *New Left Review*, 2 (March–April 1960), pp. 5–11; 'Changes of Quality', *New Left Review*, 4 (July–August 1960), pp. 3–5.
3 Taylor, 'What's Wrong with Capitalism?', p. 8.
4 Ibid., p. 9.
5 Ibid., p. 11.
6 Taylor, 'Alienation and Community', p. 13.
7 Ibid., p. 18.
8 Taylor, 'Socialism and the Intellectuals', p. 19.
9 In 'The Politics of Emigration', which documents his experience as a representative of the world student service in Austria between November 1956 and April 1957, Taylor describes the lack of understanding of socialism on the part of the young Hungarian émigrés. He observes how Marxism was a 'dead language' for them, a mere 'series of formulae which they disliked having to learn' and to which they had no attachment. Most of the émigrés, Taylor reports, were apolitical. But of those who were not, national independence was the overriding political aspiration.
10 *ULR* 4, editorial.
11 *ULR* 5, editorial.
12 And as Taylor put it sometime after the heyday of the New Left in Britain, 'without being linked to some such view of man and the ends of life, I doubt that a socialist movement can generate the power to make the changes it aims to encompass' (Taylor, 'Socialism and *Weltanschauung*', in Leszek Kolakowski and Stuart Hampshire eds, *The Socialist Idea* [1974]).
13 Taylor, 'What's Wrong with Capitalism?', p. 11.
14 See Taylor, 'Marxism and Socialist Humanism', in Robin Archer and the Oxford University Socialist Discussion Group eds, *Out of Apathy: Voices of the New Left Thirty Years On* (1989). The essay recapitulates criticisms first made by Taylor in 'From Marxism to the Dialogue Society', in Terry Eagleton and Brian Wicker eds, *From Culture to Revolution: The Slant Symposium 1967* (1968).

15 See Karl Marx, *Early Writings*, tr. Rodney Livingstone and Gregor Benton (1975).

16 See Karl Marx, *Capital*, vol. 1., tr. Ben Fowkes (1976).

17 'Charles Taylor – un philosophe enraciné dans le monde', an interview with Charles Taylor, *Le Devoir* (14 December 1992).

18 This form of argument has been deployed recently for justifying high wage increases for the directors of companies of previously publicly owned utilities. The wages, say, of the director of a privatized water company are justified on the grounds of the risks involved in the initial capital investment, on the responsibility of the job accruing from readiness to take risky decisions in correspondingly high-pressure environments. The bent of Taylor's argument, however, is that precisely the enormity and concentration of initial capital resources protects against risk. Indeed, it is this almost guaranteed profit-making outcome which attracts large investment in the first place. Moreover, concentration of capital diminishes competition, and of course the presence of serious competitors is a major source of risk. Risk is also reduced by the facility of fixing rather than suffering prices, as they are determined under conditions of capital concentration and diminished competition. So, against the argument for privatization, say, of water, tax is still being paid in the form of investment in development and research, but without any representation on the part of the taxpayer. As a result of water privatization, the citizen may pay less tax to the government. But the consumer remains the equivalent of a taxpayer, where the tax equivalent is paid to the directors of the company rather than the government, without the democratic procedures to which the latter is bound.

19 Taylor, 'A Socialist Perspective on the "70s"', *Canadian Dimension*, 5, 8 (February 1969), pp. 136–40. See also *PP* 114.

20 Taylor, 'Shared and Divergent Values', originally published in Ronald L. Watts and Douglas M. Brown eds, *Options for a New Canada* (1991).

21 For an account of the importance of the deliberative procedure in sorting out the stakes of the Canadian constitutional dispute, see Simone Chambers, 'Contract or Conversation? Theoretical Lessons from the Canadian Constitutional Crisis', *Politics and Society*, 26, 1 (March 1998), pp. 143–72.

22 Taylor concedes the errors of his previous ways in 'Alternative Futures: Legitimacy, Identity and Alienation in Late-Twentieth-Century Canada', in Alan Cairns and Cynthia Williams eds, *Constitutionalism, Citizenship, and Society in Canada* (1985), reprinted in *RS*.

23 See John Horton, 'Charles Taylor: Selfhood, Community and Democracy', in April Carter and Geoffrey Stokes eds, *Liberal Democracy and its Critics* (1998), p. 170.

24 Ibid.

25 Taylor, 'Globalization and the Future of Canada', p. 341.

Chapter 8   Modernity, Art and Religion

1   Taylor, 'Inwardness and the Culture of Modernity', in Alex Honneth, Thomas McCarthy, Claus Offe and Albrecht Wellmer eds, *Philosophical Interventions in the Unfinished Project of Enlightenment* (1992), p. 88. See also Taylor, 'Two Theories of Modernity', *Hastings Center Report* (March–April 1995), p. 24.
2   Taylor, 'Inwardness and the Culture of Modernity', p. 89.
3   The task is resumed, for instance, in Taylor's 1999 Gifford Lectures, 'Living in a Secular Age' (forthcoming).
4   See among other works T. W. Adorno and M. Horkheimer, *Dialectic of Enlightenment*, tr. John Cumming (1972); M. Foucault, 'What is Enlightenment?', tr. Catherine Porter in P. Rabinow ed., *The Foucault Reader* (1986); J. Habermas, *The Philosophical Discourse of Modernity*, tr. Frederick G. Lawrence (1987); J.-F. Lyotard, *The Postmodern Condition*, tr. Geoff Bennington (1984); A. MacIntyre, *After Virtue* (1984); A. Honneth et al eds, *Philosophical Interventions in the Unfinished Project of Enlightenment*.
5   For an influential early formulation of these types of reason, see Max Horkheimer, *The Eclipse of Reason* (1947). For a more refined taxonomy, see Habermas, *Theory of Communicative Action*, 2 vols, tr. Thomas McCarthy (1984, 1987).
6   I draw here from chs 13–16 of *SS* as well as Taylor's discussion of the 'anthropocentric turn' in 'Living in a Secular Age'.
7   See Habermas, *The Philosophical Discourse of Modernity*, lecture one.
8   See above, ch. 4, n. 16.
9   While Taylor alludes to the broader social and cultural transformations accompanying the changes in '*idées-forces*' in *SS*, he examines them in more detail in 'Living in a Secular Age'. He discusses some of them in 'Die Moderne und die säkulare Zeit', in Krzysztof Michalski ed., *Am Ende des Milleniums. Zeit und Modernitäten* (1999).
10   In the 'Preface' to *SS*, Taylor states the two aims of his enterprise: to show how modern 'ideals and interdicts . . . shape our philosophical thought, our epistemology and our philosophy of language'; and to provide a platform for a 'renewed understanding of modernity' (*SS* ix). My point is that a theory of modernity which is at the same time an explication of the ideals and interdicts that motivate epistemology etc. is bound to suffer from a certain 'idealism' or 'intellectualism'.
11   See Daniel Bell, *The Cultural Contradictions of Capitalism* (1976); Allan Bloom, *The Closing of the American Mind* (1987); Christopher Lasch, *The Culture of Narcissism* (1978).
12   See Martha Nussbaum, 'Our Pasts, Ourselves', *New Republic* (9 April 1990), pp. 27–34.

13 Stephen Mulhall makes this suggestion in 'Sources of the Self's Senses of Itself: The Making of a Theistic Reading of Modernity', in D. Z. Phillips ed., *Can Religion be Explained Away?* (1996).

14 See J. Habermas, *Justification and Application* (1993), p. 74. Curiously enough, Habermas appeals to the authority of Adorno and Derrida here, as discussed by Christoph Menke in *Die Souveränität der Kunst* (1988), available in English translation as *The Sovereignty of Art* (1998).

15 See Richard Rorty, 'Taylor on Truth', in J. Tully ed., *Philosophy in an Age of Pluralism* (1994).

16 Ibid., p. 20. For an attempt at marrying Taylor's interpretation of moral sources with Rorty's pragmatism, see Gary Gutting, *Pragmatic Liberalism and the Critique of Modernity* (1999).

17 It also requires community with other human beings: 'being made in the image of God, as a feature of each human being, is not something that can be characterised just by reference to this being alone. Our being in the image of God is also our standing among others in the stream of love, which is that facet of God's life we try to grasp, very inadequately, in speaking of the Trinity' (*CM* 35).

18 See, for instance, Quentin Skinner, 'Modernity and Disenchantment: Some Historical Reflections', in Tully ed., *Philosophy in an Age of Pluralism*, p. 47; and Stephen K. White, *Sustaining Affirmation* (2000), p. 69. This theme was widely taken up by reviewers of *SS*, as Michael L. Morgan notes in 'Religion, History and Moral Discourse', also in Tully ed., *Philosophy in an Age of Pluralism*, p. 50.

19 Taylor, 'Foreword' to Marcel Gauchet, *The Disenchantment of the World*, tr. Oscar Burge (1997), p. xv.

20 See Bernard Williams, 'Republican and Galilean', *New York Review of Books* (8 November 1990), p. 47.

21 See Mulhall, 'Sources of the Self's Senses of Itself'. For other discussions of the theological implications of Taylor's work, see Morgan, 'Religion, History and Moral Discourse'; and Anne Fortin, 'Identités religieuses et changement de paradigme', in Guy Laforest and Phillipe de Lara eds, *Charles Taylor et l'interprétation de l'identité moderne* (1998). Taylor weaves philosophical and theological motifs in *CM*, and for an expression of his youthful theological outlook, see 'Clericalism', *Downside Review*, 78 (1960), pp. 167–80.

22 Taylor, 'Reply and Re-articulation', in Tully ed., *Philosophy in an Age of Pluralism*, p. 228.

23 See Taylor, 'The Immanent Counter-Enlightenment', in Ronald Beiner and Wayne Norman eds, *Canadian Political Philosophy* (2000). Besides Nietzsche, Taylor puts Bataille, Foucault and Derrida in this camp.

24 See René Girard, *Violence and the Sacred* (1984).

25 For a very brief discussion of the 'levelling' problems arising from the demise of 'complementarity' in the modern world, see Taylor, 'What's Wrong with Foundationalism?', in Mark Wrathall and Jeff Malpas eds, *Heidegger, Coping and Cognitive Science* (2000). For a more detailed

account of the levellings involved in the secular experience of time, see 'Die Moderne und die säkulare Zeit', in Krzysztof Michalski ed., *Am Ende des Milleniums. Zeit und Modernitäten* (1999).

Conclusion

1 Taylor also owes the idea that human knowledge is conditioned by a non-thematizable 'background' to his reading of Michael Polanyi and the later philosophy of Wittgenstein. See Michael Polanyi, *The Tacit Dimension* (1966), and Ludwig Wittgenstein, *Philosophical Investigations* (1953).

2 On this change in climate, see Stephen K. White, *Sustaining Affirmation* (2000).

3 Karl Marx, 'Letter to A. Ruge', September 1843, in Marx, *Early Writings* (1975).

Bibliography

The following bibliography includes works cited in the text and occasional references to other useful sources. A comprehensive bibliography of Taylor's works is available on the world wide web at http://www.netidea.com/~whughes/taylor.html. This site, maintained by William Hughes, also contains an extensive list of secondary works on Taylor.

Works by Taylor

'Socialism and the Intellectuals', *Universities and Left Review*, 2 (Summer 1957), 18–19.

'The Politics of Emigration', *Universities and Left Review*, 2 (Summer 1957), 75–6.

'Marxism and Humanism', *New Reasoner*, 2 (Autumn 1957), 92–8.

(with Michael Kullman) 'The Pre-Objective World', *Review of Metaphysics*, 12 (1958), 103–32.

'Alienation and Community', *Universities and Left Review*, 5 (Autumn 1958), 11–18.

'Phenomenology and Linguistic Analysis', *Proceedings of the Aristotelian Society*, supplementary volume, 33 (1959), 93–124.

'What's Wrong with Capitalism?', *New Left Review*, 2 (March–April 1960), 5–11.

'Changes of Quality', *New Left Review*, 4 (July–August 1960), 3–5.

'Clericalism', *Downside Review*, 78 (1960), 167–80.

The Explanation of Behaviour (London: Routledge and Kegan Paul, 1964). Abbreviated as *EB*.

Review of *La Philosophie Analytique*. *Cahiers de Royaumont*, *Philosophical Review*, 73 (1964), 132–5.

'Genesis', review of *The Structure of Behaviour* by Maurice Merleau-Ponty, *New Statesman*, 70 (3 September 1965), 326–7.

'Neutrality in Political Science', in P. Laslett and G. Runciman, eds, *Philosophy, Politics and Society*, 3rd series (Oxford: Blackwell, 1967). Reprinted in *PHS*.

'Nationalism and Independence', *Canadian Dimension*, 4, 3 (March–April 1967), 4–11.

Review of *The Primacy of Perception* and *Signs* by M. Merleau-Ponty, *Philosophical Review*, 76, 1 (1967), 113–17.

'Psychological Behaviorism', in Paul Edwards, ed., *The Encyclopaedia of Philosophy* (New York: Macmillan, 1967).

'From Marxism to the Dialogue Society', in Terry Eagleton and Brian Wicker, eds, *From Culture to Revolution: The Slant Symposium 1967* (London: Sheed and Ward, 1968).

'A Socialist Perspective on the '70's', *Canadian Dimension*, 5, 8 (February 1969), 36–41.

The Pattern of Politics (Toronto: McClelland and Stewart, 1970). Abbreviated as *PP*.

'The Explanation of Purposive Behaviour', in R. Borger and F. Cioffi, eds, *Explanation in the Behavioural Sciences* (Cambridge: Cambridge University Press, 1970), with 'Reply' to Borger.

'Explaining Action', *Inquiry*, 13 (1970), 43–89.

'Interpretation and the Sciences of Man', *Review of Metaphysics*, 25, 1 (September 1971), 3–51. Reprinted in *PHS*.

'How is Mechanism Conceivable?', in Marjorie Grene, ed., *Interpretations of Life and Mind: Essays Around the Problem of Reduction* (London: Routledge and Kegan Paul, 1971). Reprinted in *HAL*.

'What is Involved in a Genetic Psychology?', in Theodore Mischel, ed., *Cognitive Development and Epistemology* (New York: Academic Press, 1971). Reprinted in *HAL*.

'The Agony of Economic Man', in L. Lapierre et al., eds, *Essays on the Left* (Toronto: McClelland and Stewart, 1971).

'The Opening Arguments of the Phenomenology', in Alasdair MacIntyre, ed., *Hegel: A Collection of Critical Essays* (Garden City, N.Y.: Doubleday, 1972).

'Peaceful Coexistence in Psychology', *Social Research*, 40, 1 (1973), 55–82. Reprinted in *HAL*.

'Socialism and *Weltanschauung*', in Leszek Kolakowski and Stuart Hampshire, eds, *The Socialist Idea* (London: Weidenfeld and Nicolson, 1974).

Hegel (Cambridge: Cambridge University Press, 1975). Abbreviated as *H*.

'What is Human Agency?', in T. Mischel, ed., *The Self* (Oxford: Blackwell, 1977). Reprinted in *HAL*.

'The Validity of Transcendental Arguments', *Proceedings of the Aristotelian Society*, 79 (1978–9), 151–65. Reprinted in *PA*.

Hegel and Modern Society (Cambridge: Cambridge University Press, 1979). Abbreviated as *HMS*.

'Atomism', in Alkis Kontos, ed., *Powers, Possessions and Freedom* (Toronto: University of Toronto Press, 1979). Reprinted in *PHS*.

'What's Wrong with Negative Liberty', in A. Ryan, ed., *The Idea of Freedom* (Oxford: Oxford University Press, 1979). Reprinted in *PHS*.

'Sense Data Revisited', in G. F. MacDonald, ed., *Perception and Identity* (Ithaca, N.Y.: Cornell University Press, 1979).

'Theories of Meaning', *Proceedings of the British Academy*, 66 (1980), 283–327. Reprinted in *HAL*.

'Understanding in Human Science', *Review of Metaphysics*, 34, 1 (September 1980), 25–38.

'Discussion with Hubert Dreyfus and Richard Rorty', *Review of Metaphysics*, 34, 1 (September 1980), 47–55.

'Growth, Legitimacy and Modern Identity', *Praxis International*, 1, 2 (July 1981), 111–25.

'Rationality', in Martin Hollis and Steven Lukes, eds, *Rationality and Relativism* (Oxford: Blackwell, 1982). Reprinted in *PHS*.

'Social Theory as Practice', in Charles Taylor, *Social Theory as Practice* (Delhi: Oxford University Press, 1983). Reprinted in *PHS*.

'Understanding and Ethnocentricity', in Charles Taylor, *Social Theory as Practice* (Delhi: Oxford University Press, 1983). Reprinted in *PHS*.

'The Significance of Significance: The Case of Cognitive Psychology', in S. Mitchell and M. Rosen, eds, *The Need for Interpretation* (London: Athlone Press, 1983). Reprinted in *HAL*.

'Alternative Futures: Legitimacy, Identity, and Alienation in Late-Twentieth-Century Canada', in Alan Cairns and Cynthia Williams, eds, *Constitutionalism, Citizenship and Society in Canada* (Toronto: University of Toronto Press, 1985). Reprinted in *RS*.

Human Agency and Language. Philosophical Papers, 1 (Cambridge: Cambridge University Press, 1985). Abbreviated as *HAL*.

Philosophy and the Human Sciences. Philosophical Papers, 2 (Cambridge: Cambridge University Press, 1985). Abbreviated as *PHS*.

'Les pourquoi d'un philosophe', interview with Georges-Hébert Germain, *L'Actualité* (June 1986), 13–17.

'Dialektik Heute, oder: Strukturen der Selbst-negation', in D. Henrich, ed., *Hegel's Wissenschaft der Logik: Formation und Rekonstruktion* (Stuttgart: Klett-Cotta, 1986).

'Overcoming Epistemology', in Kenneth Baynes, James Bohman and Thomas McCarthy, eds, *After Philosophy* (Cambridge, Mass.: MIT Press, 1987). Reprinted in *PA*.

'Inwardness and the Culture of Modernity', in Axel Honneth, Thomas McCarthy, Claus Offe and Albrecht Wellmer, eds, *Zwischenbetrachtungen Im Prozess der Aufklärung* (Frankfurt: Suhrkamp, 1988). Reprinted in Axel Honneth, Thomas McCarthy, Claus Offe and Albrecht Wellmer, eds, *Philosophical Interventions in the Unfinished Project of Enlightenment* (Cambridge, Mass.: MIT Press, 1992).

Review of *Logics of Disintegration* by Peter Dews, *New Left Review*, 170 (1988), 110–16.

Sources of the Self: The Making of the Modern Identity (Cambridge: Cambridge University Press, 1989). Abbreviated as *SS*.

'Cross-Purposes', in Nancy L. Rosenblum, ed., *Liberalism and the Moral Life* (Cambridge, Mass.: Harvard University Press, 1989). Reprinted in *PA*.

'Explanation and Practical Reason', in *Wider Working Papers*, World Institute for Development Economics Research of the United Nations University, Helsinki, August 1989. Amended version in M. Nussbaum and A. Sen, eds., *The Quality of Life* (Oxford: Clarendon, 1993). Reprinted in *PA*.

'Balancing the Humours: Charles Taylor talks to the Editors', *Idler*, 26 (November and December 1989), 21–9.

'Où est le danger?', *Liberté*, 83 (June 1989), 13–16.

'Marxism and Socialist Humanism', in Robin Archer and the Oxford University Socialist Discussion Group, eds, *Out of Apathy: Voices of the New Left Thirty Years On* (London: Verso, 1989).

'Embodied Agency', in Henry Pietersma, ed., *Merleau Ponty: Critical Essays* (Washington, D.C.: University of America Press, 1989). First published in German translation as 'Leibliches Handeln', in Alexandre Metraux and Bernhard Waldenfels, eds, *Leibhaftige Vernunft* (Munich: Fink, 1986).

'Comparison, History, Truth', in Frank Reynolds and David Tracey, eds, *Myth and Philosophy* (Albany: State University of New York Press, 1990). Reprinted in *PA*.

'Invoking Civil Society', Working Paper (Chicago: Centre for Psychosocial Studies, 1990). Reprinted in *PA*.

'Irreducibly Social Goods', in Geoffrey Brennan and Cliff Walsh, eds, *Rationality, Individualism and Public Policy* (Canberra: Australian National University, 1990). Reprinted in *PA*.

'Shared and Divergent Values', in Ronald Watts and Douglas Brown, eds, *Options for a New Canada* (Toronto: University of Toronto Press, 1991). Reprinted in *RS*.

'The Stakes of Constitutional Reform', English translation of 'Les enjeux de la reforme constitutionnelle', submission to the *Commission sur l'Avenir Politique et Constitutionne du Québec* (Québec: Québec Government Publication, 1991), in *RS*.

'Language and Society', in Axel Honneth and Hans Joas, eds, *Communicative Action* (Cambridge: Polity, 1991). First published in German translation in Axel Honneth and Hans Joas, eds, *Kommunikatives Handeln* (Frankfurt: Suhrkamp, 1986).

'The Importance of Herder', in Edna Margalit and Avishai Margalit, eds, *Isaiah Berlin: A Celebration* (Chicago: University of Chicago Press, 1991). Reprinted in *PA*.

The Malaise of Modernity (Toronto: Anansi Press, 1991). Abbreviated as *MM*. Republished as *The Ethics of Authenticity* (Cambridge, Mass.: Harvard University Press, 1992).

'The Dialogical Self', in J. Bohman, David R. Hiley and Richard Shusterman, eds, *The Interpretative Turn: Philosophy, Science, Culture* (Ithaca, N.Y.: Cornell University Press, 1991).

'Philosophy of Mind', in J. O. Urmson and Jonathan Rée, eds, *The Concise Encyclopaedia of Western Philosophy and Philosophers*, second revised edition (London: Routledge, 1991).

Multiculturalism and 'the Politics of Recognition' (Princeton: Princeton University Press, 1992). Republished with additional commentaries as *Multiculturalism: Examining the Politics of Recognition*, ed. Amy Gutmann (Princeton: Princeton University Press, 1994). Abbreviated as *MPR*.

'Charles Taylor – un philosophe enraciné dans le monde', interview with Jean Pichette, *Le Devoir* (14 December 1992).

'Heidegger, Language and Ecology', in Hubert Dreyfus and Harrison Hall, eds, *Heidegger: A Critical Reader* (Oxford: Blackwell, 1992). Reprinted in *PA*.

Reconciling the Solitudes: Essays on Canadian Federalism and Nationalism (Montreal: McGill-Queens University Press, 1993). Abbreviated as *RS*.

'The Motivation behind a Procedural Ethics', in Ronald Beiner and William James Booth, eds, *Kant and Political Philosophy* (London: Yale University Press, 1993). First published in German translation as 'Die Motive einer Verfahrensethik', in Wolfgang Kuhlmann, ed., *Moralität und Sittlichkeit* (Frankfurt: Suhrkamp, 1986).

'Modernity and the Rise of the Public Sphere', *The Tanner Lectures on Human Values*, ed. Garth B. Peterson (Salt Lake City: University of Utah Press, 1993).

'Reply to Commentators', contribution to a symposium on *Sources of the Self*, *Philosophy and Phenomenological Research*, 54, 1 (March 1994), 203–14.

'Reply and Re-articulation', in James Tully, ed., *Philosophy in an Age of Pluralism: The Philosophy of Charles Taylor in Question* (Cambridge: Cambridge University Press, 1994).

'Can Liberalism be Communitarian?', contribution to a symposium on *Liberalism, Community and Culture* by Will Kymlicka, *Critical Review*, 8, 2 (Spring 1994), 257–62.

Philosophical Arguments (Cambridge, Mass.: Harvard University Press, 1995). Abbreviated as *PA*.

'Two Theories of Modernity', *Hastings Center Report*, 25, 2 (March–April 1995), 24–33.

'A Most Peculiar Institution', in J. E. J. Altham and Ross Harrison, eds, *World, Mind and Ethics* (Cambridge: Cambridge University Press, 1995).

'Les ethnies dans une société "normale" (1)', *La Presse* (21 November 1995), B3.

'Les ethnies dans une société "normale" (2)', *La Presse* (22 November 1995), B3.

'A Qualified No: Message to the Rest of Canada: Quebecers Still Want Change', *Montreal Gazette* (28 September 1995), B3.

'Charles Taylor en entrevue à *La Presse'*, interview with Gérard Leblanc, *La Presse* (16 September 1995).

'Sharing Identity Space', in John E. Trent, Robert Young and Guy Lachapelle, eds, *Quebec–Canada: What is the Path Ahead?* (Ottawa: University of Ottawa Press, 1996).

'Les sources de l'identité moderne', in Mikhaël Elbaz, André Fortin and Guy Laforest, eds, *Les Frontières de l'identité: Modernité et postmodernisme au Quebec* (Sainte-Foy: Presses de l'Université Laval, 1996).

'Iris Murdoch and Moral Philosophy', in Maria Antonaccio and William Schweiker, eds, *Iris Murdoch and the Search for Human Goodness* (Chicago: University of Chicago Press, 1996).

'A World Consensus on Human Rights?', *Dissent*, 43, 3 (Summer 1996), 15–21, 143. Expanded version in B. Bauer and Daniel A. Bell, eds, *The East-Asian Challenge to Human Rights* (Cambridge: Cambridge University Press, 1999).

'Nationalism and Modernity', in Robert McKim and Jeff McMahan, eds, *The Morality of Nationalism* (Oxford: Oxford University Press, 1997).

'Foreword' to Marcel Gauchet, *The Disenchantment of the World: A Political History of Religion*, tr. Oscar Burge (Princeton: Princeton University Press, 1997).

'Leading a Life', in Ruth Chang, ed., *Incommensurability, Incomparability and Practical Reason* (Cambridge, Mass.: Harvard University Press, 1997).

'From Philosophical Anthropology to the Politics of Recognition: An Interview with Charles Taylor', *Thesis Eleven*, 52 (February 1998), 103–12.

'Le fondamental dans l'histoire', in Guy Laforest and Philippe de Lara, eds, *Charles Taylor et l'interpretation de l'identité moderne* (Paris: Centre Culturel International de Cerisy-la-Salle, Cerf; Sainte Foy: Les Presses de l'Université Laval, 1998).

'Modes of Secularism', in Rajeev Bhargava, ed., *Secularism and its Critics* (Oxford: Oxford University Press, 1998).

'Globalization and the Future of Canada', *Queen's Quarterly*, 105 (1998), 331–42.

A Catholic Modernity?, ed. James L. Heft (Oxford: Oxford University Press, 1999). Abbreviated as *CM*.

'Democratic Exclusion (and its Remedies?)', in Alan C. Cairns, John C. Courtney, Peter Mackinnon and David E. Smith, eds, *Citizenship, Diversity and Pluralism* (McGill: Queen's University Press, 1999).

'Glaube und Identität: Religion und Gewalt in der modernen Welt', *Transit*, 16 (1999), 21–37.

'Die Moderne und die säkulare Zeit', in Krzysztof Michalski, ed., *Am Ende des Milleniums. Zeit und Modernitäten* (Stuttgart: Klett-Cotta, 1999).

'Living in a Secular Age', the 1999 Gifford Lectures (publication forthcoming).

'What's Wrong with Foundationalism? Knowledge, Agency and World', in Mark Wrathall and Jeff Malpas, eds, *Heidegger, Coping and Cognitive Science* (Cambridge, Mass.: MIT Press, 2000).

'The Immanent Counter-Enlightenment', in Ronald Beiner and Wayne Norman, eds, *Canadian Political Philosophy at the Turn of the Century* (Oxford: Oxford University Press, 2000). First published in German translation as 'Die Immanente Gegenaufklärung' in Krzysztof Michalski, ed., *Aufklärung heute* (Stuttgart: Klett-Cotta, 1997).

'Foundationalism and the Inner–Outer Distinction', in Nicholas H. Smith, ed., *Reading McDowell: On Mind and World* (London: Routledge, forthcoming).

Other Works

Abbey, Ruth, *Charles Taylor* (Teddington: Acumen, 2000).

Adorno, T. W. and Horkheimer, M., *Dialectic of Enlightenment*, tr. John Cumming (New York: Herder and Herder, 1972).

Anscombe, G. E. M., 'Mechanism and Ideology', *New Statesman*, 5 February 1965, p. 206.

Archer, Robin, and the Oxford University Socialist Discussion Group, eds, *Out of Apathy: Voices of the New Left Thirty Years On* (London: Verso, 1989).

Ayer, A. J., *Part of My Life* (London: Collins, 1977).

Ayer, A. J., et al., *The Revolution in Philosophy* (London: Macmillan, 1957).

Beiser, Frederick C., *The Cambridge Companion to Hegel* (Cambridge: Cambridge University Press, 1993).

Bell, Daniel, *The Cultural Contradictions of Capitalism* (New York: Basic Books, 1976).

Berlin, Isaiah, et al., *Essays on J. L. Austin* (Oxford: Clarendon Press, 1973).

Benhabib, S. and Passerin d'Entreves, M., *Habermas and the Unfinished Project of Modernity* (Cambridge: Polity, 1996).

Bernstein, Richard J., *Praxis and Action* (Philadelphia: University of Pennsylvania Press, 1971).

Bloom, Allan, *The Closing of the American Mind* (New York: Simon and Schuster, 1987).

Bohman, James, *New Philosophy of Social Science: Problems of Indeterminacy* (Cambridge, Mass.: MIT Press, 1991).

——, David R. Hiley and Richard Shusterman, eds, *The Interpretive Turn: Philosophy, Science, Culture* (Ithaca, N.Y.: Cornell University Press, 1991).

Borger, R. and Cioffi, F., eds, *Explanation in the Behavioural Sciences* (Cambridge: Cambridge University Press, 1970).

Chambers, Simone, 'Contract or Conversation? Theoretical Lessons from the Canadian Constitutional Crisis', *Politics and Society*, 26, 1 (March 1998), 143–72.

Clark, George, 'Second Wind – The Story of the Campaign and the Committee of 100' (London: Workshop Publications, 1963).

Cooke, Maeve, 'Authenticity and Autonomy: Taylor, Habermas and the Politics of Recognition', *Political Theory*, 25, 2 (April 1997), 258–88.

Driver, Christopher, *The Disarmers: A Study in Protest* (London: Hodder and Stoughton, 1964).

Durfee, Harold A., ed., *Analytic Philosophy and Phenomenology* (The Hague: Nijhoff, 1976).

Ferrara, Alessandro, *Reflective Authenticity: Rethinking the Project of Modernity* (London: Routledge, 1998).

Flanagan, Owen, *Self-Expressions* (Oxford: Oxford University Press, 1996).

Flanagan, Owen and Rorty, Amelie O., eds, *Identity, Character, and Morality* (Cambridge, Mass.: MIT Press, 1990).

Fortin, Anne, 'Identités Religieuses et Changement de Paradigme', in Guy Laforest and Phillipe de Lara, eds, *Charles Taylor et l'interprétation de l'identité moderne* (Paris: Centre Culturel International de Cerisy-la-Salle, Cerf; Sainte Foy: Les Presses de l'Université Laval, 1998).

Foucault, M., 'What is Enlightenment?', tr. Catherine Porter, in P. Rabinow, ed., *The Foucault Reader* (Harmondsworth: Penguin, 1986).

Frankfurt, Harry, 'Freedom of the Will and the Concept of a Person', *Journal of Philosophy*, 67, 1 (1971), 5–20.

Gadamer, Hans-Georg, *Hermeneutik 1: Wahrheit und Methode – grundzüge einer philosophischen Hermeneutik* (1960). Published in English translation as *Truth and Method*, tr. Joel Weinsheimer and Donald G. Marshall (London: Sheed and Ward, 1993).

Geertz, Clifford, 'The Strange Estrangement: Taylor and the Natural Sciences', in J. Tully, ed., *Philosophy in an Age of Pluralism* (1994). Reprinted in Geertz, *Available Light: Anthropological Reflections on Philosophical Topics* (Princeton: Princeton University Press, 2000).

Girard, René, *Violence and the Sacred* (Baltimore: Johns Hopkins University Press, 1984).

Gonick, C. W., 'Taylor's Socialism for 1970: A Comment', *Canadian Dimension*, 5, 8 (February 1969), 41–3.

Grene, Marjorie, *Philosophy In and Out of Europe* (Washington, D.C.: Center for Advanced Research in Phenomenology and University Press of America, 1987).

Gutting, Gary, *Pragmatic Liberalism and the Critique of Modernity* (Cambridge: Cambridge University Press, 1999).

Habermas, Jürgen, *Theory of Communicative Action*, 2 vols, tr. Thomas McCarthy (Cambridge: Polity, 1984, 1987).

——, *The Philosophical Discourse of Modernity*, tr. Frederick G. Lawrence (Cambridge: Polity, 1987).

——, *Moral Consciousness and Communicative Action*, tr. Christian Lenhardt and Shierry Weber Nicholson (Cambridge: Polity, 1990).

——, *Justification and Application: Remarks on Discourse Ethics*, tr. Ciaran Cronin (Cambridge: Polity, 1993).

——, 'Struggles for Recognition in Constitutional States', *European Journal of Philosophy*, 1, 2 (1993), 128–55.

——, *Between Facts and Norms: Toward a Discourse Theory of Law and Democracy*, tr. William Rehg (Cambridge, Mass.: MIT Press, 1996).

Hartmann, Klaus, 'Hegel: A Non-Metaphysical View', in Alasdair MacIntyre, ed., *Hegel: A Collection of Critical Essays* (Garden City, N.Y.: Doubleday, 1972).

Hegel, Georg W. F., *Phenomenology of Spirit*, tr. A. V. Miller (Oxford: Oxford University Press, 1977).

Heidegger, Martin, *Being and Time*, tr. John Macquarrie and Edward Robinson (Oxford: Blackwell, 1962).

——, *Poetry, Language, Thought*, tr. Albert Hofstadter (New York: Harper and Row, 1971).

Honneth, Axel, 'Nachwort', in Charles Taylor, *Negative Freiheit?*, tr. Hermann Kocyba (Frankfurt: Suhrkamp, 1988).

——, *The Struggle for Recognition*, tr. Joel Anderson (Cambridge: Polity, 1995).

——, 'Pathologies of the Social: The Past and Present of Social Philosophy', in David Rasmussen, ed., *The Handbook of Critical Theory* (Oxford: Blackwell, 1996).

——, Thomas McCarthy, Claus Offe and Albrecht Wellmer, eds, *Philosophical Interventions in the Unfinished Project of Enlightenment* (Cambridge, Mass.: MIT Press, 1992).

Horkheimer, Max, *Eclipse of Reason* (New York: Oxford University Press, 1947).

Horton, John, 'Charles Taylor: Selfhood, Community and Democracy', in April Carter and Geoffrey Stokes, eds, *Liberal Democracy and its Critics* (Cambridge: Polity, 1998).

Houlgate, Stephen, *Freedom, Truth and History: An Introduction to Hegel's Philosophy* (London: Routledge, 1991).

Hoy, David Couzens, 'Is Hermeneutics Ethnocentric?', in James Bohman, David R. Hiley and Richard Shusterman, eds, *The Interpretive Turn: Philosophy, Science, Culture* (Ithaca, N.Y.: Cornell University Press, 1991).

—— and McCarthy, Thomas, *Critical Theory* (Oxford: Blackwell, 1994).

Inwood, Michael, *Hegel* (Oxford: Oxford University Press, 1985).

Kant, Immanuel, *Kritik der reinen Vernunft* (Frankfurt: Suhrkamp, 1974 [1787]). Published in English translation as *Critique of Pure Reason*, tr. Norman Kemp Smith (London: Macmillan, 1929).

Kenny, Michael, *The First New Left: British Intellectuals After Stalin* (London: Lawrence and Wishart, 1995).

Kolb, David, *The Critique of Pure Modernity* (Chicago: University of Chicago Press, 1986).

Kymlicka, Will, *Liberalism, Community and Culture* (Oxford: Clarendon Press, 1989).

——, *Contemporary Political Philosophy* (Oxford: Oxford University Press, 1990).

Laforest, Guy and de Lara, Philippe, eds, *Charles Taylor et l'interprétation de l'identité moderne* (Paris: Centre Culturel International de Cerisy-la-Salle, Cerf; Sainte Foy: Les Presses de l'Université Laval, 1998).

Lamey, Andy, 'Francophonia For Ever: The Contradictions in Charles Taylor's "Politics of Recognition"', *Times Literary Supplement* (23 July 1999), 12–15.

Lamoureux, André, *Le NDP et le Quebec 1958–1985* (Quebec: Editions du Parc, 1985).

Lasch, Christopher, *The Culture of Narcissism* (New York: Norton, 1978).

Levinas, Emmanuel, *Otherwise than Being or Beyond Essence*, tr. Alphonso Lingis (Dordrecht: Kluwer, 1991).

Locke, John, *Two Treatises of Government*, ed. Peter Laslett (Cambridge: Cambridge University Press, 1960).

Lovibond, Sabina, *Realism and Imagination in Ethics* (Oxford: Blackwell, 1983).

Lyotard, J.-F., *The Postmodern Condition*, tr. Geoff Bennington (Manchester: Manchester University Press, 1984).

MacIntyre, Alasdair, *After Virtue*, second edition (Notre Dame: University of Notre Dame Press, 1984).

Malcolm, Norman, 'Explaining Behaviour', *Philosophical Review*, 76 (1967), 97–104.

——, 'The Conceivability of Mechanism', *Philosophical Review*, 77 (1968), 45–72.

Martin, Michael, 'Taylor on Interpretation and the Sciences of Man', in Michael Martin and Lee C. McIntyre, eds, *Readings in the Philosophy of Science* (Cambridge, Mass.: MIT Press, 1994).

—— and McIntyre, Lee C., eds, *Readings in the Philosophy of Science* (Cambridge, Mass.: MIT Press, 1994).

Marx, Karl, *Early Writings*, tr. Rodney Livingstone and Gregor Benton (Harmondsworth: Penguin, 1975).

——, *Capital*, vol. 1, tr. Ben Fowkes (Harmondsworth: Penguin, 1976).

Mays, Wolfe and Brown, S. C., eds, *Linguistic Analysis and Phenomenology* (London: Macmillan, 1972).

McKim, Robert and McMahan, Jeff, eds, *The Morality of Nationalism* (Oxford: Oxford University Press, 1997).

Menke, Christoph, *Die Souveränität der Kunst* (Frankfurt: Suhrkamp, 1988). Published in English translation as *The Sovereignty of Art*, tr. Neil Soloman (Cambridge, Mass.: MIT Press, 1998).

Merleau-Ponty, Maurice, *Phénoménologie de la Perception* (Paris: Gallimard, 1945). Published in English translation as *Phenomenology of Perception*, tr. Colin Smith (London: Routledge, 1962).

——, *La Structure du Comportement* (Paris: Presses Universitaires de France, 1942). Published in English translation as *The Structure of Behaviour*, tr. Alden L. Fisher (Boston: Beacon Press, 1963).

Minnion, John and Bolsover, Philip, eds, *The CND Story: The First 25 Years of CND in the Words of the People Involved* (London: Alison and Bubsy, 1983).

Morgan, Michael L., 'Religion, History and Moral Discourse', in James Tully, ed., *Philosophy in an Age of Pluralism: The Philosophy of Charles Taylor in Question* (Cambridge: Cambridge University Press, 1994).

Morton, Desmond, *The New Democrats, 1961–86: The Politics of Change* (Toronto and London: Copp Clark Pitman and Longman, 1986).

Mulhall, Stephen, 'Sources of the Self's Senses of Itself: The Making of a Theistic Reading of Modernity', in D. Z. Phillips, ed., *Can Religion be Explained Away?* (London: Macmillan, 1996).

—— and Swift, Adam, *Liberals and Communitarians* (Oxford: Blackwell, 1992).

Nagel, Thomas, *The View from Nowhere* (Oxford: Oxford University Press, 1984).

Nathanson, M., ed., *Essays in Phenomenology* (The Hague: Martinus Nijhoff, 1966).

Nozick, Robert, *Anarchy, State and Utopia* (Oxford: Blackwell, 1975).

Nussbaum, Martha, 'Our Pasts, Ourselves', *New Republic* (9 April 1990), 27–34.

O'Neill, Shane, *Impartiality in Context* (Albany: State University of New York Press, 1997).

Pinkard, Terry, 'Interpretation and Verification in the Human Sciences: A Note on Taylor', *Philosophy of the Social Sciences*, 6 (1976), 165–73.

——, *Hegel's Dialectic* (Philadelphia: Temple University Press, 1988).

Pippin, Robert, *Hegel's Idealism* (Cambridge: Cambridge University Press, 1989).

——, *Idealism as Modernism* (Cambridge: Cambridge University Press, 1997).

——, 'Leaving Nature Behind, Or: Two Cheers for Subjectivism', in Nicholas H. Smith, ed., *Reading McDowell: On Mind and World* (London: Routledge, forthcoming).

Polanyi, Michael, *The Tacit Dimension* (London: Routledge, 1966).

Redding, Paul, *Hegel's Hermeneutics* (Ithaca, N.Y.: Cornell University Press, 1996).

Reé, Jonathan, 'English Philosophy in the Fifties', *Radical Philosophy*, 65 (Autumn 1993), 3–21.

Ricoeur, Paul, ed., *Main Trends in Philosophy* (New York: Holmes and Meier, 1979).

——, *Oneself as Another*, tr. Kathleen Blamey (Chicago: University of Chicago Press, 1992).

——, 'Le fondamental et l'historique: note sur *Sources of the Self* de Charles Taylor', in Guy Laforest and Phillipe de Lara, eds, *Charles Taylor et l'interprétation de l'identité moderne* (Paris: Centre International de Cerisy-la-Salle, Cerf; Sainte Foy: Les Presses de l'Université Laval, 1998).

——, *The Just*, tr. David Pellauer (Chicago: University of Chicago Press, 2000).

Rorty, Amelie O. and Wong, David, 'Aspects of Identity and Agency', in Owen Flanagan and Amelie O. Rorty, eds, *Identity, Character, and Morality* (Cambridge, Mass.: MIT Press, 1990).

Rorty, Richard, 'A Reply to Dreyfus and Taylor', *Review of Metaphysics*, 34, 1 (September 1980), 39–46.

——, 'Taylor on Truth', in J. Tully, ed., *Philosophy in an Age of Pluralism: The Philosophy of Charles Taylor in Question* (Cambridge: Cambridge University Press, 1994). Reprinted in Rorty, *Truth and Progress. Philosophical Papers, Volume 3* (Cambridge: Cambridge University Press, 1998).

Rosa, Harmut, *Identität und kulturelle Praxis: Politische Philosophie nach Charles Taylor* (Frankfurt: Campus, 1998).

Rosen, Michael, *Hegel's Dialectic and its Criticism* (Cambridge: Cambridge University Press, 1982).

Rouse, Joseph, *Knowledge and Power* (Ithaca, N.Y.: Cornell University Press, 1987).

Ryle, Gilbert, *The Concept of Mind* (London: Hutchinson's University Library, 1949).

Sedgwick, Peter, 'The Two New Lefts', in D. Widgery, ed., *The Left in Britain 1956–1968* (Harmondsworth: Penguin, 1976).

Siep, Ludwig, 'Hegel's Idea of a Conceptual Scheme', *Inquiry*, 34 (1991), 63–76.

Skinner, Quentin, 'Modernity and Disenchantment: Some Historical Reflections', in James Tully, ed., *Philosophy in an Age of Pluralism: The Philosophy of Charles Taylor in Question* (Cambridge: Cambridge University Press, 1994).

Smith, Nicholas H., *Strong Hermeneutics: Contingency and Moral Identity* (London: Routledge, 1997).

—— 'Reason after Meaning', *Philosophy and Social Criticism*, 23, 1 (1997), 131–40.

——, 'Levinas, Subjectivity and the Sacred', *Synthesis Philosophica*, 29–30, 1–2 (2000), 129–43.

——, ed., *Reading McDowell: On Mind and World* (London: Routledge, forthcoming).

Strawson, P. F., 'The Post-Linguistic Thaw', *Times Literary Supplement* (9 September 1960).

Trudeau, Pierre Elliot, *Memoirs* (Toronto: McClelland and Stewart, 1993).

Tully, James, ed., *Philosophy in an Age of Pluralism: The Philosophy of Charles Taylor in Question* (Cambridge: Cambridge University Press, 1994).

Urmson, James O., *Philosophical Analysis* (Oxford: Clarendon, 1956).

—— and Reé, Jonathan, eds, *The Concise Encyclopaedia of Western Philosophy and Philosophers*, second revised edition (London: Routledge, 1991).

Warnock, G. J., 'Saturday Mornings', in Isaiah Berlin et al., *Essays on J. L. Austin* (Oxford: Clarendon, 1973).

Wartenberg, Thomas E., 'Hegel's Idealism: The Logic of Conceptuality', in Frederick C. Beiser, ed., *The Cambridge Companion to Hegel* (Cambridge: Cambridge University Press, 1993).

White, Alan, *Absolute Knowledge: Hegel and the Problem of Metaphysics* (Ohio: Ohio University Press, 1983).

White, Stephen K., *Sustaining Affirmation* (Cambridge: Cambridge University Press, 2000).

Widgery, D., ed., *The Left in Britain 1956–1968* (Harmondsorth: Penguin, 1976).

Williams, Bernard, *Descartes: The Project of Pure Enquiry* (London: Penguin, 1978).

——, 'Republican and Galilean', *New York Review of Books* (8 November 1990), 45–8.

Winch, Peter, *The Idea of a Social Science and its Relation to Philosophy* (London: Routledge and Kegan Paul, 1958).

——, 'Understanding a Primitive Society', *American Philosophical Quarterly*, 1 (1964), 307–24.

Wittgenstein, Ludwig, *Philosophical Investigations*, tr. G. E. M. Anscombe (Oxford: Blackwell, 1953).

Wolf, Susan, 'Comment', in Charles Taylor, *Multiculturalism and 'the Politics of Recognition'* (Princeton: Princeton University Press, 1992).

Index